BODIES OF THE TEXT

DANCE AS THEORY, LITERATURE AS DANCE

RUTGERS UNIVERSITY PRESS
NEW BRUNSWICK, NEW JERSEY

BODIES

OF THE TEXT

Edited by

Ellen W. Goellner and

Jacqueline Shea Murphy

Library of Congress Cataloging-in-Publication Data

Bodies of the text : dance as theory, literature as dance / edited by
  Ellen W. Goellner and Jacqueline Shea Murphy.
      p.   cm.
    INcludes bibliographical references and index.
    ISBN 0-8135-2126-2 (cloth) — ISBN 0-8135-2127-0 (pbk.)
    1. Dance criticism. 2. Dancing—Philosophy. 3. Criticism.
  4. Dancing in literature. I. Goellner, Ellen W., 1956–
  II. Murphy, Jacqueline Shea, 1964–
  GV1600.B63   1994   94-14738
                                       CIP

British Cataloging-in-Publication information available

*In memory of my mother, Sarah, who knew
how good it is to dance
—E.W.G.*

*To my sister, Wendy—
my first dance partner
—J.S.M.*

Contents

DANCE IN THEORIES OF WRITING

READING WRITING ABOUT DANCE

Preface

This book grew out of a question we asked each other one hot afternoon, several summers ago, lying on our backs doing hip circles in a dance studio *Ellen leading, right leg up, open side, around* after five hours teaching in an intensive writing program. We were both writing dissertations for Ph.D.'s in literature and wondered, why is it *switch legs, left leg up, around, and reach* that no one in English departments ever talks about dance? We'd each encountered resistance—or at best bewilderment—from advisers, professors, and colleagues about taking dancing seriously, making our dance interests scholarly, thinking about dance with the literary critical-skills we had developed. We didn't get it *Jacqueline takes over, leg to the side, open out, and down* especially with all the discussion of gender, bodies, fluidity, performance, sexuality, popular culture, and multiculturalism animating literary studies *and the other leg up, out, down.* There was so much that dance seemed able to bring to literary studies *how about standing now, leg swings forward* and so much that literary studies could bring to studies of dance *other leg, and side.* We wondered *add the torso, lift, and circle backward* are we crazy? Is our interest *now, shifting, to the left* in dance *spinning out and breathing fully* unintellectual?

We have become convinced, in the years since we first asked each other these questions, that a direct consideration of dance *can* focus and enrich many of the structural and theoretical discussions taking place in literary studies. We have become equally convinced that learning to read dance as literary critics read texts—especially given dance's unstable meanings, its dense net of reference to other movements, and its complexity of structured reiterations and variations—can open new areas for dance scholars and writers. We designed this book to contribute to and foster dialogue between the fields of dance and literary studies; the book itself is a product of many dance-literary collaborations.

But how to explore? In which directions? In what ways? Putting together this volume, we sought essays that show some of what dance critics and literary critics have to teach each other, what they can usefully speak about, what scholarly questions they raise for each other. We looked for essays that not only address critical or theoretical issues beyond an individual dance or literary work, but also illuminate specific texts, dance and literary. Some of the essays here came to us through a conference call for papers; others we solicited from writers whose work has significantly advanced dance scholarship and from scholars who were asking smart, new questions about literature or dance; three are reprints of pieces we believe should be more widely available; several are parts of larger works-in-progress. The inclusion of work by assistant professors and graduate students testifies, we believe, to the relative newness of dance-literary scholarship. Our aim in bringing out this collection is not to provide an exhaustive or definitive work on the interconnections of dance and literature. We know that readers will find subjects missing from this volume: an essay on the Merce Cunningham–John Cage collaboration, for instance, or one on gothic narrative and Romantic ballet, or on Greek mythology in choreography by Martha Graham and by Mark Morris. We seek, with *Bodies of the Text*, to aid in opening dance and literary studies and to stimulate other scholars to address more fully questions that the volume's contributors raise.

Our goal in organizing the chapters was largely practical; it has been our impression that literary and dance scholars are often not sure *how* to make use in their own work of the other's theory, history, or criticism. We have, therefore, organized the essays methodologically, that is, into sections according to the ways in which they enact dialogues of dance and literature. The pieces in the first section consider dance *as text*, reading particular dances and dance in general for the theoretical/cultural/political concepts embedded (or embodied) in them. The next section shows ways that representations of dance *in* texts—fiction, drama, film—can be read and analyzed. Essays in the third section demonstrate how literary theorists have used dance as a vehicle for developing or explaining theories about writing.[1] Pieces in the final section look at analyses of dance for the ideas these writings display. Some of the essays collected here bridge methodological distinctions; our intention is not to insist upon distinct methodologies, but rather to let the essays demonstrate possible ways that scholars can fruitfully combine dance and literary interests.[2]

Many of the essays we have selected explore dance as a way of conceptualizing, reinforcing, or redressing political systems or situations. Barbara Browning's "Samba: The Body Articulate" examines how Brazilian samba, in its name, structure, and danced history, is typically described to romanticize and sexualize racial hybridization in Brazil, articulating a story of racial contact, conflict, and resistance behind that country's history of colonization. Jacqueline Shea Murphy's "Unrest and Uncle Tom: Bill T. Jones/Arnie Zane Dance Company's *Last Supper at Uncle Tom's Cabin/The Promised Land*" explores ways in which African American dance has historically been tied to the oppression of African Americans, and how a contemporary choreographer refigures this by redancing the racist oppression in Harriet Beecher Stowe's 1851 novel. J. Ellen Gainor's "'A World without Collisions': Ballroom Dance in Athol Fugard's '*MASTER HAROLD*' . . . *and the boys*" analyzes black characters' complicated relationship to and investment in European-style ballroom dance in the 1982 play and argues

Fugard's analysis of dance to be a call for racial bonding antithetical to South Africa's apartheid system. In the various political ramifications of the dancing they discuss, these pieces all address the connections between the construction of racial identity and political position.

Through many of this volume's chapters runs a concern with ways that dance can illuminate understandings of femininity, masculinity, and sexuality. In "Choreographies," the exchange between Jacques Derrida and Christie V. McDonald, Derrida returns repeatedly to dance as a way of figuring the question of what constitutes "the feminine," using dance to present ideas of unstable gender and sexual identity when there is no need to remain in/as one place or one woman. Elizabeth Dempster's "Women Writing the Body: Let's Watch a Little How She Dances" is a provocative reading of how cultural gender markings can be read on Western dancing bodies, and in concert dance traditions, over the past century. In "Douglas Fairbanks: Thief of the Ballets Russes," Gaylyn Studlar looks at the inscription of masculinity in the 1924 film *The Thief of Bagdad* and argues that Fairbanks attempted to redefine Hollywood's iconography of the American Man by borrowing movement and costume from Serge Diaghilev's Ballets Russes. Michael Moon, in "Flaming Closets," departs also from the Ballets Russes to explore the cultural representations of (homo)sexuality—and their cultural impacts—through 1910 ballets and 1963 films. Specifically, he considers the relation of various *Schéhérazade* performances to the construction of gay male subjectivity. Both Studlar's and Moon's chapters are illuminating studies of artists' attempts to remake sexuality.

Other essays offer dance as a possible model for a nonessentialist valorization of the body; to their authors, dance presents a gendered identity that is grounded in a particular, biological dancing body—carrying clear signs of sexual difference—and at the same time constructed through performance. These dances work over, play with, and exceed any notion of gender as a stable biological category. Ann Cooper Albright's "Incalculable Choreographies: The Dance Practice of Marie Chouinard" offers this analysis in her reading of the text written by and on the dancing body of Canadian performer/choreographer Chouinard. Cooper Albright filters her reading of Chouinard's performances through writings by Derrida and Hélène Cixous, discussing how these theorists turn to language of movement in their discussions of sexual difference and identity. Their use of dance, in simultaneously embodying and exploding gendered images of the body, counters arguments that deconstructionists ignore the materiality of bodies and that French feminists focus too readily on "biological" or "essentialist" bodily characteristics. Shea Murphy takes up similar lines of discussion in her analysis of sexual and racial identity in Bill T. Jones's *Last Supper* and of how that dance stages and confronts theoretical and literal limitations of bodies in the 1990s. Felicia McCarren's reading of Loie Fuller's dancing body, in "Stéphane Mallarmé, Loie Fuller, and the Theater of Femininity," considers the female body's gender identity as defined through performance. Unlike the dandy ballet-goer, whose fetishistic gaze sees the female dancing body as lacking, Mallarmé understands the dancer's femininity in rhythmic rather than visual terms. McCarren, Dempster, and Derrida all touch on the historical relation between dance and the body of the female hysteric.

McCarren's and Derrida's chapters take part in another discussion—the most explicitly theoretical—which recurs: the relationship between dancing bodies and theories of writing. Susan Foster's "Textual Evidences" reads Claude François Menestrier's (1682) and Louis de Cahusac's (1754) tracts on dance and compares the way each understands bodies to carry meaning; in doing this, Foster identifies a historical period in which written meaning was differentiated from bodily meaning, and in which, subsequently, bodies were divorced from their capacities to theorize. The schism Foster identifies becomes the implicit topic of other chapters in this volume, which discuss how to reconnect the ways writing and the ways dancing bodies mean. McCarren's linking of Mallarmé's poetics and Fuller's dancing enacts this bridging, as does Derrida's representation of the parallels between dance, which is always in a state of simultaneously tracing and deferring its own significance, and writing. Mark Franko engages Foster, McCarren, and Derrida in his discussion of Mallarmé's instrumentality in positioning dance relative to literature. In "Mimique," Franko looks at how dance becomes a model for forms of literary modernism—writing imagined as mobile, indeterminate, multiple. He compares Derrida's writing on Mallarmé with two recent books on performance in Mallarmé, which alternately show how literature can embody dance and how dance can point the way to a performative reading and writing. Ellen Goellner extends this discussion in "Force and Form in Faulkner's *Light in August*," a study of the narrative dynamics of Faulkner's novel. Rather than apply narrative theory to dance, Goellner applies dance to narrative theory and counters the psychoanalytic paradigms dominating narrative studies today, arguing that dance elements provide a more illuminating analogy for Faulkner's narrative design and for understanding the shifting racial and sexual bodily tensions in his novel. Goellner's treatment of narrative structure finds connection with Browning's reading of the story that the samba's structure tells.

Dance and literature are conventionally regarded by their critics as arts that may share metaphorical connections but that are fundamentally remote from each other. We'll see. This collection not only crosses the boundaries between dance and literature but, for its duration, dissolves those boundaries to create an undivided space wherein the respective instabilities and powers of written words and dancing bodies can mingle: neither is offstage, neglected, unnecessary. What follows is a dual articulation of literature and dance, one that releases into meaning both written language and a dancing body's heft and weave.

NOTES

1. Using dance to understand writing and reading is common in critical and theoretical works, although not all literary critics who make a dance/writing or dance/reading analogy are interested in investigating that connection. To cite two recent examples: Françoise Meltzer, *Salome and the Dance of Writing: Portraits of Mimesis in Literature* (Chicago: University of Chicago Press, 1987); and Marjorie Perloff, *The Dance of the Intellect: Studies in the Poetry of the Pound Tradition* (New York: Cambridge University Press, 1985). Perloff explains in her preface her title's origin in Ezra Pound's linking of "dance" with "intellect." Writing about a new strain in contemporary poetry which emphasizes "sound structures and verbal play" and "the denial of the unitary, authoritative ego" in the speaking subject, Pound coined the term *logopoeia* and defined it as "'the dance of the intellect among words'" (x).

2. Two themes won't be found in the essays that follow, although they are perhaps the most common literary treatments of dance we came across. One is a reading of social dance and the dancing couple in literary works—for example, in Philip Sidney, Shakespeare, or Jane Austen—as the simple vertical expression of a horizontal desire. The other is the critical unpuzzling of W. B. Yeats's famous question, "How can we know the dancer from the dance?" Not all has been said about them that might be said, but they are subjects if not already familiar to, then easily imagined by, critical readers.

Acknowledgments

We are grateful to the dance scholars who generously shared their ideas, welcomed us at their conferences, offered criticism and advice on this project, and whose dance writings paved the way for this volume, especially Joan Acocella, Sally Banes, Crystelle Bond, Selma Jeanne Cohen, Susan L. Foster, Elizabeth Kendall, Susan Manning, Randy Martin, and Nicole Plett.

Thanks, too, to the scholars and friends who read and commented on various parts of the manuscript, and who brought relevant materials to our attention, especially Alice Bullard, Bruce Burgett, Michael Cadden, Lauren Muller, Raphael Shargel, René Shepperd, Simon Stern, and Hertha Wong. We are particularly indebted to Doug Kincade for asking hard questions about the relations between dance and literature, for his astute editing, and for his unflagging support of this project.

We also thank: Beth Harrison and Princeton University's Department of English, the Princeton University Writing Program, and Herman and Lois Dinkin all for providing office space and amenities; Ze'eva Cohen for her introductions and her always-open dance studio; Frank Conley, and Matt Kursh for hi-tech help; Diana Fuss, who helped us make some of our early research public; Clay Kinchen Smith for his enthusiasm and for sharing his research; and John Wilkins for his introduction to the Bay Area dance scene.

For encouragement offered at crucial points, our special thanks to Kenny Dinkin, Cindy Franklin, Tom Hoopes, Toni Morrison, Kirsten Oeste, Kate Reed, Alice St. Claire, Kim Sargent, Cindy Schrager, Marvina White, and Andie Yellott.

We also thank our editor Leslie Mitchner for her faith in us, her helpful oversight, and her patience and good humor; Marilyn Campbell and our copyeditor, Kathyrn Gohl, for refining the manuscript; and our contributors, whose research and hard work heartened us to see this project through.

BODIES OF THE TEXT

Introduction: Movement Movements

Ellen W. Goellner
and Jacqueline Shea Murphy

In the early 1980s, various lines of literary criticism began moving into areas that intersected with dance: literary critics had adopted deconstructionist approaches that understood meaning and identity to be, as they are in dance, always in flux or in motion, and French feminist notions of *écriture féminine* had based an understanding of writing on the rhythms and responses of a heralded female body.[1] As the decade progressed, representations and understandings of "the body"—the medium of dance—became the focus of increased attention in literary and cultural studies. New Historicists turned to representations of the body in various historical epochs as a way of interpreting both bodies and texts.[2] Poststructuralist questionings of categories such as "race" and "gender" forced reconsiderations of the "biological" meanings assigned to bodies—questionings that performing, dancing bodies could be seen both to inhabit and refute.[3] Increased awareness of how masculinity, femininity, and sexuality are embodied in texts focused attention on questions with which concert dance has been associated. Increased attention to multicultural and anthropological approaches in literary studies affirmed the importance of questioning the assumption that "texts" must be written and of studying oral and performed literatures.[4] The growth of film and cultural studies demonstrated that visual, temporal, nonwritten "texts," such as dance, could provide material for astute critical analyses of, for example, issues of gender and identification, visuality, and the gaze;[5] renewed interest in narrative theory, especially considerations of textual dynamics and of the inscription of performance elements in written narrative, likewise provided an opening for a consideration of dance structures.[6] By the 1990s, dance, offering a fresh and relevant perspective to scholars outside the field of dance, could enliven discussions of the academy's new historicisms, poststructuralisms, gender and queer theories, multiculturalisms, film and performance studies, and popular culture studies.

Dance scholarship had also been developing during this time. Compared with literary studies, however, the field of dance studies was virtually brand-new. Dance studies in the United States did not begin to cohere as a discipline until the 1960s and 1970s; only in the last fifteen years or so have dance scholars joined the academy in significant numbers, teaching history, criticism, and theory, and only with the current generation of dance writers has scholarly dance criticism begun to look, feel, and behave like other academic writing.[7] If, as we believed, considerations of dance could further literary studies, it quickly became apparent that dance scholarship, struggling to find a theoretical language of its own, could benefit from the critical and theoretical rigor that literary studies had developed.[8] For most of its life, the field of dance studies had largely been divided in its research methodologies between history, movement analysis, anthropology, and aesthetics. A work that broke from these approaches was Susan Foster's *Reading Dancing*.[9] This 1986 study of the poetics of dance and the semiotics of the meaning-generating and meaning-subverting forces in choreographic works demonstrated the congeniality of Roland Barthes's physical and dynamic concept of textuality to dance theory and analysis. Foster showed how dance, like the literary text, goes down in "language."

For close watchers and describers of dance in search of theory and methodology, literary studies theorists who have labored after the new aesthetic concepts of play, desire, power, tension, contest, genealogy, intertext, and margin-and-center offer an already rich vocabulary. Because literary analysis has long been busy reflexively questioning its own rhetoric and critical strategies, it can aid dance critics in further examining the nature and function of their many narratives about dance—histories, reconstructions, concert reviews, and other descriptive accounts of what dance happened, might have happened, or might yet happen. Narrative theory, in its structurally descriptive mode, can provide dance scholars with finely tuned descriptions of dance's representational qualities: its mimicry of lived movements; its notable "figures"; its retrospectives and onrushings; its pace, measure, points of view. The tools of narrative theory could help, for example, in the analysis of plotted dances such as Marius Petipa's *Sleeping Beauty* or Martha Graham's *Cave of the Heart*, or in the wholly different use of verbal narrative in works such as Pina Bausch's *Palermo Palermo* or Mark Morris's verbal-movement punning in *Dido and Aeneas*.

The entrance of cultural studies critics into literary arenas of debate offers yet another critical framework for dance scholars and raises new questions for scholarly investigation.[10] Some of these critics have called attention to the limited cultural writings about concert dance in general and American dance in particular.[11] Until recently, interpretive readings of the male dancing body or of "exotic" dance in American popular culture[12]—for example, studies of the transformation and commodification of the Hawaiian hula or of belly dancing—and critiques of normative readings of classical and Romantic ballets have been slow to emerge, as have critical accounts of the notions of "high" and "low" (or "popular") dance forms as they are practiced, gendered, raced, funded, marketed, consumed, and reviewed.[13] Writings about other arts are already heading this way: for instance, in music, with pioneering works such as Jacques Attali's *Noise*, Susan McClary's *Feminine Endings*, Wayne Koestenbaum's *The Queen's Throat*, and Tricia Rose's *Black Noise*; and in art history with such works as the ambitious multi-volume *Image of the Black in Western Art* and Linda Nochlin's *Women, Art, and Power and Other Essays* (including her seminal 1971 essay, "Why Have There Been No Great Women Artists?").[14] The burgeoning of cultural studies brings dance into contact with other fields that have intersected with literary studies for some time, particularly, gender and women's studies, but also American studies, film studies, African American studies, and ethnic studies.

That dance studies might need to catch up with critical developments in other humanities fields should not surprise. Long viewed as unintellectual, intuitive, and uncritically expressive, dance did not easily emerge as a scholarly discipline within the text-centered university, in part because of how dance was introduced to university curricula. Dance studies entered the academy, if not through the back door, then through a side door—a gym door, to be precise. Modern dance first appeared in colleges and universities in the United States in physical education departments, beginning with Margaret H'Doubler's efforts at the University of Wisconsin, which offered the first dance major in 1926, and with Sarah Lawrence College, where dance was offered as a course of study beginning in 1926, when the college opened. Modern dance as practiced within the academy, in accordance with the educational reform ideals of John Dewey and his followers, filtered from Wisconsin to P.E. departments at other schools. The opening of the Bennington School of Dance at Bennington College in the summer of 1934 focused and cemented the alliance of dance and education, the school becoming a major institution and advocate in the development of modern dance in the United States. Other colleges, particularly women's colleges, continued to develop and promote modern dance programs, although for decades dance would remain in their P.E. departments. Tours of these colleges by visiting dance groups and soloists in the 1930s were called—with little affection—the "gymnasium circuit." Guest dancers performed on the sprung floors of the college gymnasiums before student audiences seated in bleachers. Informal as they were, these events, occurring on the margins of both the academic and the concert dance worlds, nurtured collaboration, dedication, and artistic and imaginative flexibility; their very marginality gave venue to innovative encounters between artists and audiences.

Even smaller matters of institutional structuring played a role in effecting dance's second-class membership in the academy. Many general reference rooms in college and university libraries, for instance, had no dance holdings at all, although they carried reference works for art history, music, theater, and film studies. Nor was it uncommon for the scholarly dance books that libraries did own to be cataloged and shelved with books on sports and physical education or under "recreation" along with books on chess and power-boating.

Thus the institutional sanction of dance studies, the acceptance of it as an academic discipline in its own right, is a relatively recent and still developing phenomenon. The "dance boom" in the late sixties and early seventies saw some of the institutional obstacles to dance scholarship begin to come down, especially as dance programs began to engineer their separation from P.E. departments.[15] The history of dance at Wesleyan University—now an important center for dance and dance studies—provides a case in point: although Wesleyan offered a dance concentration in 1971 and a dance major in 1976, a full-fledged dance department was not instituted until 1986, and it did not receive full funding from the university until 1991. The development of graduate programs specifically in dance writing, history, theory, and criticism (as distinct from dance performance or dance education) has been even more recent. The University of Chicago sponsored an NEH-funded series of graduate seminars in dance history and criticism for three summers beginning in 1974; many students who attended the seminars, run by Selma Jeanne Cohen, went on to build dance studies programs across the country. York University in Toronto offered a master's degree in dance history and criticism in 1976, and the Performance Studies Department at New York University's Tisch School of the Arts has offered a Ph.D. with a concentration in dance since the early 1980s.[16] The first Ph.D. program in dance history and theory was finally approved in 1993, at the University of California, Riverside.[17]

Even though dance studies successfully established an institutional grounding—however tentative—outside P.E. departments, scholarly prejudices against theoretical considerations of dance continued to hinder development of the field. Writing about dance was sometimes seen as deauthenticating, as though analyzing it or theorizing about it would detract from the evanescent meaning of the movement. More frequently, dance history, theory, and criticism were simply assumed not to require much rigor and were left to studio instructors with little formal scholarly training or research and writing experience. Behind these prejudices, in large part, was dance's grounding in physical bodies and in the now-familiar conceptions about and distrust of the body and bodily practices held by Western scholars working in a logocentric tradition. (This despite the common experience that the *physical* act of writing articulates, that is, gives distinct bodily form to, ideas.) As feminist philosopher and social theorist Iris Marion Young explains, "Dualism so structures our thinking that the appearance of the term 'body' seems typically to distinguish itself from mind, consciousness, imagination, etc. The body is a person's 'physical' aspect, the biological, the material complex chemical and mechanical processes. . . . The body is meaningless and deterministic."[18] The gendering of this binary—in which the "feminine" and irrational body is set against the loftier "masculine" mind—has further marginalized dance as a legitimate subject of philosophical and critical inquiry. As both a body-centered art and a field of critical inquiry, dance has been marked as "feminine" and "homosexual" and easily dismissed.[19] (Excluding access to "feminine" and "sexualized" studies—in addition to excluding actual women—has been, of course, a common university strategy from its earliest days; much of the arts curriculum has at one time or another been excluded, often on such grounds.) Along with many dance scholars, however, we see dance bridging the separation between mind and body; indeed, the field of dance studies today seems—somewhat paradoxically, perhaps—uniquely capable of challenging the dichotomy that historically privileges verbal, particularly written, language over bodily or kinesthetic knowledge and language.[20]

Interesting theoretical and practical issues arise when the ephemerality of dance gets caught up in the "permanence" of the written word. That dance cannot be frozen, held, stilled is its very essence. Dance writers are thus, even more than literary scholars, always confronted with the great difficulty of reducing the realities of motion to verbal formulas. As such, the language of dance criticism may help literary critics discover fresh ways to describe flux: narrative movements, interpretive gestalt shifts, and more. Dance's ephemerality as an art form also means that a choreographed or improvised work vanishes as soon as it is performed. The preservation of choreographed works has for centuries involved elaborate systems of notating body effort and shape, dance steps, and floor patterns and has relied heavily on the personal transmission of dances from generation to generation—a kind of oral-and-bodily tradition. The development of video and film technologies affords a new tool in the preservation and reconstruction of dances and can provide a fairly accurate and permanent visual record of specific dance performances.[21] In making specific works and performances available to students and scholars, video has been a pedagogical boon to dance studies, particularly in the development and spread of dance history and criticism courses. Including the ephemerality of dance in contemporary critical debates could help scholars working outside the field of dance examine long-held assumptions about the permanence of art and the cultural significance of works recited, sung, danced, or otherwise performed.

The political climate in the United States has also played a role in both fostering and curtailing the critical development of dance studies. The "dance boom" of the 1960s and 1970s, marked on one end by the 1965 establishment of the National Endowment for the Arts and on the other by the steep funding cuts for that organization in the 1980s, enabled an expansion nationally of professional dance companies—which in turn significantly increased audiences for concert dance—and triggered a jump in the amount of space alotted in newspapers and magazines for dance performance announcements and reviews.[22] For these reasons, much of the best writing on dance was not being produced by dance instructors in colleges and universities; American dance writing matured largely as journalism.

Dance criticism was undertaken by journalist-critics writing regularly for dailies, weeklies, and magazines, beginning with John Martin, dance critic and editor for the *New York Times* from 1927 to 1962. An early and powerful advocate of modern dance, Martin lectured and wrote several books on dance, as well as writing dance reviews in his regular column.[23] Edwin Denby's writings, revered by the journalist-critics who began their careers in the sixties and seventies, offer stunning descriptions of dancing bodies and their effects on the viewer. A poet and former dancer-choreographer, he began as a writer for *Modern Music,* then became a daily dance critic at the *New York Herald Tribune* during World War II when Walter Terry was drafted. Preferring to write longer essays, Denby left his position at the *Tribune* after the war, but continued to write about dance for a variety of publications through the early 1960s. A strong supporter of both ballet and modern dance, Denby was posthumously awarded the 1987 National Book Critics Circle Award for his dance criticism.[24]

With the dance boom in the 1960s, a new generation of dance critics emerged. Some shifted the attention of dance criticism toward the avant-garde: Jill Johnston of the *Village Voice,* a critic committed to promoting the avant-garde performances and happenings at the Judson Dance Theater in the 1960s, developed a style wholly different from Denby's lyrical and analytic description. Providing a key moment in the history of dance criticism, the Judson performances—often collaborations of dancers, visual artists, and musicians, and their engaged art-world audiences—shaped critical practices by demanding new interpretive strategies.[25] Arlene Croce, whose admiration for George Balanchine's work brought her to dance criticism, began as a film critic. Determined to write about dance, Croce founded *Ballet Review* in the 1960s, galvanizing journalist-critics on ballet. A protegée of Pauline Kael, film critic for the *New Yorker,* Croce became dance critic for that magazine in 1973. In her dance reviews, she shares with Denby a concern for describing the structure, theme, style, and rhythm of a choreographed work, and she regularly includes discussion of a dance's relationship to earlier works or the influences on it of other art forms.

Other leading journalist-critics today, such as Deborah Jowitt (writing for the *Village Voice*) and Marcia B. Siegel (currently writing for the *Hudson Review*), have continued the strong formalist concerns of Denby and Croce while extending the range of the dance critic's review. Intelligent, insightful critics of ballet, modern dance, postmodern dance, and today's avant-garde performances, Jowitt and Siegel produce verbal records of what happens onstage; Siegel in particular writes as a reporter and teacher for her dance audiences, with little interest in issuing critical verdicts. Jowitt and Siegel are both important to the development of American dance writing not only for their eloquent dance reviews but also for the many dance writers inside and outside the academy they have influenced and mentored; both helped launch the Dance Critics Association in the mid-1970s and helped establish DCA's annual critics workshop.[26]

Understandably, the scholarly and theoretical investigations informing literary studies have remained beyond the scope and mission of journalistic dance writing, which concerns itself mainly with description, interpretation, and evaluation. But the distinction between scholar-critics and journalist-critics of dance is more blurred today than is the distinction between literary scholar-critics and book reviewers. Between dance journalist-critics and scholars exist a mutual respect and reciprocity not usually found among literary critics. Dance scholars routinely cite the writings of their journalist colleagues, and many writers from both groups belong to the same professional organizations.

Some of the obstacles to a scholarly exchange between dance and literary critics have been erected by dance writers, journalistic and scholarly, wary of uncritically adopting literary theory models. There is, of course, no uniform understanding of "the body" among those who write about dance, much less among writers and choreographers; some writers as well as some choreographers view academic analysis as overly invested in the mind at the expense of the body. Others worry that dance studies, if overly theorized, could lose sight of its central subjects—dancing bodies and the choreographed text—especially when concern exists, even among literary scholars, that the production of theory has become its own politico-philosophical industry, one quite divorced from the study of specific works of literature. Of perhaps greatest concern, however, are "writings by scholars in other fields," dance historian Selma Jeanne Cohen explains, "who have not bothered to learn enough about dance."[27] These hesitations by dance writers insist that any "theory" of dance grapple with the meaning in physical, present, dancing bodies. They add also to general concerns about the practical and political effects of exalting theory in academic studies—about whom such privileging shuts out and what it can whitewash or ignore—and they challenge literary theorists to continue questioning their own critical assumptions.

If Western cultural views of the body provide a broad philosophical and cultural context for understanding the marginal place of dance in the academy, practical impediments within the university continue to influence the development of dance studies. Because of the continued marginality of dance studies and the dearth of dance faculty positions at many colleges and universities, dance scholars often work and publish outside the academy.[28] Those scholars who are members of dance faculties are frequently expected to provide studio training (like that found in conservatories) as well as teach dance history, theory, and criticism, an expectation not usually found in other humanities fields. (This is comparable to requiring a Strindberg scholar to teach introductory acting or set design, or a scholar of Renaissance art to teach figure drawing or etching.)[29] Such institutional expectations underscore ways that dance studies confounds academic separation between theory and practice.

Dance faculty interested in research frequently struggle to obtain time and funding that faculty in other departments often take for granted, and scholars who write about dance from nondance departments—literature, theater, philosophy, anthropology—are spread throughout a university or among disparate professional organizations and have no ready rubric for communication. Nevertheless, the important role that cross-disciplinary programs and consortia have played in other newly formed fields, such as cultural studies or film studies—and even more so in identity-based fields such as African American studies and women's studies—testifies to the importance of institutional sanction to the development of an emerging field of study.[30] That dance studies can and does cut across many academic fields and interests challenges departmental boundaries for inter-disciplinary dialogue. Moreover, although in many instances the obstacles out-lined above have hindered the development of dance studies, institutional resistance has also sparked scholarly innovation in the field and created a strong mentoring system at the graduate level.

Various signs point to dance studies truly coming into its own as an inter-disciplinary yet autonomous field of inquiry. Scholarly presses, for instance, cru-cial to the development of any academic field, have shown a growing interest in dance scholarship.[31] Because mainstream periodicals, however high or original the quality of the journalistic work they produce, have limited sway in the aca-demic world of refereed journals, exams, and canonical structures of codified knowledge, scholarly publishing opportunities are particularly important to dance writers.[32] Academic journals, in contrast to scholarly presses, seek out and publish few articles on dance.[33] As one result of this state of affairs, humanities scholars outside dance are generally not familiar with dance studies publications (or conferences) and vice versa; this is particularly clear in the recent outpouring of work on hip-hop dance.[34]

But cross-disciplinary, literary-dance investigations are underway. For ex-ample, the 1994 annual meeting of the American Studies Association included a full session, organized by Susan Manning, on "Revisionary Narratives of Ameri-can Dance." In his discussion of the body in action and the modern novelistic tradition, *Body Work: Objects of Desire in Modern Narrative* (1993), Peter Brooks recognizes the significance of dance to narrative theory in general and its importance to studies of modernist literary expression in particular. Brooks looks only briefly at E.T.A. Hoffmann's *Der Sandmann* and Arthur Saint-Léon and Léo Delibes's ballet *Coppélia;* he sketches the engagement of such literary fig-ures as Théophile Gautier, Honoré de Balzac, Stéphane Mallarmé, and W. B. Yeats with Romantic ballet or the performances of Loïe Fuller and La Cornalba. However, even this attention to concert dance by a leading theorist shows dance capable of literary-critical consideration alongside other complex and valued cul-tural productions.

In dance studies, professional organizations for scholars and critics founded over the past few decades have begun to pose critical and theoretical topics for conferences, sometimes joining literature, history, or other humanities depart-ments to treat issues of mutual interest.[35] Various dance scholars—some of whose work appears in this volume—have begun to publish works that take on the critical problems raised by literary and culture theory. For instance, several recent books engage in reading choreographic texts and dance practices as things-in-relation rather than as things-in-themselves. These groundbreaking works seem to be ushering in a new era of dance writing: Lynn Garafola's *Dia-ghilev's Ballets Russes* (1989); Randy Martin's *Performance as Political Act: The Embodied Self* (1990); Cynthia Novak's *Sharing the Dance: Contact Impro-*

visation and American Culture (1990); Mark Franko's *Dance as Text: Ideologies of the Baroque Body* (1993); Susan Manning's *Ecstasy and the Demon: Feminism and Nationalism in the Dances of Mary Wigman* (1993); and Sally Banes's *Greenwich Village 1963: Avant-Garde Performance and the Effervescent Body* (1993).[36] Younger dance writers have also begun to apply questions frequently raised by literary critics to dance in illuminating ways: Leslie Satin, for example, uses recent theory on autobiography to study the representation of self in works by contemporary female choreographers, and Ann Daly has written some of the earliest and best feminist critiques of ballet.[37] With an increased recognition among dance scholars that race, gender, class, sexuality, and national association enter into the formal making of concert as well as popular dance, there has been a concomitant realization that these can underlie not only a dance's themes, character, and subjects but its very language of movement.

The way participants in a recent forum on George Balanchine sidestepped issues of race dramatized both the importance of these lines of inquiry and the limitations they still face in the field of dance studies. In connection with the New York City Ballet's eight-week 1992–1993 retrospective of Balanchine's ballets, the Dance Collection of the New York Public Library for the Performing Arts held a series of symposia on Balanchine and his work. One of these, "Rethinking the Balanchine Legacy: Balanchine, Jazz, and Popular Dance," promised to consider the influence of, among others, black dance forms on Balanchine's work.[38] It also provided a moment when literary theory could help ask an important question in the critical "rethinking" of Balanchine's work: What, exactly, do black dancing bodies signify in the choreographic imagination of one of the twentieth century's major dance figures? Sally Banes's keynote paper, "Balanchine and African American Dance," set out this project, providing biographical information on Balanchine's contact with popular African American dances of the 1910s and 1920s and with African Caribbean dance, through contact with black dancers, most notably Katherine Dunham. Banes also described Balanchine's enthusiasm for things American, including popular American dance, and Balanchine's original vision of an American dance company, which comprised four each of black and white women, and black and white men.[39]

Virtually all the presentations and discussion that followed Banes's, however, were delicately unhinged from the project of "rethinking" Balanchine's work in light of his choreographic encounters with African American and Caribbean dance forms. The reluctance of program participants to discuss the racially inflected movement in Balanchine dances produced the nagging suspicion that silence on this topic was part of a larger worry that any explicit talk of race in connection with ballet, with the choreography of Balanchine, even in connection with traditional modern dance, might diminish the standing, or our appreciation, of those dance forms. What was clear that day, however, was that the reluctance to speak of a black presence in Balanchine's work comes at a high cost; that this sort of critical blindness forecloses debate and precludes valuable insight, impoverishing our understanding of Balanchine's choreography. Later, after the day's presentations, writer and critic Toni Morrison's arguments about noticing came to mind. According to Morrison, one source of critical blindness in regard to matters of race is that "the habit of ignoring race is understood to be a graceful, even generous, liberal gesture," and in this climate of critical discourse, "silence and evasion have historically ruled."[40] Morrison observes in closing her book *Playing in the Dark* that "all of us, readers and writers, are bereft when criticism remains too polite or too fearful to notice a disrupting darkness before its eyes" (91).

In regard to a critical rethinking of Balanchine's legacy, however, "noticing" is exactly what is needed: noticing the racially inflected movement in his dances; noticing that Balanchine's early vision of a racially defined American dance company was never realized (why not?) and that his "leotard dances," as they are sometimes called (regarded by many as among his most brilliant), are also called the "black and white" dances.[41] And we must go from all this noticing to asking how that racially inflected movement, borrowed from a decidedly "other"—that is, nonballetic—dance form, works in a Balanchine dance, how incorporation of that movement helped shape Balanchine's creation of an American dance, or how and why Balanchine transformed movements from the popular black dance idiom in the particular ways he did.[42]

Maurice Merleau-Ponty countered the mind-body binary that structures so much Western thinking by locating consciousness in the body.[43] In so doing, he opened a way for us to understand bodies as capable of generating ideas in structures of movement as well as in habitual bodily being. For too long within the academy, bodies have been static metaphors for unknown and mysterious forces and have been allowed only to signify hidden desires, irrational impulses, the unconscious.[44] Reclaiming the body-subject, exploring the body's discursive meaning—its "perceptions, action, and responses that are not linguistically constituted" (Young 12–13)—is, in part, the work of dance studies. Thinking bodies. Dancing bodies. All require an exploration of the body's nonverbal expression to the verbal world, academic and otherwise, which it also inhabits.

NOTES ⎯ ⎯ ⎯ ⎯ ⎯ ⎯ ⎯

We are indebted to Selma Jeanne Cohen, Susan L. Foster, Elizabeth Kendall, Susan Manning, Gay Morris, and Nicole Plett, all of whom were generous with their time and knowledge in responding to versions of the introduction. They brought to our attention material we would have otherwise missed, and they caught and corrected many of our factual errors. For their editorial suggestions, we thank Cindy Franklin, and, especially, Doug Kincade and Barbara Lamb for the pains they have taken to improve the style of this essay. Errors that remain are our responsibility alone.

1. For a discussion of French feminism, see Ann Cooper Albright's analysis in this volume of Hélène Cixous's writing. See also Diana Fuss, *Essentially Speaking: Feminism, Nature and Difference* (New York: Routledge, 1989); and Ann Rosalind Jones, "Writing the Body: Toward an Understanding of *L'Ecriture Feminine*," in *The New Feminist Criticism: Essays on Women, Literature, and Theory*, ed. Elaine Showalter (New York: Pantheon Books, 1985), 361–377.

2. For general introductions to New Historical methods see H. Aram Veeser, ed., *The New Historicism* (New York: Routledge, 1989); and Lynn Hunt, ed., *The New Cultural History* (Berkeley: University of California Press, 1989).

3. For example, see Eve Kosofsky Sedgwick, *Between Men: English Literature and Male Homosocial Desire* (New York: Columbia University Press, 1985); Henry Louis Gates, ed., *"Race," Writing, and Difference* (Chicago: University of Chicago Press, 1986); and Judith Butler, *Gender Trouble: Feminism and the Subversion of Identity* (New York: Routledge, 1990).

4. For two examples, see Trinh T. Minh-ha, *Woman, Native, Other: Writing Postcoloniality and Feminism* (Bloomington: Indiana University Press, 1989); and Mary Margaret Steedly, *Hanging without a Rope: Narrative Experience in Colonial and Postcolonial Karoland* (Princeton: Princeton University Press, 1993). See also Walter Ong, *Orality and Literacy: The Technologizing of the Word* (New York: Methuen, 1982).

5. Laura Mulvey, *Visual and Other Pleasures* (Bloomington: Indiana University Press, 1981), and Kaja Silverman, *The Acoustic Mirror: The Female Voice in Psychoanalysis and Cinema* (Bloomington: Indiana University Press, 1988), are two of the many recent works that discuss these issues.

6. See Seymour Chatman, *Story and Discourse: Narrative Structure in Fiction and Film* (Ithaca, N.Y.: Cornell University Press, 1978); W. J. T. Mitchell, ed., *On Narrative* (Chicago: University of Chicago Press, 1981); and Peter Brooks, *Reading for the Plot: Design and Intention in Narrative* (New York: Random House, 1985).

7. A pioneering academic discussion on the aesthetics of dance, for example, is Selma Jeanne Cohen, *Next Week, Swan Lake: Reflections on Dance and Dancers* (Middletown, Conn.: Wesleyan University Press, 1982). In this brief book, Cohen considers what and how dance represents, the meaning of style, the significance of movement. Writing after Cohen, Francis Sparshott attempts a more taxonomic consideration of the art of dance, in *Off the Ground: First Steps to a Philosophical Consideration of Dance* (Princeton: Princeton University Press, 1988).

8. For a similar assessment of the state of dance scholarship by a dance writer, see the opening pages of Jane Desmond, "Dancing Out the Difference: Cultural Imperialism and Ruth St. Denis's 'Radha' of 1906," *Signs: Journal of Women in Culture and Society* 17.1 (1991): 28–49. The Society of Dance History Scholars' 1994 national conference, "Retooling the Discipline: Research and Teaching Strategies for the Twenty-First Century," included panels on literary theory applied to historical dance, gender studies and dance history, and expanding methodological perspectives in dance studies (February 10–13, Brigham Young University, Provo, Utah).

9.   Susan L. Foster, *Reading Dancing: Bodies and Subjects in Contemporary Dance* (Berkeley: University of California Press, 1986).

10.   For brief and insightful discussions of the use of culture for the study of literature, see Vincent B. Leitch, "Cultural Studies," in *The Johns Hopkins Guide to Literary Theory and Criticism*, ed. Michael Groden and Martin Kreiswirth (Baltimore: Johns Hopkins University Press, 1994), 176–182; and Stephen Greenblatt, "Culture," in *Critical Terms for Literary Study*, ed. Frank Lentricchia and Thomas McLaughlin (Chicago: University of Chicago Press, 1990), 225–232.

11.   For example, Sue-Ellen Case (English, University of California, Riverside), Wahneema Lubiano (English, Princeton University), Susan Manning (English, Northwestern University), Randy Martin (Sociology, Pratt Institute), Patricia Rose (American Studies, Rutgers University), and Andrew Ross (American Studies, New York University).

12.   For recent work on the male dancing body, see Michael Moon's and Gaylyn Studlar's chapters in this volume; Susan L. Foster, "That Frightful Danseuse of the Male Sex," typescript; Mark Franko, "Where He Danced: Cocteau's Barbette and Ohno's 'Water Lilies,'" *PMLA* 107.3 (May 1992): 594–607.

For recent work on "exotic" dance forms, see Desmond 28–49; Aeko Sereno, "Images of the Hula Dancer and 'Hula Girl': 1778–1960," *Dissertation Abstract International* 52 (1990): 0580A; Deborah Jowitt, "Sphinxes, Slaves, and Goddesses," in *Time and the Dancing Image* (Berkeley: University of California Press, 1988), 103–147; Wendy Buonaventura, *Belly Dancing: The Serpent and the Sphinx* (London: Virago Press, 1983).

13.   An interesting early work problematizing ballet is Joann Kealiinohomoku, "An Anthropologist Looks at Ballet as a Form of Ethnic Dance," in *What Is Dance?* ed. Roger Copeland and Marshall Cohen (New York: Oxford University Press, 1983), 533–549. Recent work by June Vail also raises important questions about the "high" and "low" status of dance forms; see, for example, Vail, "Watching American Critics Watch World Dance," in *Looking Out: Perspectives on Dance and Criticism in a Multicultural World*, ed. David Gere, Lewis Segal, Patrice Koelsch, and Elizabeth Zimmer (forthcoming).

Elizabeth Kendall's *Where She Danced: The Birth of American Art-Dance* (Berkeley: University of California Press, 1979) was among the first efforts to contextualize the development of dance—in this case, of American modern dance—within American culture. Jowitt's *Time and the Dancing Image*, an iconographic history of ballet and modern dance, finds cultural meaning in Western concert dance by contextualizing the development of its key images.

14. Jacques Attali, *Noise*, trans. Brian Massumi (Minneapolis: University of Minnesota Press, 1985); Susan McClary, *Feminine Endings: Music, Gender, and Sexuality* (Minneapolis: University of Minnesota Press, 1991); Wayne Koestenbaum, *The Queen's Throat: Opera, Homosexuality, and the Mystery of Desire* (New York: Poseidon Press, 1993); Tricia Rose, *Black Noise: Rap Music and Black Culture in Contemporary America* (Middletown, Conn.: Wesleyan University Press, 1994); *The Image of the Black in Western Art*, Ladislas Bugner, gen. ed. (Cambridge: Menill Foundation, 1976); Linda Nochlin, *Women, Art, and Power and Other Essays* (New York: Harper and Row, 1988).

15. During this period, Barnard College first offered an arts major with a concentration in dance; Oberlin College instituted a major and a minor in dance through its theater and dance department; Wesleyan University offered a dance concentration; Ohio State sanctioned an M.A. in dance; Wisconsin's dance department began offering B.S., M.A., and M.F.A. degrees in dance, and its P.E. department offered a Ph.D. with a dance concentration.

16. Selma Odom started York University's master's program in dance. The performance studies department at New York University, largely influenced by Richard Schechner's interdisciplinary performance theory work, is one of the most fertile sites for theoretical innovation in dance study. See Richard Schechner, *Essays on Performance Theory, 1970–1976* (New York: Routledge, 1988). NYU's performing studies dance faculty includes journalist-critic Marcia B. Siegel.

17. The information in the paragraph above is drawn, in large part, from telephone conversations with dance program administrators (spring and summer 1993), from Margaret Lloyd, *The Borzoi Book of Modern Dance* (1949; reprint, New York: Dance Horizons, 1987), and from Nancy Smith, "Twenty-Five Years of Dance," *Wesleyan* 75 (Summer 1992): 14–26.

18. Iris Marion Young, "Introduction," in *Throwing Like a Girl and Other Essays in Feminist Philosophy and Social Theory* (Bloomington: Indiana University Press, 1990), 4.

19. The Romantic ballet's ballerina cult offers an example. Ballerinas of the Paris Opéra were encouraged to become mistresses of rich male patrons by the Opéra's male presenters. For more on this, see Ivor Guest, *Romantic Ballet in Paris* (Middletown, Conn.: Wesleyan University Press, 1966); and Suzanne Gordon, *Off Balance: The Real World of Ballet* (New York: McGraw-Hill, 1983). Writing of the similar perception of female ballet dancers in mid-nineteenth-century America, Elizabeth Kendall observes: "Whether or not it was true, all [American 'pick-up' ballet girls] were assumed to be at the disposal of gentlemen who hired them for club celebrations and bachelor dinners. A former ballet girl could not enter domestic service or work in a shop once she had been in that sort of theater work" (*Where She Danced* 7). Lynn Garafola notes another such connection in *Diaghilev's Ballets Russes* (New York: Oxford University Press, 1989). She observes how, with the rise of popularity of concert dance in the early part of this century with Diaghilev's Ballets Russes, "ballet became a magnet for homosexual [audiences]" (xii).

See also Garafola, "The Travesty Dancer in Nineteenth-Century Ballet," *Dance Research Journal* 17.2 and 18.1 (1985–86): 35–40; and Abigail Solomon-Godeau, "The Legs of the Countess," *October* 39 (Winter 1986): 65–108, especially the section titled "The Bazaar of Legs," which explores the sexual economy of nineteenth-century ballet and male balletomanes' fetishizing of ballerinas' legs. For a broader discussion of the historical gendering of dance, see Elizabeth Dempster's chapter in this volume.

20. Francis Sparshott addresses just these issues in "Why Philosophy Neglects the Dance," in *What Is Dance?*, 94–102. However, he dismisses the ideas that dance has been neglected by "the learned and literary worlds at large" either because dance is culturally aligned in the West with the feminine or because "dance is corporeal, and philosophers fear and hate the body" (95). He argues that, historically, the objection to dance "was not to its physicality but to its lack of meaning" (97). (For the fuller treatment Sparshott gives these matters, see "Why the Aesthetics of Dance Has Been Neglected," chapter 1 in *Off the Ground*, 3–82.) The dancing body's ostensible "lack of meaning," however, is not a cause but a consequence of dominant views holding that bodies and their movements can only be signifiers with no inherent significance or language of their own—exactly the view we argue against in this book. Sparshott's argument is limited by its having preceded so much important work in feminist theory and the recent interdisciplinary reconsiderations of "the body" crucial to theorizing dance.

21. The limitations of capturing live dance on video are well known. Video fixes the viewer's perspective, and the flattened surface quality of video distorts the choreography and significantly diminishes the impact of live dancers.

22. Susan Manning, personal communication, spring 1993; Randy Martin, "Reasserting Dance in the Public Sphere: Toward a Critical View of Reconstruction," paper; Sally Banes, "Criticism as Ethnography," in *On the Edge: Challenges to American Dance*, comp. Janice Ross and Stephen Cobbett Steinberg, proceedings of the 1989 Dance Critics Association conference, 4–9; Susan Foster, personal communication, spring 1993.

23. As a theorist and critic, Martin held modern dance to be the expression of emotional experiences that cannot be expressed by rational or intellectual means; see, for example, John Martin, *The Modern Dance* (1933; reprint, New York: Dance Horizons, 1969). Although this view clearly does not describe all modern dance, much less postmodern dance, Martin's work is important in the development of dance writing and the changing perceptions of dance in America.

24. *Edwin Denby: Dance Writings, 1936–1965*, ed. Robert Cornfield and William McKay (New York: Knopf, 1986).
25. For a discussion of the Judson Dance Theater and its importance to American dance, see Sally Banes, *Democracy's Body: Judson Dance Theater, 1962–1964* (Ann Arbor: UMI Research Press, 1983); and idem, *Terpsichore in Sneakers: Post-Modern Dance* (Middletown, Conn.: Wesleyan University Press, 1977).
26. For collections of dance reviews, see Jill Johnston, *Marmalade Me* (New York: E. P. Dutton, 1971); Arlene Croce, *Afterimages* (New York: Knopf, 1977); idem, *Going to the Dance* (New York: Knopf, 1982); and idem, *Sightlines* (New York: Knopf, 1987); Deborah Jowitt, *Dance Beat: Selected Views and Reviews, 1967–1976* (New York: Marcel Dekker, 1977); idem, *The Dance in Mind* (Boston: David R. Godine, 1985); Marcia B. Siegel, *At the Vanishing Point: A Critic Looks at Dance* (New York: Saturday Review Press, 1968); idem, *Watching the Dance Go By* (Boston: Houghton Mifflin, 1977); and idem *The Tail of the Dragon: New Dance, 1976–1982* (Durham, N.C.: Duke University Press, 1991).
27. Selma Jeanne Cohen, personal communication, October 10, 1993.
28. Typically, they are journalist-critics, editors, professional dance notators, or they hold positions in arts foundations, help stage dance reconstructions, or work with dance and theater archives.
29. Some colleges and universities do, of course, hold such expectations of their humanities faculty, though these tend to be the exception. There are certainly dance scholars who enjoy teaching studio courses as well as history and criticism, as there are scholars in drama and music who enjoy teaching studio and performance courses. Our concern here is with institutional expectations.
30. Two relatively new groups now work to disseminate dance history and scholarship. Devoted in part to making material in major dance repositories more accessible, the Dance Heritage Coalition assists with the surveying and archiving of dance collections and offers an electronic clearinghouse for dance documentation and preservation. And the National Initiative to Preserve American Dance recently launched a three-year, one-million-dollar national grant program to expand and secure the permanent record of American dance. Susan Manning has observed that one question those interested in dance studies and theory now consider is how the development of degree programs in dance studies compares with the development of more cross-disciplinary councils, centers, and consortia (personal communicaton, spring 1993). One of the most recent of such consortia, "Choreographing History: The Construction of Dance's Past," was sponsored by the Humanities Research Institute at the University of California, Irvine, in 1993. Another recent example is the Princeton Atelier, conceived and coordinated by Toni Morrison and under the auspices of the Council of the Humanities, which brings together artists from different genres to collaborate with Princeton University faculty and students; the 1994 guest artists were choreographer Jacques d'Amboise and critic-novelist Antonia Byatt.

31. Chief among them are Wesleyan University Press (which has long had a commitment to publishing scholarly books on dance), Routledge, and the university presses of Oxford, University of California, Duke, Indiana, New England, Cambridge, University of Wisconsin, Princeton, and with this volume, Rutgers.

32. *Dance Research Journal, Studies in Dance History, and Dance Research* are the leading scholarly journals devoted solely to dance studies. Unfortunately, articles published in them are not regularly included in yearly humanities indexes and bibliographies.

33. Some notable exceptions: *Salamagundi* 33–34 (Spring–Summer 1976) devoted a special issue to dance writing; *Raritan* published Vernon Shetley's "Merce Cunningham," 9 (Winter 1989): 72–90; the 1991 issue of *Signs* already cited published a rare dance piece with Desmond's essay, "Dancing Out the Difference"; the May 1992 issue of *PMLA* was devoted to performance and carried on its cover a photograph of Rudolph Nureyev and Merle Park in Balanchine's *Apollo*, but no accompanying essay inside; Mark Franko's essay "Where He Danced," analyzing performance pieces including the theater dance butoh, was published in that *PMLA* issue. Theater and dramatic arts journals, in particular, *TDR, The Drama Review* and *Theatre Survey*, more regularly publish essays on dance. See also the *Journal of Aesthetics and Art Criticism*.

34. The most thorough and theoretically sophisticated treatment of hip-hop culture to date is Tricia Rose's *Black Noise*.

35. For example, the 1991 Congress on Research in Dance (CORD) conference, "Dance as Discourse," was co-hosted by the University of Iowa's writing program. The 1992 CORD conference coordinated with the Association for Theatre in Higher Education to explore "Dance Theatre in a Multicultural Context." The 1992 annual meeting of the Society of Dance History Scholars was held back to back with the multidisciplinary conference "Choreographing History," hosted by the University of California, Riverside. The 1993 Dance Critics Association conference, "Moving Across Words," focused on performance, movement observation, and scholarly and journalistic writing.

36. See also Sally Ann Ness, *Body, Movement, and Culture: Kinesthetic and Visual Symbolism in a Philippine Community* (Philadelphia: University of Pennsylvania Press, 1992), written from an ethnographic perspective.

37. Leslie Satin, *"One and Another*: Walking through Time with Sally Gross," paper delivered at Narrative: An International Conference, Rensselaer Polytechnic Institute, April 1993, from her dissertation, "Bodies, Texts, and the Dancing Self." Ann Daly, "Classical Ballet: A Discourse of Difference," *Women in Performance* 3.2 (1987/1988a): 57–66; idem, "At Issue: Gender in Dance," *Drama Review* 31 (Spring 1987): 22–24; idem, "The Balanchine Woman," *Drama Review* 110 (Summer 1986): 8–12. For a feminist reading of modern American dance figures, see Ann Daly, "Dance History and Feminist Theory: Reconsidering Isadora Duncan and the Male Gaze," in *Gender in Performance:*

The Representation of Difference in the Performing Arts, ed. Laurence Senelick (Hanover, N.H.: University Press of New England, 1992), 239–259.

38. For a general discussion of the complexities of identifying "black dance," see Zita Allen, "What Is Black Dance?" in *The Black Tradition in American Modern Dance* comp. Gerald E. Meyers and Stephanie Reinhart, a pamphlet produced for American Dance Festival's 1991–1992 season.

39. Reported by Lincoln Kirstein in Nicholas Fox Weber, *Patron Saints: Five Rebels Who Opened America to a New Art, 1928–1943* (New York: Knopf, 1992), 179–180; and in Francis Mason, *I Remember Balanchine: Recollections of the Ballet Master by Those Who Knew Him* (New York: Doubleday, 1991), 116.

40. Toni Morrison, *Playing in the Dark: Whiteness and the Literary Imagination* (Cambridge: Harvard University Press, 1992), 9. Morrison's concerns are not with dances but with canonical works of American fiction by white writers. Her criticism seems representative (in large part) because her essays range widely over African American literary theory, certain feminist theories, reader-response theory, structuralist, semiotic, and hermeneutic theory. It is relevant because liberal politeness, in its many forms, is a potent force in the dynamics of academic work and arts writing today.

41. The dancers in these works are costumed in what appear to be a mixture of black and white practice clothes. Most notable among the black-and-white dances is *Agon*, a pas de deux created for Diana Adams (a white woman) and Arthur Mitchell (a black man).

42. Brenda Dixon was one of the first to address an African American influence in Balanchine's work; see Dixon, "Up from Under: The Afrocentric Tradition in American Concert Dance," proceedings of the Hong Kong International Dance Conference, July 15–28, 1990, pp. 169–183).

To rethink Balanchine's choreography in light of these critical problems does not necessitate a move toward or neccessarily entail an Afrocentric reading of Balanchine's dance movement. Nor are we concerned here with pointing out racist or nonracist moments in Balanchine's (or any choreographer's) works. That is, we can talk about a racially inflected movement in the dances of white choreographers without employing Afrocentric critiques.

The questions we are asking raise issues different from those raised in important recent works that focus on African American choreographers, dances, and dancers: Richard Long, *The Black Tradition in American Dance* (New York: Rizzoli Publishers, 1990); *Black Choreographers Moving: A National Dialogue*, ed. Julinda Lewis-Ferguson and comp. Halifu Osumare (Berkeley: Expansion Arts Services, 1991); *The Black Tradition in American Modern Dance*, the pamphlet produced for American Dance Festival's 1991–1992 season; and the pamphlet produced for their 1992–1993 season, *African-American Genius in Modern Dance*.

43. Merleau-Ponty's description of lived body experience posits a universal white male body, which feminist phenomenologists and others have challenged. See, for example, Young's essay "Throwing Like a Girl," and Vivian Sobchak, *The Address of the Eye* (Princeton: Princeton University Press, 1992).

44. For discussion of these meanings that bodies have carried, see Susan L. Foster, "Introduction," *Choreographing History* (Bloomington: Indiana University Press, forthcoming 1995), a collection of interdisciplinary essays.

READING DANCE AS TEXT

Women Writing the Body: Let's Watch a Little How She Dances

Elizabeth Dempster

Asked what he thought of a new school principal, a Central African responded to Carrington: 'Let's watch a little how he dances.'
—Walter Ong, *Orality and Literacy*

THE DANCING PROFESSOR

On the inside back sleeve, where they usually have the head-and-shoulders shot of the author, there is a photo of Susan Leigh Foster, author and academic, dancing—midflight in fact. *Reading Dancing* is a book about dance,[1] a book about a theory of dance, and just as sometimes a book about gardening featuring the author in action in a vegetable patch, so this photograph of the author-as-dancer has, we might presume, been chosen to establish a certain credibility with respect to the subject at hand. But there is more at play, and at stake, in this image.

It is this author-dancer's intention to place two practices, two unlike bodies, of writing and dancing, in dialogue. In *Reading Dancing* a distinctly formulated body, a body which has been shaped to a precise physical articulation, is identified as the site of discourse. The author's body asserted as dancing presence exceeds the smooth surface of the page. Her body intervenes and demands that the reader become spectator. In articulating a vision of the body's movement as an act of writing, and picturing herself as dancer, Foster reminds us of the bodily ground of all these acts of reading, writing, dancing, and watching dancing.

STUMBLING, (ST)UTTERING, AND OTHER DISORDERS

In the original presentation of this essay another coupling of bodies, more disjunctive than harmonious, was proposed. The paper was presented in the form of a dance in two parts, one spoken, one moved through. It was a duet between speaking body and dancing body, between muteness and loquacity.

A play of two voices was intended, a play in which both were to some degree suppressed, and this suppression was symptomatic of a disordering of relations between the body and speech. However, in presenting dancing and speaking as polarities, the dance/paper appeared to confirm the impossibility of dialogue between the two practices. Stumbling and stuttering, the author-as-dancer unwittingly pictured herself as an unspeakable presence and as a site of nostalgia.

The dancer is a place of mourning where readers search for another lost body of pleasure and innocence. Dance is a mythical site where the body, speechless and thus uncorrupted, plays. This is, of course, nonsense. Dancing, like speaking, is a social act, produced by and within given discourses.

———

Laleen Jayamanne: When you moved from dance to film, you made a comment to the effect that the body alone is no longer sufficient.

Yvonne Rainer: What the body can say without verbal language is limited, which is why I so frequently used language in my dances . . . to tell stories mostly. I would speak or project texts and later used more elaborate scripts, including multi-media. But I guess I grew impatient with the limitations of the body's expressivity. That is why I no longer involve myself in the kind of "physical research" I had done through my body.[2]

Martha Graham: [The body] is an instrument with which to express great truths of life; it must be prepared for the ordeal of expressiveness.

Movement never lies.[3]

The contrasting choreographic projects of Martha Graham and Yvonne Rainer are emblematic of two distinctive periods and genres in twentieth-century dance—the modern and the postmodern. Graham, ascribing to the body a superfluity of expression, created dances which are descriptive of such a condition. For Rainer the insufficiencies and limitations of the body's speech necessitate a relocation; the body and its movement are contextualized by other more overtly discursive practices.

———

The object of this lengthy but introductory play of terms—speech, writing, text, body—is to delineate a space of inquiry where one might ask not only "What does the body speak?" but also "How is the body written in dance?" And "Whose stories are told and what bodies are silenced in this process of inscription?"

In recent years the question of "the body," the way the body has been inscribed with cultural codes, has been a focus within feminist theory. Strangely, this questioning of the body and its representation—which has played such a significant role in the development of new critical strategies—has rarely been brought to bear upon the practice of dance, surely the most bodily of cultural productions. My intention in this chapter is to present an overview of the ways in which the body is being written in dance, and the ways in which dance, within the Western theatrical tradition, has defined and redefined bodies, particularly women's bodies. I offer a survey and a reading which are necessarily schematic, at best a preliminary diagnosis—a few lines drawn across the surface of a large and silent body, marking points of entry for future and deeper incisions.

—

Bodies and dances are not only legible but comprehensible. I have chosen to borrow, in a somewhat illegitimate manner, terms and methods drawn from contemporary literary theory in order to establish the dancing body as a location of signifying practices and to foreground the reflexive relationship existing between the dancing/speaking subject and the dance/language. Because dances have no existence except through the body/bodies which produce and reproduce them, they can be considered as texts written of and through precisely inscribed bodies.

But the dancer's body is not merely a written-upon page; it is more accurately described as an artifact, of blood, flesh, organs, bone and skin, arduously and meticulously constructed. Social and political values are not simply placed or grafted onto a neutral body-object like so many old or new clothes. On the contrary, ideologies are systematically deposited and constructed on an anatomical plane, that is, in the neuromusculature of the dancer's body, and a precise reading of this body can only proceed if the reader/spectator's gaze is not deflected by, but penetrates beneath, the brilliance of the body's surface.

—

And simultaneously with its attraction, we find testimony to the fear and loathing that that body has inspired: beautiful but unclean, alluring but dangerous, woman's body (can we say that it is always in some sense, the mother's body?) has appeared mysterious, duplicitous—a source of pleasure and nurturance, but also of destruction and evil.[4]

In the Western theatrical tradition, certainly since the Romantic era, often termed the "age of the ballerina," dance has been closely associated with the female body. In this cultural context the dancing body is constructed as a female, feminized, and sexualized body, a body which is site and source of powerful and conflicting passions. Curt Sachs's *World History of the Dance* opens with the statement, "The dance is the mother of the arts"; in *The Principles of Art*, Robin G. Collingwood identifies dance as "the mother of all language"; for choreographer George Balanchine ballet is a "woman, a garden of beautiful flowers."[5] The dancer's body is conceptualized as the ground, the soil, from which all these beauties spring. Ancient themes: woman's body, mater, and matter.

If dance is the space of "the feminine" and "the maternal," it follows within the logic of a patriarchal social order that its power and the power of the body must be controlled, constrained, disguised, or denied. Dancer and choreographer Russell Dumas has spoken of the regulatory mechanisms which are brought to bear upon the body and its representations:

> The body and the dance images which are presented through the body are subject to immense social control. The control over the body which is apparent in particular areas of dance, for example the Royal Academy of Dance system of examination and accreditation in classical ballet, is one aspect of what is a much more pervasive surveillance and control over the body in our society.
>
> Part of the reason why dance is marginalized and trivialized, and why the body is satirized, is that such measures control the body and delimit and reduce its potency.[6]

Dance has been represented as a secondary, derivative, diversionary and minor art, an art which does not generate its own meanings. It has traditionally been defined in relationship to the male-identified art forms of music and drama, and its communicative potential, force, and action are commonly misrepresented as dependent upon those relationships. In this (false) representation, the body is dispossessed of its capacity for mindful action. The "male" arts of music and drama commandeer the space of mind and spirit; the female-identified art of dance is relegated to the nether regions of an unthought and unthinking body. Dance may be the mother of all manner of things but she cannot know or speak of herself.

Dance is identified with a body which has been defined as a dependent, contingent object, lacking autonomy, lacking the capacity to speak of or otherwise represent itself and lacking a transcendent symbology and function.[7] This conception of the body denies its capacity, and by extension that of dance, to allude to other realities or to create new fictions. As I have argued in my profile of Dumas, "dance is in the world, refers to that world, but also creates its own reality. It is not simply reflective of a current social reality but can be a gesture towards some other; it is able to project other possibilities, alluding to a future, to a past, and to another present" (48).

Dance can be thoughtful action, a movement of embodied mind. It offers the possibility of a distinctive mode of action, a mode of action embracing a conception of the body which is not shadowed by habits of thought based on Cartesian dualism. But when dance is not regarded as a signifying practice in its own right and when it is assigned a minor role within a cultural economy, this distinctive capacity remains disguised, delimited, and reduced. Some dancers are innocent of the cultural economy, and reduced. Some dancers are innocent of the cultural economy of which their work is part; others recognize and are willing to accept the parameters of dance practice—the shape, scale, and status of dance, as determined by that economy. Ann Daly, discussing the work of Balanchine, analyzes the encoding of gender-dichotomized difference in classical ballet. She asserts that the "ballerina is not simply an innocuous, isolated theatrical image" but an icon of femininity which not only reflects but inscribes gender behavior in every-day life.[8]

The ballet is identified by Daly as "one of our culture's most powerful models of patriarchal ceremony." The ballerina, by her compliant participation in the enactment of this ceremony, in effect contributes to her own oppression and "ratifies her own subordination." Daly argues that the gender prescription evident in the ballet's representation and deployment of the female body is fundamental to the ballet form. Ballet would not be ballet without these gender demarcations. She concludes that women are inscribed by but cannot represent themselves in the classical ballet. It is a form which denies the female dancer her own agency. For the balletomane these may be controversial and unwelcome assertions, but in my judgment Daly's analysis is acute, persuasive, and salutary. I return to some of the issues she raises later in this chapter.

If, as Daly implies, there are dancers who are compliant with existing conceptions and definitions, there are others who challenge such prescription and who seek transformation of the terms of exchange to which they have been subject. Some of the most remarkable art of the twentieth century has been produced by women working in the medium of dance. These dancers and choreographers have written and continue to write the body in distinctive and diverse ways, projecting "other possibilities" through and for the body. Although Western theatrical dance has rarely been subjected to rigorous sociopolitical scrutiny, it is nonetheless a social practice which is inevitably and profoundly political. So any history of dance, even if it simply be a tracing of the changing imagery of the body's deployment in space and time, will contain fragments of a political history of the body. It requires a careful reading, but the history of Western theatrical dance can be interrogated in such a way as to reveal the residues of political actions and representations upon, through, and of the body.

In "Towards a Sexual Politics of Contemporary Dance," Roger Copeland introduces the work of a number of women dancer/choreographers who have vigorously challenged established dance practices (45–50). He emphasizes the political significance of the aesthetic innovations in dance over this century by linking developments in modern and postmodern dance with various stages and styles of feminist thinking. The following survey of three major genres of concert dance—classical, modern, and postmodern—takes up some of the themes touched upon in Copeland's reading of twentieth-century dance.

The history of dance is conserved and continually renewed in contemporary bodies. Multiple texts and multiple bodies coexist in the present time, and, although dance forms are adaptive and subject to redefinition, contemporary examples can still usefully be studied as historical texts in which the social, cultural, and political values of the time in which they originated are encoded. The three genres under consideration are based on strongly contrasting conceptions of the body and strongly contrasting modes of representation and training practices. It is through participation in the given discourse of a genre, constituted by dance classes, rehearsals, and performances, that the body characteristic of that genre is constructed and inscribed. This is not to imply that the dancer's body is solely a function of discursive procedures, or, expressed differently, that an appropriately inscribed body can be achieved by training alone. The classical ballet body, for example, is predicated upon a "natural" body of particular anatomical characteristics and dimensions. The introduction of the proscenium arch marked the transition from the allegorical aesthetic of late Renaissance dance to the pictorial aesthetic of the neoclassical dance of the eighteenth century. Neoclassical dance, elevated and framed, presented "perfected pictures of human society" articulated through an ideal or set of ideal bodily forms.[9] A pictorial aesthetic continues to characterize the ballet genre and governs the presentation and definition of "perfected bodies."

The classical ballet posits an ideal and idealized world, and it is an overtly synthetic construct, utilizing a system of precisely coded, highly patterned abstract movement and incorporating the stylized gesture and deportment of the sixteenth-century French court. All traces of the "natural," the unschooled, the mundane or contemporary gesture are erased from the body in a lengthy and rigorous training which begins in childhood. The classical dancer's body is defined by achievement of the greatest degree of frontal legibility as established in the turn-out, by a commitment to the vertical, to lightness and speed and, in the words of Lincoln Kirstein, by a commitment to "the conquest against gravity of aerial space."[10]

The turn-out established in the five positions of the feet is the root of ballet training and is fundamental to the ethos and image of the ballet form:

> for 'turning-out' means that the dancer, whatever the convolutions of the dance, continually shows as much of herself as possible to the spectator.
>   In ballet the human passions are expressed by the gradual uncontorted curves and straight lines of the extended human body. There is no residuum, no veil. The human body is purged of atmosphere. All is shown.[11]

The classical dancer's body is a body orientated to display and to a celebration of outwardness, but this disclosure is highly regulated and ordered. The dancer's training begins at an early age when the body and the mind are most impressionable, and it is a training directed to a re-creative purpose—the reproduction of masterworks. Her body is subjected to intense scrutiny as it strives for achievement of the already existent and long-established lexicon of some two hundred steps which determine the range of its permissible movement. If, as Ann Daly states, the ballet is a cultural institution which ceremonially inscribes patriarchal ideology, then this training process is the female dancer's initiation into a patriarchal symbolic order, that is, into the language of the father.

The classical body is a highly disciplined, highly regulated one, and the female dancer enjoys a very limited degree of autonomy with respect to the deployment and representation of her body in performance. A transition into a position of greater independence, such as that offered in choreographic work, is rare for the female dancer in this tradition. Indeed, orthodox ballet training tends to suppress precisely those qualities of independent judgment and self-definition considered essential to choreographical development and innovation.

George Balanchine has described the choreographic process as an activity of the male mind ordering and transforming "raw nature" as incarnated in the bodies of women. In the ballet tradition, choreography, that is, the *writing* of movement, is almost exclusively the province and privilege of men. The traditional ballet company structure, although foregrounding the female performer, continues to delimit her participation in the definition and extension of that form and perhaps, considering Daly's analysis, a situation of fuller participation is a logical impossibility. If dichotomized gender-imaging is fundamental to the ballet form, any major redefinition which redresses gender-based inequalities would produce dances no longer recognizable as ballet.

One of the most striking paradoxes of the classical ballet genre is that this most athletic, physically demanding of dance forms harnesses the considerable strength, stamina, and will of the female dancer in service of narratives representing female passivity, dependence, and frailty. Critic Chris Savage-King wonders why a form that promotes the female is treated with disdain by feminist observers.[12] She suggests that we should look to the dancer and the dance, and not, as it were, to the distractions of the drama. But the context of the dancer's labor cannot so easily be put aside. While the skill and talent of many ballerinas are formidable and indisputable, their display appears to be, at center, controlled and guided by a male hand and a male eye. The ballerina's power is more apparent than real. Although her body enunciates with great vibrancy and vitality, she is granted no authorial rights over performance texts.

Major innovation in dance has occurred largely outside the ballet academy. The radical redefinition of concert dance which began at the turn of the century was a movement initiated by women artists working independently of traditional structures to develop new languages of physical expression. Early modern dance was a repudiation of the tenets of nineteenth-century ballet, including its emphasis on spectacle and virtuoso display. It was an avowedly female-centred movement, both with respect to the manner in which the body was deployed and represented and in the imagery and subject matter employed. The early modern dancers were asking that the body and its movement, along with the place and context of dance, be looked at in new ways. They inherited no practice; the techniques and the choreographic forms they developed were maps and reflections of the possibilities and propensities of their own originating bodies.

In the early 1900s, dancers such as Isadora Duncan, Loie Fuller, Maud Allen, and Ruth St. Denis constructed images and created dances through their own unballetic bodies, producing a writing of the female body which strongly contrasted with classical inscriptions. These dancers, creating new vocabularies of movement and new styles of presentation, made a decisive and liberating break with the principles and forms of the European ballet. The modern dance genre is now most closely identified with the choreographic output of the second generation of modern dancers—Mary Wigman, Doris Humphrey, Martha Graham—and the training systems they developed. It is to this body of work that the following discussion refers.

Modern dance is not a uniform system, but a corpus of related though differentiated vocabularies and techniques of movement which have evolved in response to the choreographic projects of individual artists. Common to these contrasting styles of dance—and it is this that allows us to group otherwise disparate works under the banner of "modern dance"—is a conception of the body as a medium and vehicle for the expression of inner forces. The spatial and temporal structure of these dances is based on emotional and psychological imperatives. The governing logic of modern dance is not pictorial, as in the ballet, but affective.

For the modern dancer, dance is an expression of interiority—interior feeling guiding the movement of the body into external forms. Doris Humphrey described her dance as "moving from the inside out";[13] for Graham it was a process of "making visible the interior landscape."[14] This articulation of interior (maternal) spaces creates forms which are not, however, ideal or perfected ones. The modern dancer's body registers the play of opposing forces, falling and recovering, contracting and releasing. It is a body defined through a series of dynamic alternations, subject both to moments of surrender and moments of resistance.

In modern dance the body acts in a dynamic relationship with gravity. For Humphrey the body was at its most interesting when in transition and at a moment of gravitational loss, that is, when it was falling. Modern dance has often been termed "terrestrial," that is, floor-bound, and inward-looking. As such it has been negatively compared to the ballet and the aerial verticality and openness of that form. But as Graham has stressed, "the dancers fall so that they may rise." It is in the *falling,* not in being down, that the modern body is at its most expressive.

The modern body and the dance which shapes it are a site of struggle where social and psychological, spatial and rhythmic conflicts are played out and sometimes reconciled. This body—and it is specifically a female body—is not passive but dynamic, even convulsive, as Deborah Jowitt sees it:

> In many of [Graham's] important works of the forties and fifties, you felt the dancing shuddering along in huge jerks, propelled by the violently contracting and expanding bodies. When I first saw Graham in 1955, I was stunned by the whiplash of her spine; by the way, as Medea in *Cave of the Heart*, she writhed sideways on her knees—simultaneously devouring and vomiting a length of red yarn.[15]

Jowitt concludes that Graham's dancing was like no other she had witnessed, "a body language consisting solely of epithets."

Modern dance posits a natural body in which feeling and form are organically connected. Graham, for example, conceived the body as a conduit, a responsive channel through which inner truths are revealed. The body has a revelatory potential, and technique is the means by which the outer manifestations of the body are brought into alignment with the inner world of the psyche.

> Through all times the acquiring of technique in dance has been for one purpose—so to train the body as to make possible any demand made upon it by that inner self which has the vision of what needs to be said. No one invents movement; movement is discovered. What is possible and necessary to the body under the impulse of the emotional self is the result of this discovery.[16]

The function of technique in modern dance is, as Graham has described it, to free the socialized body and clear it of any impediment which might obscure its capacity for "true speech." Ironically, perhaps, this concept of the "natural" body was expounded in support of highly systemized and codified dance languages and training programs which inscribe relationships—necessarily conventional and arbitrary—between the body, movement, and meaning.

Modern dance's valorization of the "natural" and its positing of an individualized presymbolic subject are not features of the classical system of training. Ballet training shapes, controls, improves upon, and perfects the body's given physical structure; in this process both the natural body and the individualized subject are erased. As the principles of modern dance have become progressively codified into systematic techniques, the concept of a "natural" body, preexisting discourse, can no longer be sustained. Modern dance, now distant from its creators' originating ideas, is passed on through highly formalized training programs; like the classical system, this training involves erasure of naturally given physical traits and processes of reinscription.

How are the body and "the feminine" inscribed by the female-devised languages of modern dance? Graham's dances sacralize and mythologize the female body, a body shown to be subject to forceful emotional, unconscious, and libidinal impulses. In Foster's reading it is the body of the hysteric:

> The action begins in the abdomen, codified as the site of libidinal and primitive desires. The symbolic contents of the abdomen radiate through the body, twisting and overpowering the body with their message. Graham's characters seem to be subject to the psychological mechanism of repression. The powerful message from the unconscious makes its way only with difficulty through the emotional and intellectual centers of the person and into the world. Graham depicts the tense conflict between corporeal and psychological elements. (81)

Graham's location of "the feminine" may seem uncomfortably close to the space traditionally ascribed to the body, women, and dance within patriarchy. Her choreographies, however, represent the inner world as a dynamic, outward-flowing, conflictual force; "the feminine" is not passive but voluptuously and sometimes violently active. It is a force which shapes the outer world. Graham's work reflects the psychoanalytic preoccupations of her time, but the public and performative nature of Graham's articulation of these concerns, and the power she ascribes to the female body, significantly distinguish her representation of the feminine from that associated with clinical practice.

As early as the 1930s, Graham and her fellow artists were presenting a newly defined dance practice in the public arena, and in so doing they created spaces for dance and for women which had not existed before. But this form of dance, once an oppositional practice, is now offered as a second language supplementing classical ballet in the training of the professional dancer. In my judgment, modern dance's gradual codification, its identity as a formularized technique, has rendered it susceptible to colonization; it is this codification rather than any inherent ideological complicity which permits elements of modern dance to be subsumed into the ballet.

Lincoln Kirstein, the founding father of the New York City Ballet, has cursorily dismissed modern dance as a "minor verse" of theater. He considers it timebound, nostalgic, and lacking the "clear speech acts" and universal legibility of the ballet. He is one of a number of critics who have argued that ballet is the only enduring Western concert dance form.[17] In Kirstein's view, ballet's preeminence is assured because modern dance has failed to produce a stable lexicon and is therefore lacking in consequence.

But modern dance has clearly developed vocabularies and syntactical conventions, and Kirstein's perceptions are misplaced. He would be less inaccurate if his subject had been postmodern dance. The postmodern is not a newly defined dance language but a strategy and a method of inquiry which challenge and interrogate the process of representation itself. Once the relation between movement and its referent is questioned, the representational codes and conventions of dance are opened to investigation. Analysis, questioning, and manipulation of the codes and conventions which inscribe the body in dance are distinguishing features of the postmodern mode.

In the 1940s, Merce Cunningham had already begun to demonstrate that dance could be primarily about movement. In contrast to the expressionism of modern dance, in which movement is presumed to have intrinsic meaning, Cunningham choreographies emphasize the arbitrary nature of the correlation between signifier and signified. In his deconstruction of existing choreographic codes, Cunningham challenged the rhetoric of "the natural" which surrounded modern dance. The political dimensions of this deconstructive project have been addressed more directly in the work of some of the later postmodern choreographers.

Susan Foster defines two stages/modes of postmodern dance practice: objectivist and reflexive. The first is the precondition for the second, but the two modes were coextensive in the 1960s and 1970s and together constitute the genre. Foster differentiates the two stages of postmodern dance as follows:

> Objectivist dance focuses on the body's movement, allowing any references to the world to accrue alongside the dance as a byproduct of the body's motion. The reflex-

ive choreography . . . assumes that the body will inevitably refer to other events, and because of this asks how those references are made. Whereas objectivist dance has laid bare the conventions governing representations to allow the body to speak its own language, reflexive choreography works with these same conventions to show the body's capacity to both speak and be spoken through in many different languages. (188)

Like Cunningham, the postmodern choreographers emerging in the 1960s distinguished themselves from both the classical tradition and the then firmly established modern dance in that their focus was on the fundamental material and medium of dance, the moving body itself. The body was no longer to be trained to the task of interpreting or illustrating something other than its own material reality. Postmodern dance does not present perfected, ideal or unified forms, nor bodies driven by inner imperatives, but bodies of bone, muscle, and flesh speaking of and for themselves. According to Foster, "The dances are about what they look like. Because [objectivist dances] simply present individual people in motion, the dancers clearly do not presume to represent idealized experience or experience that might be common to all people" (185).

In *Work 1961–73*, Yvonne Rainer writes of her "chunky" body not conforming to the traditional image of the female dancer. Elsewhere she recalls a Boston reviewer, writing in the 1960s, disdainfully commenting on the "slack" bodies of (the later-termed) postmodern dancers.[18] A democratization of the body and of dance was heralded in the postmodern work of the 1960s and 1970s. While Cunningham pursued a deconstruction of choreographic conventions through technically trained bodies—bodies which maintained the "look" of the dancer—postmodern works of this period featured both trained and untrained performers, in short, "any-old-body." Widely used choreographic devices such as rule games, task-based and improvisational structures provided a frame for the perception and enjoyment of bodies in action—trained or untrained, old or young, thick or thin, male or female.

The play of oppositions and the gender stereotyping embodied in the ballet and perpetuated in modern dance traditions were systematically deemphasized in the postmodern work of this era. Within the selection, structuring, and performance of movement, strong contrasts and oppositions were reduced or eliminated. Rainer speaks here of *The Mind Is a Muscle, Trio A* (1966):

The limbs are never in a fixed, still relationship and they are stretched to the fullest extension only in transit, creating the impression that the body is constantly engaged in transitions. Another factor contributing to the smoothness of the continuity is that no one part of the series is made any more important than any other. For four and half minutes a great variety of movement shapes occur, but they are of equal weight and are equally emphasized.[19]

The postmodern dancer's range and style of movement were not determined by gender, and sex-specific roles were rare—notable exceptions being a number of works by Yvonne Rainer in which issues of gender, sexual identity, and seduction in performance were addressed directly.[20] The early postmodern focus on nonhierarchial and nongenderized use and organization of the body and its movement continues in current postmodern dance.

Postmodern dance, as Foster has indicated, also involves the reworking and reassessment of earlier forms of bodily inscription—drawing from, quoting, subverting, and manipulating classical and other lexicons. Referring to Rainer's *Trio A* (1966) and Trisha Brown's *Accumulation* (1971), *With Talking* (1973) and *Plus Watermotor* (1977), Foster has noted the tensions which arise when (at least) two disparate modes of representation are juxtaposed or brought into dialogue (186). In these works the body is present as an instrument concerned simply with physical articulation, but at the same time it also alludes to other discourses: Rainer's *Trio A* contains references to earlier dance forms, and Brown's dance presents speaking and dancing as simultaneous but independent texts. The play of contrasting discourses and the use of quotation in postmodern compositional process produce layered and complex dance works open to multiple readings. Yvonne Rainer, in conversation with Trisha Brown, discusses this effect in Brown's *Glacial Decoy* (1979):

> The costumes bring in another dimension . . . of, not exactly a persona, but an association with personae created elsewhere and earlier, somewhere between *Les Sylphides* and *Primitive Mysteries*, maybe even *Antic Meet*, which has that take-off on *Primitive Mysteries*. And it is the dress that produces this association. There's a recurring, fleeting transformation from a body moving to a flickering female image. I think that because the dress stands away from the body the image is never totally integrated or unified, so one goes back and forth in seeing movement-as-movement, body-inside-dress, dress-outside-body, and image-of-woman/dancer, which is not the same thing as seeing or not seeing your work in terms of your being a woman. Femaleness in *Galcial Decoy* is both a given, as in your previous work, and a superimposition.[21]

The processes of deconstruction and bricolage commonly associated with postmodern dance also describe an attitude to physical training. The development of what might be termed the postmodern body is in some sense a deconstructive process, involving a period of detraining of the dancer's habitual structures and patterns of movement. The dancer brings intelligence to bear on the physical structure of her/his body, focusing close attention upon the interaction of skeletal alignment and physiological and perceptual processes. Through this process the dancer reconstructs a physical articulation based on an understanding of what is common to all bodies and what is unique to her/his own. Our bodies evolve in dialogue with a complex physical and social world, so the training systems which have informed postmodern dance are based on a conceptualization of the body as an organism in flux. The postmodern body is not a fixed, immutable entity, but a living structure which continually adapts and transforms itself. It is body available to the play of many discourses. Postmodern dance directs attention away from any specific image of the body and toward the process of constructing all bodies.

If postmodern dance is a "writing" of the body, it is a writing that is conditional, circumstantial, and above all transitory: it is a writing that erases itself in the act of being written. The body, and by extension "the feminine," in postmodern dance is unstable, fleeting, flickering, transient—a subject of multiple representations.

When the written and written-upon body dances, what is spoken and what is received? Laura Mulvey's analysis of the dynamics of male spectatorship relative to narrative cinema has been usefully applied to narrative ballet and its audience.[22] A feminist critique, such as Ann Daly's, focuses on analysis of the ways in which the act of displaying and viewing the female body in dance reinstates male power. But what of the female spectator? When a women is watching another woman dancing, what happens?

Ambivalence toward the body and judgment against one's own can be part of the terms of exchange operating between dancers and spectators. Dancer and writer Shona Innes has argued that orthodox ballet training prepares and conditions the young female dancer to fail.[23] The would-be ballerina is encouraged to compare herself (unceasingly) to an image of a never-to-be-attained perfection. This conditioning to failure underlies what I have elsewhere termed an economy of shame.[24]

In the classical dance the spectator is invited to gaze upon a distanced, ideal world where the female dancer is traced as sylph and cipher, a necessary absence. The perception of the body as a natural, physical entity is obstructed and suppressed by distance; the mundane body has no place here. The classical ballet thus creates conditions conducive to self-forgetfulness. In the body of the ballerina the watcher might seek another transformed body; in the contemplation of distanced virtuosity a space of forgetfulness opens, a space in which her own present imperfect body is subsumed in the perfected body of the other.

In contrast, dancing located in the space opened by postmodernist practice demands not a forgetting but a heightened awareness of the commonality of all bodies and the particularity of each. The dance, which plays across, puts on, and takes off a variety of modes of symbolic discourse, is written through a pedestrian body. It is a dancing which stresses the materiality, the fleshliness—and therefore the vulnerability and mortality—of all bodies: the dancer's and, by a reflexive action, the spectator's.

Postmodern dance presents the potentialities of the mundane body; an ordinary body of bone and flesh, common to spectator and dancer alike, is posited as the locus of dancing. The presence of the pedestrian body as the ground of danced action invalidates the exclusionary participant criteria of ballet and challenges the limits and conditions encoded in that form. There is in postmodern dance no image of perfection or unity, no hierarchy and no failure.

A final distinction: in the classical genre the specificity of the female body is obscured. The dancer's body is regularized and abstracted; difference is reduced to sameness. Postmodern dance foregrounds the kinaesthetic and the tactile and denies the privilege of a universalizing gaze. In asserting the materiality of the dancing body, it affirms the specificity of each dancing presence, of each body's lived experience. The postmodern body is plural, polyvalent, mutable. When a woman watches this dancing, what happens?

The dancing body is a cultural production, dynamically interacting with the sociocultural matrix of which it is a part, and dances are projected images, not mere mirror reflections of already existing social realities. Dance's capacity to project images of the body's action in the world marks it as powerful means of enculturation. As I indicated earlier, certain dance forms and training practices tend to reinforce patriarchal and phallocentric modes of social and sexual interaction. The enduring popularity of recreational ballet classes among preadolescent girls is an indication perhaps of the continuing influence of this dance form in female socialization. But it is also the case that the body, dancing, can challenge and deconstruct dominant cultural inscription. The early modern dance proposed a feminist dance practice which would return the real female body to women. The work of Isadora Duncan, perhaps the most mythologized of the early moderns, has been linked with the women's emancipation movement of the 1900s. For Duncan the dancing body was a paradigm of freedom. The loosening of the fetters which bound the body itself (Duncan danced uncorseted and barefoot) was part and parcel of her vision of the social and political liberation of women. As she wrote in *The Dancer of the Future* around 1902:

> The dancer of the future . . . will dance not in the form of a nymph, nor fairy, nor coquette, but in the form of a woman in her greatest and purest expression. She will realize the mission of woman's body and the holiness of all its parts. She will dance the changing life of nature, showing how each part is transformed into the other. From all parts of her body shall shine radiant intelligence, bringing to the world the message of the thoughts and aspirations of thousands of women. She shall dance the freedom of women.[25]

As expressed by Isadora Duncan, the goal of the "free dance," as it was termed in the 1900s, was to provide a pure reflection of the natural, unwritten body of woman. However, as Mary Ann Doane points out in discussion of the representation of the female body in feminist film, "The ideological complicity of the concept of the natural dictates the impossibility of a nostalgic return to an unwritten body. For it is precisely the massive reading, writing and filming of the female body which constructs and maintains a hierarchy along the lines of a sexual difference assumed as natural."[26] Duncan's vision of the dance of the future presumes an unproblematic return to a body of untainted naturalness and to an essential purity which she believed was fundamental to women. To recognize that

Duncan's vision is unrealizable and perhaps, from today's perspective, in some degree complicit with the concept of "natural" sexual difference is not to deny the power of her rhetoric nor to dismiss the considerable impact her dancing had upon audiences of her time.

Later modern dancers continued to employ the rhetoric of the "natural," yet they were prolific in their production of distinctive—and one could argue decidedly "unnatural"—female languages and texts. It seems that modern dance might once have been a viable mode of self-representation for the women who wrote and spoke it into being, but once codified—one woman's speech becoming "women's language"—it became vulnerable to colonization. Although modern dance's representation of the feminine stands in contrast to that of the ballet, it has become in its own way as prescriptive as the system it originally sought to challenge. Because postmodern dance is not a newly defined dance language but an interrogation of language itself, it presents the possibility of an interventionist practice.[27] Postmodern dance acknowledges the specificity of each dancing body—as that body is constituted naturally, that is, as a physical entity with given anatomical and physiological characteristics, and as it is constituted within particular discourses. The body, not disciplined to the enunciation of a singular discourse, is a multivocal and potentially disruptive force which undermines the unity of phallocratic discourse. Postmodern dance does not eschew the dance of the past but suggests tactical procedures by which the dancer might keep a hop, skip, and a jump ahead and away from reductive and normalizing prescriptions.

Contemporary practice in dance as represented in the three genres briefly discussed here is a rich and virtually untapped field for feminist inquiry. It is a repository of past images, a measure of the present, and a site where new images of the body (and images of a new body) are being drawn. This preliminary sketch of the terrain is offered in the hope that other bodies, other readers, writers, and dancers will also say: "Let's watch a little how she dances."

But what if the object began to speak.[28]

Dance contains within itself gestures toward a dissolution of the dichotomous pairing of terms fundamental to the Western philosophical tradition. In moments of dancing the edges of things blur and terms such as mind/body, flesh/spirit, carnal/divine, male/female become labile and unmoored, breaking loose from the fixity of their pairings. This vision of dance is not utopian but a felt experience, occurring fleetingly, elusively, in many styles and occasions of dance. It is a potential not so much unrealized as unrepresented. Throughout this chapter I have borrowed terminology from literary theory, but dances are not books and the body is not a written-upon page. Dance requires its own close watching. It takes time, and the "reading" of dance is an undertaking which may necessitate the development of new critical strategies. Literacy in dance, from which a political reading proceeds, must begin with attention to the body and to the gravity, levity, spatiality, and rhythms of its movement. When the object speaks, when the body dances, perhaps it is not a watching but a listening which is required. Or if it is watching, it is watching with an eye that glides under the surface of skin and rests there, listening without expectation. We need to learn to look critically at the body in dance and to resist the seduction of the glittering surface, of old stories and old bodies in new clothes. I have likened this vigilant watching to a process of dissection: it is an incisive glance which destroys the deceptive unity of the dancing body. But in this act of incision another, evanescent body is born.

The realm of the "proper" is his body, his dance, his speech. To speak his tongue she leaves her mother and hands her body over to the academy. For the rest of us, we have no option but to be "improper," to speak pidgin, to mutter, to stammer, and to block up our ears against his bitter scorn. But sometimes in an unguarded moment a fissure opens in a once silent body and from it flows an unstoppable, uncontainable speaking as we cast our bodies without thinking into space.

NOTES — — — — — — — —

This essay first appeared in Susan Sheridan, ed., *Grafts: Feminist Cultural Criticism* (London: Verso, 1988).

1. Susan Leigh Foster, *Reading Dancing: Bodies and Subjects in Contemporary American Dance* (Berkeley, 1986).

2. Laleen Jayamanne with Geeta Kapur and Yvonne Rainer, "Discussion: Modernity, 'Third World,' and *The Man Who Envied Women,*" *Art and Text* 23.4 (1986): 41–51.

3. Martha Graham, "Martha Graham Speaks," *Dance Observer*, April 1963, p. 53.

4. Susan Rubin Suleiman, *The Female Body in Western Culture* (Cambridge and London, 1986): 1.

5. Curt Sachs, *World History of the Dance* (New York, 1937); Robin Collingwood, *The Principles of Art* (Oxford, 1938). Roger Copeland cites Balanchine's "notorious proclamation" as follows: "The ballet is a purely female thing; it is a woman, a garden of beautiful flowers, and the man is the gardener." Roger Copeland, "Towards a Sexual Politics of Dance," *Contact Quarterly* 7.3/4 (1982): 48.

6. Elizabeth Dempster, "Profile: Russell Dumas," *New Theatre Australia*, no. 1 (1987): 47–49.

7. See Luce Irigaray, *Divine Women* (Sydney, 1986).

8. Ann Daly, "The Balanchine Woman: Of Hummingbirds and Channel Swimmers," *Drama Review* 31.1 (1987): 8–22.

9. For a detailed discussion of the modes of representation and choreographic conventions in Renaissance and neo-classical dance, see Foster, *Reading Dancing*.

10. Lincoln Kirstein, "Classic Ballet: Aria of the Aerial," *Playbill*, May 1976. Reprinted in Roger Copeland and Marshall Cohen, eds., *What Is Dance?* (Oxford, 1983), 239.

11. Adrian Stokes, *Tonight the Ballet* (New York, 1935). Reprinted in Copeland and Cohen, *What Is Dance?* 247.

12. Chris Savage-King, "Classical Muscle," *Women's Review*, no. 2 (1985): 28.

13. See Selma Jeanne Cohen, *Doris Humphrey: An Artist First* (Middletown, Conn., 1972).

14. Martha Graham, "Martha Graham Is Interviewed by Pierre Tugal," *Dancing Times*, October 1950, pp. 21–22.

15. Deborah Jowitt, "Monumental Martha," in *Dance Beat: Selected Views and Reviews, 1967–76* (New York, 1978).

16. Martha Graham, "The Modern Dancer's Primer for Action," reprinted in Selma Jeanne Cohen, ed., *Dance as a Theatre Art* (London, 1974), 139.

17. See Lincoln Kirstein, *Dance: A Short History of Classical Theatrical Dancing* (New York, 1935).

18. Trisha Brown and Yvonne Rainer, "A Conversation about *Glacial Decoy*," *October*, no. 10 (Fall 1979): 29–37.

19. Yvonne Rainer, *Work 1961–73* (New York, 1974), 67.

20. See Rainer's *Work 1961–73* for descriptions and scores of *In the College* (1972), *Lives of Performers* (1972), and *This is the story of a woman who . . .* (1973).

21. *Les Sylphides* (1909), Fokine; *Primitive Mysteries* (1931), Graham; *Antic Meet* (1958), Cunningham, Brown and Rainer 32.

22. Laura Mulvey, "Visual Pleasure and Narrative Cinema," *Screen* 16.3 (Autumn 1975): 6–18.

23. See Shona Innes, "The Teaching of Ballet," *Writings on Dance*, no. 3 (*Of Bodies and Power*) (Summer 1988): 36–47.

24. Elizabeth Dempster, "The Economy of Shame," *Spectator Burns*, no. 1 (October 1987): 24–27.

25. Isadora Duncan, "The Dancer of the Future," reprinted in Cohen, *Dance as a Theatre Art*, 129.

26. Mary Ann Doane, "Woman's Stake: Filming the Female Body," *October*, no. 17 (1981): 24.

27.   Postmodern compositional strategies are not in themselves oppositional. In her discussion of reflexive choreographic structures Susan Foster distinguishes between resistive and reactionary forms of postmodern dance. A resistive form of postmodern dance is concerned with a critical deconstruction of tradition; it questions rather than exploits cultural codes. A mainstream and reactionary postmodern (the work of Twyla Tharp is Foster's example) plays across dance languages and traditions uncritically, exploiting conventional codes, but not questioning them.

28.   Luce Irigaray, *Speculum of the Other Woman* (Ithaca, N.Y., 1985).

Samba:
The Body Articulate

Barbara Browning

Samba is the dance of the body articulate. What does it mean to speak with the body? In Portuguese, one says that the skilled sambista is able, and obliged, to *dizer no pé*—"speak with the feet."[1] No other language is required: song is redundant, words are superfluous. One recognizes this at the Rio *carnaval*: there is an eloquence in the white shoes, in the silver high heels scraping the asphalt. You can see it daily in the familiar shantytowns pocking the hills around white moneyed neighborhoods, in the bare feet stamping down on a concrete floor. In the samba, in fact, not only the feet speak. The dance is a complex dialogue in which various parts of the body talk at the same time and in seemingly different languages. The feet keep up a rapid patter, while the hips beat out a heavy staccato and the shoulders roll a slow drawl. It is all funky with message. To articulate means, of course, to flex at the joints, and samba may seem both fluid, jointless, and at the same time entirely disjointed. The message is simultaneously narrative and lyrical. That is, it spins itself out over time, increasing in meaning as it recounts its origins, and yet it compresses its significance in a momentary image. Samba narrates a story of racial contact, conflict, and resistance—not just mimetically across a span of musical time, but synchronically, in the depth of a single measure.

When we speak of narration, we assume an element of linearity.[2] A story or history takes place in and over a span of time. Our telling of it, similarly, takes place over time. But the sequence of events, be they real or fictional, does not necessarily correspond to the sequence of their telling. Analysts of narrative distinguish between the two time lines and assign significance not only to those events recounted (and, perhaps particularly, to those unrecounted), but also to the divergence in their order. In musical terms, one might describe such divergence as polymeter—the layering of rhythmic times. In narrative terms, this is diachrony; it is what complicates all accounts of historical events, such as the

FIG. 1. Photo: B. Browning

colonization of Brazil, the suppression of indigenous peoples and cultures, and the period of the enslavement of African peoples, which lasted longer in Brazil than in any other nation in the New World. The preceding sentence is itself a kind of supercompressed narrative, which could use some spinning out here.

The Portuguese began importing African slaves to Brazil in the mid-sixteenth century. While abolition did not take place officially until 1888, black Brazilians frequently refer to that date as the inception of a *falsa abolição,* when Afro-Brazilians merely shifted from one kind of slave quarters to another—the *favelas.* Historical documents, including records of the importation of Africans, were destroyed at the time of abolition in a gesture intended by the governing class to erase the shame of slavery.[3] Of course destroying the text could not abolish the story. It is important not only to recover that lost narrative, but also to understand the story as it persists in the present.

The physical destruction of historical records is not the only gap in the narrative of the history of blacks in Brazil. Subsequent social histories have been notoriously reticent about discussing the hardships inflicted on nonwhites.[4] Given the economic destitution of the vast majority of Brazilian blacks and the virtual absence of major political figures of color in Brazil, it is perhaps hard to fathom the durability of the popular myth of Brazilian racial equity. Discrimination exists, one is told, but it is on the basis of class, not race.

So why are all the blacks so terribly poor? The Brazilian establishment concedes class discrimination, but race has effectively been erased as a term from discussions of postabolition society, up to the present. Erasure is precisely the word here because it is the metaphor behind the ideology of color which has led to these accounts full of holes. From early in this century, social theorists have suggested that mixed-race Brazilian society was undergoing a continual process of "whitening": miscegenation was thinning out the black population, while European immigration reinforced the trend toward whiteness. Early arguments of this type explicitly stated that such a trend was favorable, given the innate "superiority" of the white race.[5] In the 1930s the sociologist Gilberto Freyre countered this racist theory of whitening with a seemingly more benign version: if black and mixed-race Brazilians appeared to be a "mongrel" lot, it was due to their economic oppression, not to white racial "superiority."[6] Freyre's racially mixed Brazil was, in fact, a brave new world, enhanced by its cultural diversity. When Freyre first proposed his theories, they were viewed as progressive and clearly antiracist, but in the decades to follow they were taken up by a governing class that was all too eager to obfuscate questions of racial inequality. Also, Freyre's progressive origins have obscured the reactionary uses to which his writings have been put. By the 1960s a vocal group of intellectuals (destined to be censored and forced into exile by the military regime) was attacking Freyre as "inevitably dated and anachronistic."[7] They were right, yet Freyre's ideas still have tremendous currency among the population at large. It was he who formulated the supposed existence of a "Brazilian racial democracy" which is so dear to unpoliticized blacks and whites alike. He extended the humanistic principle that it is poverty, not racial inferiority, which degenerates men, and he argued that in Brazil, consequently, discrimination falls along economic, not color, lines. Today the phrase "Brazilian racial democracy" functions primarily to exclude race from political discussion.

The erasure of race from Brazil's political history has been remarkably continuous—from the ostensibly humanistic destruction of slavery documents, through the ostensibly humanistic avowal of racial democracy. Still, since the 1970s, a steady tide of resistance has been rising among young blacks who get the big picture. They've been telling each other another story. Popular accounts of race relations in Brazil, which hold that abolition never took place in a meaningful way (a "false abolition" leading to the *favela* as a modern slaves' quarters), are grounded in historical and demographic realities. It might be argued that these accounts operate on a figural level, as slavery is no longer literally, legislatively, a reality. But the insidiousness of these word games is all too apparent. The stunning poverty and virtually complete economic dependance of black Brazilians are hardly a metaphor. Yet the poor black tenant of a *favela,* who is employed as a domestic servant but who calls herself a slave, is aware of the power of the word and of her own articulateness in saying it. She reads herself in relation to her African antecedent as both a representation of a woman erased from Brazilian history and a continuation of the same woman's story. I do not mean to diminish the power of this gesture by suggesting it is lyrical as well as narrative. This is a strong lyricism grounded in racial identification. These are the bare feet stamping down on a concrete floor. A person can say these things in so many words. Or a person can speak with the body.

The lyricism of the samba is its incorporation of figures that flash across time. Dance ethnography has often referred to such figures as African or indigenous "survivals"—gestures in contemporary dances that can be traced or inferred to preslavery and precolonial sources. The term *survival* acknowledges the fact of cultural repression, but it fails to recognize that African and indigenous culture in the New World has not merely held on, but has grown and developed subsequent to the moment of historical rupture. In the case of Brazil, backward-looking projects of inference are often confounded by the lack of textual sources. We have the nineteenth-century engravings of Debret, Rugendas, and Martius and Spix, which show freeze-frame gestures and dance configurations. We have spotty written depictions of indigenous dances of Brazil and West Africa at the point of first contact with Europeans, although these are written from the perspective of viewers completely unfamiliar with the rhythmic and gestural vocabularies they attempt to describe. Examining contemporary dances of relatively isolated indigenous communities in Brazil and Africa is a shot in the dark. A direct comparison of these dances with the samba would not take into account the contemporaneous modifications which have taken place over centuries in these communities. Dance ethnography can never be convincing historiography.[8] Rhythmic and gestural vocabularies—the language of the body—can endure, but they are not frozen in time. They can themselves refer to ruptures in historical time—rhythmic disjunction—and they can figure themselves in relation to their past, as the *favelada* figures herself in relation to her ancestor. It doesn't mean they do the same dance. Even if the gestures are the same, they have accrued a double, self-reflexive significance. My project here is to locate the space between a narrative or figural reading of Brazilian dance. This is neither a purely historical nor a purely semiotic analysis.[9] I mean, rather, to allow for a synthesis of time and signs, which would be the only way to account for the complex speaking of the body in Brazil.

The body says what cannot be spoken. Musically, this can be explained as syncopation. Samba is a polymeter, layered over a 2/4 structure. But the strong beat is suspended, the weak accentuated. That suspension leaves the body with a hunger that can only be satisfied by filling the silence with motion. Samba, the dance, cannot exist without the suppression of a strong beat. Polymeter is a manner of describing rhythmic structures which combine various ways of counting. It is the dominant mode of all Pan-African music, and it is what distinguishes this music from Western forms in which harmonic and melodic progression predominate. A person schooled in the European musical tradition may, on encountering a polymeter, find it either incomprehensibly complex, or may apprehend a surface texture which seems not to *go* anywhere—hence the complaint of monotony. The problem is, in a sense, not the indirection of the music but the misdirection of the listening. The interest of harmonic/melodic music is in its pattern across time: the way the line varies, or harmonies change. The interest of polymetric music is in the simultaneous patterns which are established in a single measure. One reads Western music, on the page, from left to right. If polymetric music is notated, one must read it vertically in order to perceive its complexity. This is not to say that it doesn't change over time. In fact, the breaks in rhythmic structure, the ruptures in the pattern, are the points at which the full complexity of the original pattern becomes evident. But the break precisely points out all that was inherent or potential in the texture before the tear.

Western musical notation is inadequate for inscribing polymeters. Samba cannot be convincingly programmed into a computerized drum machine, as it contains rhythms bent so slightly that their variation can't be broken down even into sixty-fourths. But an inaccurate inscription is perhaps the only way to represent here the exigencies of reading the rhythm synchronically—up and down. The basic texture of samba requires that these patterns be in place:

Fig. 2.

These two bars represent the basic phrase. In the first, two strong beats are established. In the second, these beats are suspended in the *clave* part, the final line in this notation. *Clave* is Spanish for "key," and it is the term generally used to refer to the rhythmic pattern fundamental to any polymeter. In a sense it is analogous to the European notion of a clef or key which organizes harmonic relations. The clave is a regular irregularity. For those unfamiliar with polymeters, the clave is generally the part most difficult to make heads or tails of. It appears arbitrary, seems to come in and out of rhythm. In order to play it, one must let go of the downbeat. The clave in its capriciousness assumes a quality that seems melodic. It is, effectively, the *song* of any polymeter. And it is the key, in the sense that it opens all the other patterns which might otherwise appear locked. The clave of the samba breaks the count of one-x-two-x-one-x-two into one-two-xx-one-two-three-xx. That three-count brings into relief the tighter, rapid triplets of the second line of the notation. These are not, in fact, true triplets, as one beat is slightly weighted—generally, the second of each set. This is the bending of rhythm to which I referred. The bottom-heavy center triplet sets the strong beat off balance—an imbalance recomplicated by the clave's trip-step.

The basic samba step appears to articulate the triplets. It requires levity, speed, and dexterity, and accuracy, but not in the sense of hitting the rhythm on the mark. It must locate itself *between* rhythms. The dance is on a three-count—right-left-right/left-right-left—but it also weights one count, either the first *or* the second triplet. It may accentuate or contradict the weighting of the triplets in the music. As one triplet is heavier, the step slides toward the first line of rapid sixteenth-notes. The stronger step gives almost two sixteenths to itself and hints at that doubleness by, in an instant, shifting the weight from the ball of the foot to the heel—a double articulation or flexing at the joint. The step is *between* a triplet set and four sixteenth-notes. The relation between the feet and the rhythm might be approximately notated as:

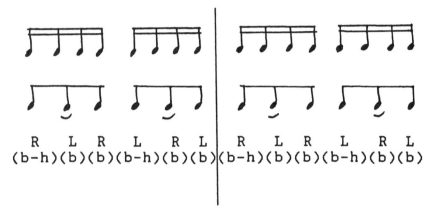

R   L   R   L   R   L   R   L   R   L   R   L
(b-h)(b)(b)(b-h)(b)(b)(b-h)(b)(b)(b-h)(b)(b)

FIG. 3.

On each step marked b-h (ball-heel), the weight of the body is pitched slightly forward, while the next two steps (ball-ball) are a mere lifting up and back in preparation for the next pitch forward. The dance that I have inscribed here is a simple version in which the pitching-forward occurs on the initial beat. A funkier version of the step would pitch forward rather on the second beat of each set of triplets. That is a recomplication of the rhythm which most Western students find more difficult, although it is merely a resituation of the same step within the rhythmic structure—another dislocation of the downbeat.

If you are reading this chapter hoping to learn the dance, this is the moment at which you will shake your head in exasperation. It will only make things worse if I tell you that while all this is happening, the hips—particularly if you are a woman—must lag slightly behind the feet such that their triplet, while it follows the same right-left-right pattern, will accentuate or weight a beat slightly after that of the feet, while your shoulders (strange quietude over this cacophony) will simply roll on the one and two of the third line of my original notation. I have taught Brazilian dance for years, and if ever I had prefaced a class with this description I would have lost even the most agile of my students. Western students of polymetric music and dance often request that the rhythms be broken down, but a complete breakdown results in just that—the rhythm breaks down. Our frequent admonition—stop thinking and dance—isn't to say that the motion is unthinkable. It's to say that the body is capable of understanding more things at once than can be articulated in language. One has no choice but to *think with the body*.

The dancer may be able to accommodate more simultaneous rhythms than the individual musicians in a samba ensemble. Robert Ferris Thompson coined the phrase "apart-playing" to describe the way in which individual musicians work together to create a polymeter.[10] Each player concentrates on his part (I use the masculine pronoun here as it most realistically represents the gender of the players in most Brazilian percussion groups), and the separate lines of thought coincide at the beginning of each phrase. But the *meaning* of these separate lines only becomes apparent when they come together. The dancer may make reference to all of them with different parts of her body. This is a synthetic quality of Pan-African dance generally. John Miller Chernoff has noted that African drummers say they *understand* a polymeter by knowing how to dance it: "In African music, it is the listener or dancer who has to supply the beat: the listener must be *actively engaged* in making sense of the music."[11] When one watches a sambista dance, one is watching a gesture of making significance.

I said that samba is layered over a 2/4 structure. In the notation, that fundamental beat can be read in the third line. In the instrumentation of a modern samba band, the fundamental 2/4 beat is played by an instrument called the *surdo,* an enormous bass drum which is strapped over the shoulder. *Surdo,* which means "deaf" in Portuguese, can be understood as referring to the effect of the deep pounding on the player or the listener. But it might also be understood as the quality of sound produced by the drum. The surdo is so extremely deep in tone, so very bass, that its effect is like a negative utterance. It seems in a sense to erase or negate that moment in sound. Samba as a rhythm not only suspends its downbeat through the clave, but even in its stressing of that beat blacks it out. The accompanying dance can fill the gap with a strong step or can reinforce its dislocation with another kind of suspension. But marking the absense of the downbeat is another way of indicating it. However the samba is danced, *it is the suspension or silencing of a beat which provokes movement.*

The same can be said of samba historically. Samba is a dance that generally attracts attention for its frenetic exuberance. It is regarded as a secular form, neither religious nor overtly political. Known as the Brazilian national dance, it has contributed to a world image of that country as one of exaggerated elation, in which joyous movement is considered meaningful in and of itself. But samba means more than this. And if its steps can only be called forth by syncopation, its deeper meanings can only be evoked by another kind of suppression, which is racial, cultural, and political. Those who would promote samba as a purely aesthetic form, the "Brazilian national dance" in its most harmless sense, are also those who have long promoted the fiction of a "Brazilian racial democracy"—a fiction which began to be inscribed with the destruction of the documents of slavery. This is another form of negative articulation, an erasure of a historical moment which in fact brings that moment into relief. This fiction has silenced a history of cultural and political repression of blacks and indigenous peoples. Samba speaks that history.

I said that samba narrates racial contact synchronically, not across time like most fictions or histories. But there is a fiction sometimes used to explain the history of samba—*a história do negro e da índia*, "the story of the black man and the 'Indian' woman." (I use here and elsewhere the term *Indian,* as opposed to indigenous Brazilian, to refer not to a literal and culturally significant people, but rather to the highly figurative image constructed by colonists and appropriated and ironized by the blacks in Brazil, as is discussed below.) The story goes that in the early days of colonization, an escaped black slave encountered a *cabocla*—an Indian woman—in the bush. As both were tired of life among the Portuguese, they set up housekeeping there in the wild, and their children began a *mestiço* race. The only difficulty was the parents' inability to communicate in each other's language, so their arguments took place in stomps, shakes, and shudders—the samba. The word (of uncertain origin) *zamba* means a mestiço child, offspring of an African father and an indigenous mother. But few ethnologists suppose that this is the real source of the term *samba* as it refers to a particular rhythm and style of dance. This narrative of the birth of samba is obviously fictional, but it serves to illustrate precisely to what degree the encounter between Africans and indigenous Brazilians has had to be fictionalized by white society in order to diminish its political potential. The identification of the two races in their resistance against whites was and is threatening. The reduction of the encounter to a benign love story culminating in samba is a manner of defusing the threat. But ironically, it is samba which tells the story left silent in the fictional version.

If *zamba* is not the source of the term, what is? I will begin with one of the less popular hypotheses. Baptista Siqueira notes that in the seventeenth century, Jesuit missionaries recorded the term *samba* among the Cariri people of Brazil in reference to a kind of wild tortoise, which was a delicacy served at festive gatherings. The meaning of the word later expanded to signify the physical space of communal festivities. Siqueira cites a journalistic account from the turn of the century that seems to incorporate the Cariri in a fictional construct that resembles the story we've already heard:

> the dance is a function of dances: the samba is a mixture of the *jongo* of the African percussive ensembles, of the Sugarcane dance of the Portuguese and of the *poracé* of the Indians. The three races are melded in the samba, as in a crucible. The *samba* is the *apoplexy* of the court, it is the pyrrhic victory of the bedroom. In it, the heavy sovereign conquers the light *mameluca* [a woman of mixed African and indigenous race]. In it are absorbed the hatreds of color. The *samba* is—if you will permit me the expression—a kind of pot, into which enter, separately, dark coffee and pale milk,

and out of which is poured, homogeneous and harmonic, the hybrid *café-com-leite*: coffee with milk.[12]

The *índia* of the story is here replaced by the *mameluca*, the *zamba* with *café-com-leite*. The proliferation in Brazil of terms for highly specified kinds of racial mixing is truly mind-boggling. Dozens of designations are in popular use.[13] It is of no surprise that in the fictional constructions, the woman is the one figured as source or product of miscegenation. For obvious historical reasons, it is more accurate to suggest that it was the mameluca who absorbed Portuguese, *male* whiteness, even if it is figured as milk. In fact, early European writings frequently figured the conquest of Brazil as a maternal process: Europe giving suck to the "savages," offering up sweet Christian humanism—the milk of human kindness. Of course colonization is never gentle. And the milk proffered by the Portuguese to both African and indigenous women was what is sometimes referred to in Brazil by the popular brand name *Leite Mocó:* semen. It is doubtful whether racial *hatred* was absorbed in quite the "homogeneous and harmonic" way described here. The erotic undertones of this story, however, point to the way racial difference has been romanticized in Brazil. It is particularly the woman of mixed race who figurally absorbs the fear of racial resistance in her sexual conquerability.

This mameluca, like the cabocla of the earlier story, is of course fictional, yet there has been a fascinating appropriation of the Indian as a figure within black cultural expressions in Brazil. This is not to say no literal indigenous influence on black music and dance forms has occurred. In fact, it is difficult to separate the literal from the figurative influence. Siqueira's thesis is of interest because he attempts to ground the figurative cabocla in a literal historical account—based on etymology—which would reaffirm an indigenous cultural presence in popular forms. Certainly samba as it is danced in interior regions of northeastern Brazil, where many people are of indigenous descent, resembles closely the descriptions we have of seventeenth-century indigenous dances. The posture is more stooped toward the ground, and the feet shuffle in a minute pattern that is more earth-bound than those of the springy coastal forms.

Most Brazilian folklorists derive the word *samba* not from the Cariri, but from an African source. The Ki-Kongo word *semba* is translated in Portuguese as *umbigada,* meaning "a blow struck with the bellybutton." In the earliest documented forms of the dance in Brazil, this gesture was used by the dancer in the center of a circle of spectators to call the next dancer to take a turn. Edison Carneiro argues that this gesture unifies almost all variations on the samba in Brazil.[14] The same gesture was also recorded by the Portuguese among Angolans in Africa during the period of slavery. Since the work of Arthur Ramos and Carneiro, the dominant school of Brazilian ethnologists is profoundly Africanist and has tended to obscure indigenous influences on the culture. Hence, in the literature on samba, Siqueira's thesis sticks out like a sore thumb.

Based on similarities to rhythms and dances recorded in Angola, it is probably fair to say that samba is essentially a Kongo rhythm and expression. But it has certainly absorbed other cultural influences. It has also absorbed the eroticization of miscegenation. And while samba is even popularly regarded as essentially African, the women who dance it professionally—in the carnaval or in tourist shows—are all called *mulatas,* regardless of their color. I myself am white and blue-eyed, and I have danced with shining jet-black women, but in the context of our dancing samba we were all mulatas. When I have danced particularly well, I have always been told that this is evidence of some black blood. This statement is not a literal misapprehension of my race. It is a statement of belief that the meaningfulness of race is culture and that a commitment to culture can result in an accrual of racial spiritual energy. *Mulatto* is a term which in this country has recently come to be regarded as not merely a racial but a racist designation. Opposition to the word is based on its etymology: from Spanish *mulato, mulo;* from Latin *mulus,* "mule." The mule is a freak of nature, mismatched hybrid, useful for labor but unable to sustain itself as a line. The mule is incapable of reproducing. The mulata of the samba is eroticized, of course, but does she really embody the ideals of racial miscegenation in Brazil? Or is she perceived as that which does not produce or reproduce its own color, but absorbs the European Leite Mocó in a sensuality which allows for not only progressive whitening, but also a dissolution of the potential for racial anger? This may be the underlying perception or desire in white depictions of samba. But popular samba perceives—and constantly reaffirms and *reproduces*—its color.

It seems obvious that these ways of talking about race are highly figurative and that the stories told about samba's racial history are fairy tales. But none of this is so far from the typical discussion of the significance of race in Brazil. Miscegenation is central to Brazilians' self-conception.

Even the deepest, heaviest African traditions in Brazil have an intricate language for speaking of race. Traditional African religions as they are practiced in Brazil go by a number of names. In Bahia, where the communities of worship of West African gods are most pervasive, the religion is known as *candomblé.* Derived from the beliefs and practices of the Yoruba people of southwestern Nigeria, candomblé is an ancient, complex, and powerfully beautiful belief system in which spirituality is expressed through sophisticated rhythmic structures, and divinity makes itself present in the bodies of dancers. This is what is commonly referred to as "possessional dance," but I am disinclined to use the term because of its connotations of violence or violation. The dancer in the candomblé studies for an extended period of time in order to be able to open her body to the divinity which will serve and be served by her community.

The houses of candomblé which appear to have remained closest to Yoruba tradition are said to be of the *kêto* or *nagô* "nation." The word *nation* was used during the period of the slave trade to identify not the land of origin of Africans arriving in Brazil, but rather the port out of which they had been shipped. The "nations" were in effect trade names. But the Africans in Brazil reclaimed the terms as a way of identifying cultural affinities. Blacks in Brazil today can often specify the nation of their great-grandparents. Differences in candomblé practice are marked by nation, although the members of the houses may be descended from other areas of Africa. While relatively small in number, the kêto and nagô houses are highly regarded in the religious community at large and have certainly been favored by the Africanist ethnographic community of which I have written. Far more common, however, are houses of the angola nation, or of the *candomblé de caboclo*. The pantheon of these houses is still based on that of the Yoruba gods, or *orixás*. But in these houses the figure of the "Indian" has been imbued with both spiritual and political significance. Here, the caboclo enters the canon as a figure mediating between the divine and the temporal. The caboclo spirit is, in the words of the folklorist Raul Lody, "the free hunter, true prototype of him who would not allow himself to be enslaved."[15] In other words, the caboclo is an idealized image of the resistant black.

A corresponding phenomenon in the United States is that of the black Indians of the New Orleans Mardi Gras. While some racial mixing took place between African and Native Americans in the South, it is sometimes perceived that this mixing has been exaggerated in black folklore and popular culture. Zora Neale Hurston wrote, with tongue firmly in cheek, that she was the only southern black not matrilineally descended from an Indian chief.[16] Hurston's comment suggests that an African-American claim of "Indianness" is based on a desire to assume a lighter color. But racial identification with indigenous peoples might be read as a much stronger political affiliation—one that comprehends not only color but a history of cultural and political repression. This identification is with both literal, historical indigenous people and with the mythic *type* of the Indian. During the New Orleans Mardi Gras, a highly codified event which celebrates the Creole elite, groups of black men parade in elaborate Native American costumes, singing their own songs and even speaking their own dialect. They provide a counterbalance to the aristocratic element of the festival, purposefully presenting themselves as not Creole, but black—and not just black, but black Indians. Students of Mardi Gras history note that the groups claim to have adopted Indian custom through actual cultural contact and intermarriage, but this story of a black-Indian love affair may also signify something different.[17] The costumes worn in the Mardi Gras resemble those of Plains Indians, not any southern tribe. In fact, the cultural prototype was more likely drawn from the "Wild West" carnival shows popular in the region in the late nineteenth century than from any blood relatives.[18]

If some discrepancy exists in the stories circulating around the black Indians, we shouldn't be surprised. The phenomenon, as George Lipsitz has written, "projects a cultural indeterminacy"—neither "really" Indian nor "purely" African;[19] the complexity is the point. Even its family history can't be contained. In Brazil, a person's caboclo or Indian aspect is a quality which may come not from blood inheritance, but from commitment to the ideal of freedom. My own Indian

protector spirits have been identified at moments of my most energetic and muscular dancing, or at times (often the same ones) when I evidenced a furious
protectiveness of my own sexual independence.

The dances of the candomblé, as I said, come from a Yoruba tradition—even
those designated of the angola nation. Samba appears to have been derived from
Kongo-Angolan moves. Yet there are certain similarities, the most striking being
the circle formation of the dances' participants. In the candomblé, the circle of
dancers moves counterclockwise, until one or several receive a divine spirit. At
that moment, no longer held to be a mere dancer but an incorporation of divine
energy, the entity moves to the center of the circle, which is called a *roda,* or
wheel. Each god presents a particular choreography, obliquely mimetic of a divine principle. Yemanjá, goddess of the sea, undulates, and her shoulders are
tremulous as the sea's surface.

In the *samba de roda,* the most traditional form of the dance as it is danced in
Bahia, the circle does not rotate, but the participants stand, clap, and take turns
going to the center. This tradition is separate from the roda of the candomblé. It is
only in the candomblé de caboclo that samba is considered an integral part of the
candomblé ceremony. When the caboclo spirit comes down, he sambas. The roda
is fixed. Ethnographers have been uncomfortable classifying the *samba de caboclo* with other candomblé dances, perhaps because of the purist, Africanist
tendencies in the Brazilian ethnographic community which I mentioned earlier.
But even within the religious community, the use of the term *samba* to designate
the caboclo spirit's dance seems to be a way of blurring the distinction between
the divine and the profane. Defenders of the candomblé de caboclo have argued
that the term *samba de caboclo* is a reductive or even derogatory classification.
The caboclo, however, is precisely intent on breaking down barriers, releasing
strictures such as those between the sacred and the secular.

In the candomblés which do not entertain the caboclo, samba can also occur,
but only after a ceremony has ended. The secular drumming and dancing are an
afterthought, and they may be encouraged as a way of redeeming an evening in
which the divine turnout has been disappointing. Samba in this context often
puns visually on the candomblé dances. While the dance is considered secular, it
may encode references to divine choreographies. In this way, the roda de samba
serves a complementary purpose to that of the roda de santo, or the circle formation of the candomblé. The roda here is an inclusionary (or exclusionary) boundary. So while a boundary seems to exist between the candomblé and the samba,
the latter form reinforces the boundary of the African religious community. The
ethnographer Maria Teixeira argues that this irony does not debase the notion of
a divine circle, but rather raises the human body and its motion to a sacred
ground. The roda de samba is the space in which the individual body and *its*
intelligence mediate between spheres: "The center of the Roda de Santo, through
axé, relives the mythic drama of the Orixás; it is the divinities that assume the
stage with all their refinement, potency and decorum. In the Roda de Samba, it is

the cult of the body which assumes relevance."[20] *Axé* is Yoruba for "pure potentiality, divine energy," or, in the translation of Robert F. Thompson which has always struck me as the most accurate, "the power to make things happen." When Teixeira says that axé allows divine entities to take over the stage—and the bodies of the dancers—of the candomblé, she means it is the presence of the orixás that brings significance to the dance. But in the roda de samba, the *human body* assumes a heightened level of significance.

Axé is not restricted to the context of the candomblé. The power to make things happen can exist within a secular rhythm. It is not any samba which provokes motion in the irresistible way I described earlier. A certain degree of potentiality is required. When one is dancing, the parts of the body respond to the various instruments and patterns being played. And the parts of the body respond when a given musician begins to play with particular axé, which should not be confused with volume.

I spoke above of the roda as an inclusive or exclusive boundary, and nowhere in Brazilian dance is this more powerfully represented than in the *roda de capoeira*. Capoeira is another Kongo-derived tradition, a fighting game performed to percussive music. The moves are fluid, elegant, and potentially devastating if used for effect. Blacks in Brazil trained in capoeira for defense of the *quilombos*—communities composed of escaped slaves—and its practice was prohibited by white authorities. But the roda was a protective circle for the training capoeiristas. The changing rhythm of the musicians served as a warning to fighters so that if an overseer approached, the moves were modified to appear to be "merely" a samba. Even within the game of capoeira, dance serves as a disguise. The two players at the center of the roda sway back and forth rhythmically in a step called the *ginga,* and it is only out of that seemingly imbalanced and unprotected attitude that capoeira's kicks and sweeps can be deployed.

As Muniz Sodré has observed, one of the oldest and most popular capoeira songs is an ironic twisting of the sentiments of whites in Brazil during the slavery period. The song simply repeats the phrase "cala a boca, moleque" (shut your mouth, black boy). The words are provocative and not only echo the old white attitudes but perhaps articulate a contemporary sentiment—in a slightly more complicated sense. While the overt sentiment expressed by white Brazilian society today is not only tolerance of but affection for the musicality of black culture, the unstated message given by whites is still "cala a boca moleque—e vá sambar." Shut up and dance. The provocation of the capoeira song, though, is a directive much more dangerous: If you can't speak the truth with your mouth, speak it with your feet—not in a patter of meaningless, endlessly expendable energy, but in a precisely aimed *benção,* or blessing, a kick which plants the sole of the foot on the chest of one's opponent. A blessing is a benediction, good talk, the appropriate response. Frantz Fanon wrote that this is the language of the politicization of the oppressed: "He of whom *they* have never stopped saying that the only language he understands is that of force, decides to give *utterance by force.*"[21] Capoeira has always been a language of black resistance.

Both the candomblé and capoeira were aggressively suppressed by white authorities until participation by middle-class whites became impossible to ignore. The tourist industry also saw the potential exotic appeal. Now there is official sanction and even financial support, under particular and controlled circumstances. But during the period of prohibition, both candomblé dance and capoeira were sustained in the roda de samba, through gestural and rhythmic reference.

In the layered rhythms of samba, the strong accent which is suspended is the silencing of other forms. That gap is filled by direct incorporation of candomblé and capoeira moves. The percussionists may even make reference to the rhythms and songs of these forms. In the midst of a samba, the *agôgô* bell may begin to play the clave of the orixá Xangô's rhythm, or the *atabaque* drummer may start to slap out a capoeira beat. But more likely the reference will be subtle. In the body of the dancer, it may be multiple. The feet shift rapidly in the pattern of the dance of the caboclo-identified bush divinity, Oxóssi. The hips flash the fire of the storm goddess Iansã, and the shoulders shimmer like the surface of Yemanjá's waters. The whole of the dance is seemingly set off balance in the deceptive sway of capoeira's ginga, but it hides a potential blow. Or the blow can actualize itself: mid-samba one can sweep the feet out from under one's partner in a move taken straight from capoeira. This is known as *samba duro*—hard samba.

We can narrate the interrelation of the dances by constructing another story, set perhaps on a sugarcane plantation in Bahia, where, hidden, the Yoruba formed their circles of divinity and the Kongo formed their circles of political anger. And the circles became one circle and the rhythms overlapped, and the sacred slapped its belly against the profane and samba was born. But it didn't happen like that. African and indigenous communities were dispersed. Their histories were ruptured. Their own narrative structures were shattered. The culture that grows out of violence maintains its echoes of historical and rhythmic disjunction. The rodas of candomblé, capoeira, and samba can't be straightened out into a linear account. Samba is as much a fragmentation of a holy black body as it is a healing of spiritual and political wounds.

But the rhythm is gorgeous. The body is gorgeous. It tells the story I can't tell here—one that is aesthetic, spiritual, and political. What happened next? The dancing body itself was dispersed. Some stayed in Bahia, and they still dance in a roda, swathed in the huge white skirts of the candomblé ceremonies. Some went to Rio, where they institutionalized the *escolas de samba,* carnaval samba schools where today white television soap opera stars parade topless on floats, meagerly twitching their bottoms in a weak imitation of the real thing. Some refused to ride, or would have, had they been invited: they remained on the asphalt, scraping ever-new inventiveness out of their silver shoes. It is as impossible to say which is more "authentic"—samba in Rio or Bahia—as it is to make sense of a simple historical account of how it got there. The Rio sambista in silver shoes, in all likelihood black despite her "mulata" classification, may dance consumed with axé.

I believe I came to understand the significance of the body in time only when I learned to samba. Of course as a white I have been suspect, and it was perhaps partly my tenacity in the face of this suspicion that made me understand resistance in the dance. I have been challenged. Once it happened in a house of candomblé in Bahia. The caboclo arrived and spun about furiously, then stopped abruptly and pointed at my feet. I was pushed into the roda, and I danced as if to save my life. I was fully aware that the caboclo was not so much interested in the speed of my feet as in my commitment to saying something meaningful with them. The exigency of the caboclo is the weight I feel in my bones and muscles each time I attempt to write, in words, about the significance of resistant culture.

Once the challenge happened on a little *praça* or plaza off the beach in the Flamengo section of Rio. Some members of the famous Mangueira samba school were jamming and swilling beer. A seasoned mulata, fifty-ish, short, stocky, and tanked to the gills, was decked out in the school colors: hot pink visor and t-shirt, lime-green eye shadow, hot pants, and plastic shoes. She looked me over and put me to work: I did a respectable little solo, ending with a subdued swivel and then shiver in the hips. She took her turn: a lengthy, hilarious trip-step in no rush at all, ending with pure glory. She glanced at me, licked her fingertips, and held them, wet, millimeters from the V of her hot pants as she took a deep, luxuriating grind down to the ground. She busted my chops.

For all of the anxiety which samba's eroticism causes some American women and politically sensitive men, I have found its *auto*erotic potential to be extraordinarily liberating. In a culture in which racism and sexism are articulated in each other's terms, it was perhaps my sex that allowed me a certain degree of bodily comprehension of color—what is called an accrual of black blood, or Indian protector spirits. Samba, like capoeira, does not employ full frontal blows. Part of its strength is seduction, even apparent vulnerability. But the female sambista must assume her sexuality—not as the coffeepot, receptacle of some wan Leite Moçó, but as Iansã's self-sufficient whirlwind of the hips. She takes a man if she wants one! It would be highly idealistic—and wrong—to suggest that this is the reality of a Brazilian underclass woman. But it is an ideal expressed by her in the samba.

She can be funny, terrifying, painfully beautiful, but above all she must be eloquent. She is committed to saying something that has not been and cannot be spoken. Wherever she is, whatever color she is, her feet have to speak, and they have to speak not only of beauty, but of her own belief and resistance.

NOTES

1. The anthropologist Edison Carneiro writes: "the choreography of the samba is characterized by a slippery step, by individual creativity, and by no other fixed rule than that all that the sambista feels must be *said,* must be expressed, with the feet." Carneiro, *Carta do samba* (Rio de Janeiro: Ministerio da Educação e Cultura, 1962), 11 (my translation). The expression is a commonplace.

2. For a discussion of basic narratological principles, see Tzvetan Todorov, "The Two Principles of Narrative," trans. Philip E. Lewis, *Diacritics* 1.1 (Fall 1971): 37–43.

3. See Robert Conrad, *The Destruction of Brazilian Slavery, 1850–1888* (Berkeley: University of California Press, 1972).

4. The American sociologist Thomas E. Skidmore has spent two decades calling into question the popular myth of Brazilian racial equity. See Skidmore, *Black into White: Race and Nationality in Brazilian Thought* (New York: Oxford University Press, 1974).

5. A major proponent of this theory was the mixed-race writer Francisco José de Oliveira Vianna. See Vianna, *Evolução do povo Brasileiro* (Rio de Janeiro, 1922).

6. Gilberto Freyre, *New World in the Tropics: The Culture of Modern Brazil* (New York: Knopf, 1959), 119.

7. Dante Moreira Leite, *O caráter nacional brasileiro* (São Paulo: Pioneira, 1969), 271. See also Carlos Guilherme Mota, *Ideologia da cultura brasileira, 1933–1974* (São Paulo: Editora Ática, 1978).

8. For a consideration of some of the challenges of modern dance ethnography, see Anya Peterson Royce, *The Anthropology of Dance* (Bloomington: Indiana University Press, 1989), 17–37.

9. The semiotic aspect of my analysis is greatly indebted to Muniz Sodré's small and beautiful book, *Samba, o dono do corpo* (Rio de Janeiro: Codecri, 1979). Sodré's thesis, with which I am clearly in accord, is that samba is inherently semiological and constitutes a language in response to cultural repression. He notes that the clue to this language is encoded in the name of the very first samba school of the Rio *carnaval:* Deixa Falar, or "let me speak." I hope here to expand this discussion, in order to accommodate for the development of the language over time.

10. Robert F. Thompson, "An Aesthetic of the Cool: West African Dance," *African Forum* 2.2 (Fall 1966): 93–94.

11. John Miller Chernoff, *African Rhythm and African Sensibility* (Chicago: University of Chicago Press, 1979), 50.

12. Olavo Bilac, *Kosmos* (1906), cited in Baptista Siqueira, *Origem do termo samba* (São Paulo: IBRASA, 1977), 138 (my translation).

13. Benjamin Nuñez gives thirty-five terms for persons of mixed race, in Nuñez, *Dictionary of Afro-Latin American Civilization* (Westport, Conn.: Greenwood, 1980).

14. Edison Carneiro, *Folguedos tradicionais* (Rio de Janeiro: Conquista, 1974), 35–36.

15. Raul Lody, *Samba de caboclo* (Rio de Janeiro: Funarte, 1977), 5 (my translation).

16. "I am colored but I offer nothing in the way of extenuating circumstances except the fact that I am the only Negro in the United States whose grandfather on the mother's side was *not* an Indian chief." Zora Neale Hurston, "How It Feels to Be Colored Me," in *I Love Myself When I am Laughing and Then Again When I Am Looking Mean and Impressive*, ed. Alice Walker (Old Westbury, N.Y.: Feminist Press, 1979), 152.

17. See Sam Kinser, *Carnival, American Style: Mardi Gras at New Orleans and Mobile* (Chicago: University of Chicago Press, 1990).

18. See Jason Berry, Jonathan Foose, and Tad Jones, *Up from the Cradle of Jazz* (Athens: University of Georgia Press, 1986).

19. George Lipsitz, "Mardi Gras Indians: Carnival and Counter-Narrative in Black New Orleans," *Cultural Critique* 10 (Fall 1988): 102.

20. Maria Teixeira, *O rodar das rodas: Dos homens e dos orixás* (Rio de Janeiro: Instituto Nacional do Folclore, 1985), 46–47.

21. Frantz Fanon, *The Wretched of the Earth*, trans. Constance Farrington (New York: Grove Press, 1968), 84.

Flaming Closets

Michael Moon

In memory of Jack Smith

Lost in the woods around Cummington, Massachusetts, one summer afternoon in 1981, my friend Mark and I walked in endless circles and talked desultorily, exchanging fragments of our life stories. He told me the following anecdote by way of partially explaining why he had become sexually active only late in youth. When he was twelve, he said, his mother went out shopping one Saturday afternoon and left him and his two older brothers, who were thirteen and fourteen, at home by themselves. The oldest boy proposed they have what he called a Scheherazade party in their mother's absence, and the other two readily fell in with the plan. He had recently been talking about what sounded to each of them like a funny and possibly exciting game of "playing harem," and the boys decided to seize the opportunity to try it out. Giggling, they put on a phonograph record of Rimsky-Korsakoff's *Schéhérazade* and launched into simultaneous and uproarious stripteases to the music. Once they were undressed, one of the boys ran into their parents' room and returned with three of their mother's scarves, which they tied around their by now erect penises as they resumed their hilarious "harem girl" dances. At this point their mother, having realized she had forgotten her wallet, unexpectedly returned home. The three "dancing girls" found themselves surprised by a parental whirling dervish who shouted and cursed at them, threw the phonograph record off the turntable, and then, her fury still unvented, hurled a chair through one of the living-room windows. Mark said years later that he was so embarrassed and frightened by the episode that he didn't again indulge in any form of sexual experimentation—even solo masturbation—for nine years afterward.

To the question of why Mark's mother was so upset and angry there is of course no shortage of answers or explanations: a parent's violent responses to her pubescent sons' enactment of their sexuality; a woman's—a mother's—rage at a scene of the male sexuality by which she had long felt (if only unconsciously or inarticulately) oppressed; the blind homophobic fury of an at least nominally heterosexual woman at the (to her) astonishingly casual homosexual play of her three sons. It would have been little comfort to Mark and his brothers, and perhaps even less to their mother, to have been told that their behavior in this situation paralleled in some striking ways the plot of the most celebrated Scheherazade party of them all, the 1910 Serge Diaghilev–Ballets Russes production, but I think it is of considerable interest to the student of the dynamics of homoeroticism and homophobia as constitutive elements of modern culture to notice how aspects of the scenario of Diaghilev's influential pseudo-oriental extravaganza in some ways correspond to Mark's story. In the Ballets Russes *Schéhérazade*, the shah is told by his brother that he (the shah) is being duped by his wives, that all of them are unfaithful to him. The shah, in a pet, pretends to go off hunting, and leaves his chief wife, the sultana Zobeida, and the rest of the harem to themselves. As soon as he is gone, his wives receive their various "slave" lovers, Zobeida's being the so-called Golden Slave (one of Vaslav Nijinsky's most celebrated roles). The shah returns unexpectedly, surprising his wives with their lovers, and, in a rage, orders his janissaries to slaughter the whole group. In a scene awhirl with flashing scimitars and falling bodies, Zobeida holds herself motionless, until, seeing her lover killed, she stabs herself to death. Her astonished husband bursts into tears, and the curtain falls.[1]

Diaghilev's *Schéhérazade*, starring Nijinsky and the legendary Ida Rubinstein (as the "unfaithful wife" Zobeida) and choreographed by Michel Fokine, was one of the most famous premieres in an age of opening-night *coups de théâtre*. Marcel Proust, who attended with the composer and conductor Reynaldo Hahn, his erstwhile lover, wrote afterward that the spectacle was the most beautiful he had ever seen.[2] Peter Wollen, drawing on Edward Said's *Orientalism* and related work of Perry Anderson and Arno Mayer, has deftly analyzed the implications of early twentieth-century cultural productions such as *Schéhérazade*, the fashions they inspired and the social and political attitudes they underwrote, and the fantasies that were disseminated through them.[3] These latter included racist and imperialist fantasies of white bourgeois global domination of "oriental" peoples, and depended, for the glamorous and erotic aura they exuded for many white Europeans and Americans, on other fantasies, imbricated with them, about inhabiting environments of extreme opulence in which the members of "master races" could enact with impunity "forbidden" sexual impulses on the dominated bodies of others.

Wollen focuses his analysis of *Schéhérazade* on Léon Bakst's set and costume designs, which, historians of fashion agree, revolutionized consumer perceptions throughout the bourgeois world. Bakst's use of brilliant hues of blue and green and red and orange side by side was immediately imitated in cultural productions of all kinds, in painting, jewelry design, and interior decoration. Cecil Beaton, then an acute young observer of the haute monde, wrote of the Paris of 1910 in the aftermath of *Schéhérazade* that "a fashion world that had been dominated by corsets, lace, feathers and pastel shades soon found itself a seraglio of vivid colours, harem skirts, beads, fringes and voluptuousness" (quoted in Wollen 21).

"Fringes and voluptuousness" is suggestive: in the new seraglio "look" derived from Bakst's designs, signifiers of the ostensibly trivial order of bright-colored shawls, beads, and "fringe" suddenly became ubiquitous, and included within their semiotic range a "voluptuous fringe" that lay, in a manner of speaking, just the other side of the looking glass from their wearers' ordinary lives, a phantasmagoric "oriental" margin populated by lascivious odalisques and their slave lovers, jealous masters and their terrible household executioners. When the fashionable world of 1910 donned turbans, "harem pants," oriental shawls, and beads in "shocking" quantities and color combinations, they can be seen to have been participating in a mass fantasy of joining a "voluptuous fringe" where ordinary social life took on a "barbaric splendor" and sexuality imaginarily escaped the constraints of bourgeois domestic life and took on a "savage" and many-hued intensity.

Riots did not break out at the premiere of *Schéhérazade*—that famously happened to the Ballets Russes three seasons later, at the first night of *Le sacre du printemps*. Violence was apparently largely confined to the stage in *Schéhérazade,* in the general slaughter that followed the shah's vengeful entry into the scene of orgy in his own harem. In his analysis of the potent implicit political effects of the fashions—and not least of all the fashions in fantasy—a spectacle like *Schéhérazade* fostered, Wollen emphasizes the enormous impact of Bakst's designs on popular perceptions and attitudes in this century. Interested as I am in the history of gay male subjectivity in the modern epoch, I want to consider another aspect of the "riot of fantasies" that converged on *Schéhérazade* and that it in turn reproduced and disseminated. Besides its fosterage of colonialist racist attitudes of the kind Wollen reads out of it, there are other significant ways in which the repressive violence I have spoken of as being in one sense limited to the space of the stage in *Schéhérazade* extended far beyond it. The ones I emphasize here are the misogynist and homophobic implications of the murderous disciplinary violence the piece symbolically carried out on its "stars," Rubinstein and Nijinsky, in their respective characters of Zobeida and the Golden Slave.

In a series of performances around the time of *Schéhérazade*, ranging from Saint Sebastian to Salome, Ida Rubinstein powerfully enacted a series of fin de siècle fantasies about the ostensibly "evil" potential of various modes of behavior attributed to women in some of the dominant representational regiments of the turn of the century. These ranged from phallic femininity (woman as castrator, femme fatale) to anorexic withdrawal (woman as victim, wraith). Self-styled high priestess of decadent performance in the early years of this century, Rubinstein offered to audiences sensational specularizations of some of their most resonant fantasies of gender conflict, including such complex ones as her impersonation of a "feminized" (i.e., castrated) male in her role as the protagonist of Gabriele d'Annunzio and Claude Debussy's *The Martyrdom of Saint Sebastian* (1911). *Saint Sebastian* boasted, as had *Schéhérazade* the year before, not only Rubinstein's presence but also the choreography of Fokine and the set and costume designs of Bakst.[4] In his study *Idols of Perversity*, Bram Dijkstra speaks of Rubinstein as having served as "an ambulant fetish expressive of the ideologically manipulated desires of [her] society." He emphasizes two of the possible bases for this fetishization of her poses on the part of male viewers:

> Clearly, the fetishized emaciation of iconic figures such as Rubinstein made it possible for males to respond to them in either a sadistic or masochistic fashion, depending on whether they were seen as subjects in control of their own destinies (and hence a threat to the aggressive self-identity of the men observing them) or as ultrapassive objects of aggressive desire.[5]

Although he analyzes lesbian artist Romaine Brooks's painting of Rubinstein at some length, Dijkstra limits his consideration of the possible meanings of her career almost entirely to male-centered ones. The crucial element of Rubinstein's public persona that Dijkstra fails to consider is her position as a powerful emblem for some of her lesbian admirers (these appear in his text only under the rather bland designation "her women friends") of a will to exhaust the entire repertory of binary roles through which femininity was conceived in the turn-of-the-century West. Placing predictable heterosexual male projections onto her performances to one side, one can readily imagine at least some of the ways that the more or less open secret of the lesbian sexuality she figured for some members of her audience (especially, we may assume, for lesbians themselves and for some gay male admirers) contributed to the highly charged atmosphere of her public appearances. For example, besides those aspects of her work described by Dijkstra as being in some ways compatible with contemporary male-identified fantasies of both extreme (phallic) feminine potency and no less extreme feminine passivity, the self-assertive and exhibitionistic aspects of her work also permitted her to present herself, at least liminally, as both a subject and an object of lesbian desire rendered visible to an extraordinary degree.

In her role as Zobeida in *Schéhérazade*, Rubinstein initially functions as a "threatening" embodiment of transgressive female heterosexual desire. But in the work's famous ending, which many members of its first audience, including Fokine, seem to have found its most overwhelming gesture, Rubinstein's motionless stance amid the scene of massacre around her seems to have represented an almost unbearably ambiguously charged moment. For the duration of that prolonged moment Zobeida resists enacting either her rage at her husband and master or her grief over the slaughter of her lover and her other companions, and instead gathers to herself the storm of energy swirling around her by temporarily but nonetheless forcefully adopting the position and appearance of being its still center.

Only a modicum of these tensions are resolved by the abrupt gesture with which Zobeida shatters her powerful but unsustainable pose: stabbing herself to death. The performative energies of Rubinstein's repertory of symbolic roles—the male-identified potent castrator (Judith) and violated suicide (Lucrece) as

Fɪɢ. 4. Ida Rubinstein as Zobeida in *Schéhérazade*, 1910. Photo: Bert

well as those of possible subject and object of lesbian desire—collapse incoherently as Zobeida, the temporary imaginary embodiment of all these roles, falls dead. Similarly, the positions—of being tremendously empowered and being oppressed literally to death—between which Rubinstein rapidly oscillated in the climactic moments of *Schéhérazade* are left unresolved in the case of her gay male counterpart, Nijinsky, when, after an extraordinary enactment of flight and defiance, his "slave" character is seized and executed. "How odd it is that Nijinsky should always be the *slave* in your ballets," Diaghilev's friend and musical adviser Walter Nouvel quipped to the impresario at the time *Schéhérazade* was being planned. "I hope one day you'll emancipate him" (quoted in Buckle 124). Of course, Diaghilev never did, and Nijinsky's struggle to emancipate himself was to all appearances an excruciating failure. He was to break off his relationship with Diaghilev in 1913 and to stop dancing publicly altogether by 1919, thereafter to live on in confinement, diagnosed as schizophrenic, until 1950.

At the time of *Schéhérazade,* however, he was still successfully negotiating the powerful projections of sexual contradiction onto his performances that are as notable an aspect of the record of his career as a different set of these are of his colleague Rubinstein's.[6] Fokine, for example, praised the way the dancer's "peculiar" "lack of masculinity" made him the perfect interpreter of the role of the Golden Slave. "Now he was a half-human, half-feline animal, softly leaping great distances, now a stallion," Fokine writes in a characteristic evocation of Nijinsky's supposed resolution of highly charged contradictions in his performances, in his body, and his dancing (quoted in Buckle 141). Both subhuman and superhuman, he is simultaneously perceived as an effeminate cat and a tremendous stud, but not as "masculine" in any ordinary sense. Fokine presents his decision to eliminate ordinary "masculinity" from the expressive range of Nijinsky's dancing in *Schéhérazade* as an inevitable consequence of what he saw as the peculiar strengths of Rubinstein's imperious appearance, and he does so with a stunning non sequitur. "Next to the very tall Rubinstein," he writes, "I felt that [Nijinsky] would have looked ridiculous had he acted in a masculine manner." The astonishing success of *Schéhérazade* no doubt had more than a little to do with the extraordinary energy with which it found terms for specularizing— rendering both visible and spectacular—the "scandals" of the sexualities of its two stars and of their respective ways of revealing and concealing these in performance. Fokine to the contrary, much more complicated relations had to be "adjusted" between the two principals in *Schéhérazade* than Rubinstein's height in comparison with Nijinsky's relative shortness: the whole array of conflicting sexual projections that could be made onto them and their performances had to be brought into effective relation to each other.

The main outline at least of the *Schéhérazade* scenario as it was eventually performed by the Ballets Russes had been the idea of artist and theatrical designer Alexandre Benois, and he afterward wrote of Nijinsky's performance in terms remarkably similar to Fokine's "half-this, half-that" ones: impersonating

FIG. 5. Nijinsky as the Golden Slave in *Schéhérazade*, 1911. Photo: Baron Aldolphe de Meyer

the Golden Slave, Benois said, Nijinsky had become in rapid turns "half-cat, half-snake, fiendishly agile, feminine and yet wholly terrifying" (Buckle 141). As with Rubinstein's performance, but in rather different terms, Nijinsky's was perceived as being both intensely phallic and no less intensely "feminine." The most significant difference between the affective ranges of Rubinstein's and Nijinsky's performances is that while her role permitted her to enact a fairly wide range of positions, including certain ones that were deemed "masculine," it was precisely these "ordinary" masculine positions that were excluded from Nijinsky's role. What Fokine calls Nijinsky's "peculiar" "lack of masculinity"—the constant interplay in his most characteristic performances of flashes of hypervirile and hyperfeminine effects, which make sensational impressions but can never be gotten to "add up" to "ordinary" masculinity—represents the piece's powerful negative electrical charge, at its opposite pole from the positive charge the piece locates in Rubinstein's power to enact "masculinity," at least liminally, alongside other performative modes.

Judging from available contemporary descriptions of the performance, one does not get the sense that there was any moment in Nijinsky's performance in which he was permitted to signal anything like Rubinstein's "majestic" and overwhelming gesture of prolonged motionless resistance to the murderous violence that furiously manifests itself in the piece's last scene. The strain of being a visible and intensely mystified embodiment of the open secret of male homosexuality in Paris and London in the decade or two after the epochal downfall and death of Oscar Wilde no doubt played a significant part in what was diagnosed as Nijinsky's schizophrenic disintegration in his late twenties, at the end of World War I.[7] Rubinstein, as the daughter and heiress of a rich St. Petersburg family, was able to use her successes with the Ballets Russes as Cleopatra and Zobeida to launch herself as a star in subsequent productions that she herself financed; as I have said, Nijinsky's attempts to become similarly autonomous were a disastrous failure for a variety of reasons, not the least of which, I suspect, was the relation of his fame to the specularization of the imputed "lack of masculinity" that restricted him to the margins of identities of which "ordinary masculinity" was an indispensable component.

Between Diaghilev's, Nijinsky's, Rubinstein's, and Bakst's "Scheherezade party" of 1910 and Mark's and his brothers' of the early 1960s lies a half century in which the construction of gay male subjectivity on a number of fronts has exhibited some striking—and sometimes terrible—consistencies.[8] Some of the most effective forms of resistance to homophobic oppression that gay men have developed and practiced during the same period have shown a similar kind of consistency. One of these has been the sometimes elaborately planned, sometimes spontaneously performed "Scheherazade party," staged over and over again in this century in locations ranging from the theater of the belle epoque to, fifty years later, a suburban American living room. Rather than dismissing it as trivial, I insist on its having been an important aspect of the widely various repertory of political acts gay men have practiced and by means of which we have resisted this century's depradations against us. I take the "Scheherazade party"—the conspicuous energies with which it is enacted as well as the phobic violence with which it is repressed, violence of either the explosive variety that Mark experienced or the corrosive kind that gradually disabled Nijinsky—as an emblematic expression of a perilously highly charged compromise, the energies of which both "sides" in the ongoing war for and against gay visibility, homophobic and homophile, have been effectively exploiting for most of this century.

Jack Smith, who died of AIDS on September 18, 1989, was one of the most accomplished and influential but least known producers of the extremely theatricalized, densely materialist version of urban gay male social and artistic practice which has to this point been recognized, studied, and theorized chiefly under the extremely reductive rubric of "camp."[9] In 1962 Jack Smith threw a "Scheherazade party" that has probably had more political and artistic impact, at least in the English- and French-speaking worlds, than any since the Ballets Russes's of fifty years before. Filming for seven consecutive weekends on the roof of an old movie theater, since demolished, on the Lower East Side of Manhattan, Smith and a group of friends, apparelled in various kinds of drag—"harem," vampire, Marilyn Monroe—enacted for the camera a series of scenes from an imaginary transvestite orgy. They swayed to unheard music, "vamped" each other, casually and unhurriedly exposed parts of their bodies—here a female breast, there the limp penis of one reveler casually draped over the shoulder of another seated before him. Smith edited the results, added a soundtrack of old 78s of German tango bands and Latin American pop songs, and screened the film in the spring of 1963 under the title *Flaming Creatures*.[10] It provoked a violent response. A small coterie of admirers, including Jonas Mekas and Susan Sontag,[11] praised Smith for helping inaugurate a new sexually and artistically radical film practice in this country. Other viewers enjoyed the film's dreamy insouciance about matters of sexuality and gender, but many hated and attacked it. Theaters that showed *Flaming Creatures* were raided, and prints of the film were seized by the New York police. A few favorable published responses aside, the history of the reception of the film has amounted in large part to a history of the effort to suppress it, both here and abroad. A print of the film was seized by U.S. customs as it was being returned from a screening in Vancouver, and showings in Ann Arbor and Austin were "busted" by local police in the late '60s. Film scholar Karel Rowe screened the film at Northwestern University in 1972 and unexpectedly found himself the object of a mini-riot as infuriated "jock" students, disappointed in their expectations of seeing an ordinary porn film, pounded on the projection booth and demanded refunds.[12] The maker of *Flaming Creatures* knew how to make a cultural product "guaranteed" to explode closets, he knew where and how to detonate it, and he was aware that setting people's closets on fire is not simply a liberatory act: inevitably, some people would get burned, including, quite possibly, the incendiaries themselves. Setting closets on fire in the way that a number of writers and filmmakers including Smith did throughout the decade leading up to the Stonewall rebellion, not for the homophobic purpose of intentionally injuring or destroying their inhabitants but in order to bring more people out, to try to put an end to the institution of the closet itself, was a serious and dangerous political project.

Smith's first performance piece, a "nightclub act" he did in collaboration with filmmaker Ken Jacobs in Provincetown in 1961, was called *The Human Wreckage Review*.[13] For the almost thirty remaining years of his career, Smith was involved in a fiercely unsentimental project of reclaiming his own and other queer people's energies (all kinds of queer people, including gay ones) from the myriad forms of human wreckage into which our society has tended to channel it.

In 1967, near what was to be the end of the period of his most intense involvement with film, not only as a filmmaker but also as perhaps the most frequently featured performer in underground film during that movement's most productive decade, Smith was asked in an interview what pleasure he had taken in his film performances. "I never could afford psychoanalysis," he answered, and went on to say, "it was very brave of me to take psychoanalysis in that form" (Malanga 14). The reply is in one sense instantly recognizable as a bit of period humor, but I propose to take it as more than that; I affirm Smith's judgment that he "was very brave" to attempt to carry out a self-analysis—one from which I believe many other people in comparably marginal situations who have seen his work, or that of his imitators, have benefited—in a public and highly improvisatory manner, rather than the private and privileged circumstances under which analysis is normally carried out. As he treats all his other performances as opportunities for "acting out," so does Smith treat the film-journal interview as yet another venue for both enacting and examining common anxieties—common, at least, to people like him, then and since, experimenting with renegotiating their wholly or partially closeted artistic and political existences.

To a question in the same interview about his plans for the immediate future, Smith replies not with the statement about new projects in the offing that the interviewer expects, but with the wistful, pseudo-personal utterance, "Well, I have got to try to pull myself together" (14). The comedy of the director/film star who is so neurotic, so hysterically self-absorbed, that he compulsively responds to "public" interviewing with "private" psychotherapy-style answers fits the alternately glacially ironic and self-distancing but also aggressively "deviant" and exhibitionistic milieu of New York pop culture of the '60s, a culture that first centered around Smith but soon shifted to Warhol.

It may be useful to interrogate the kinds of attributions that have generally been made to Smith and his work—"playfulness" and "innocence" as well as simple "irony" and "self-mockery"—in order better to understand how his performance career, during and after the period in which he made and/or starred in numerous films, represents an alternative to psychoanalytic theory and therapy—

in some ways consonant and in other ways in strong conflict with it. However "playful" one may choose to take Smith's undeniably ironic relation to his own performances to be, it is also undeniable that his career represents a highly serious, perhaps in some ways a painfully overserious, attempt to work out an exemplary role for himself and others on the sexual and artistic fringes. Asked in the interview just quoted what kind of film roles he might like to play that he had not yet done, Smith replied, "Well, I think I would like to play . . . Christ. But . . . maybe I never will—maybe the interest has all gone out of that, or maybe it would be too repetitious of Dracula" (15) (in Andy Warhol's film version of which he had recently starred as Batman-Dracula). Smith's fleeting equation of the role of Christ with that of Dracula is an interesting one, but more interesting for my present purposes is a shift in tone at just this point in his remarks: "But anyway the world could use a new idea—a new Christ image, and it would be fun to sort of work that out." This pronouncement was no doubt made at least partly tongue in cheek, but, just kidding or not, the remark has a magniloquence of a kind that has often been associated with delusion—in the offhand manner in which Smith speaks of giving "the world . . . a new Christ image" as a secondary career goal, as something that "would be fun to sort of work . . . out," if and when he gets around to it. The extremely casual, possibly facetious, messianic intentions Smith expresses here may well remind the student of gay male subjectivity in this century of other, more fateful engagements between the "image" of Christ and gay self-identifications and self-representations. (Nijinsky, for example, engaged in extensive debate with himself as to whether he was or was not Christ, in the diary he kept at the time of his breakdown, the crisis that marked the end of his performing career and the onset of his ostensible madness.)[14] Far from abandoning his public self-analysis when he ceased to make films, Smith continued in his subsequent work as a performance artist to "act out" fantasies of his imaginary identities as well as critiques of these fantasies.

Part of the success of the assault on the closet Smith's work makes is a consequence of the virtuosic fluency with which he negotiates the undulating waves of images not only across genders but also across "perversions." Successfully negotiating just such perilous performative modes—as Rubinstein in her time seems to have found ways of doing while Nijinsky did not—Smith and other featured performers in *Flaming Creatures* move insouciantly and triumphantly around and through a whole repertory of proscribed behaviors—transgressions which it would be reductive to describe as simply "transvestite," since a man's wearing feminine garb is only one of the numerous culturally enforced "police lines" Smith's performances frequently cross. Smith seems to have performed the roles of the "sheik" or the (presumably male) "vampire" at least as frequently as he did those of the "vamp" or "harem girl" in '60s films. He played all these roles, and directed others to play them, in ways that short-circuit their relations to the heterosexualized representational regimes from which they derive. What is compelling about these figures in Smith's films is not the sheik's enactment of virility or the harem girl's of femininity; nor is it simply the reversal of these roles, as it might be if Smith's were simply another version of traditional transvestite comedy. To underestimate or dismiss the real erotic appeal Smith's "comedies" have had for many gay viewers is to ignore the primary source of their power: his films are incitements to his audience not only to play fast and loose with gender roles but also to push harder against prevailing constraints on sexuality.

From its inception Smith's film practice seems to have derived much of its energy from his identification with the movie star and belated vamp Maria Montez, and from what he saw as *her* identification with the definitively kitsch epics she acted in during her brief but stellar ten-year film career—the same length as Smith's of two decades later, as it turned out. Smith, like many other gay men of

FIG. 6. Maria Montez in a publicity shot for *Cobra Woman*.

his generation, was particularly fascinated by the five Universal Studios vehicles in which Montez starred with the athletic but wooden leading man Jon Hall: *Arabian Nights, White Savage, Ali Baba and the Forty Thieves, Sudan,* and, above all, *Cobra Woman,* where Montez played twin "queens of the jungle," one good, one evil.[15] Smith began his career collaborating with Ken Jacobs, and their earliest joint effort appears to have been a film called *Little Cobra Dance* (the third part of *Saturday Afternoon Blood Sacrifice: TV Plug: Little Cobra Dance,* 1957), in which Smith, dressed as an "exotic" Spanish lady, launches into a wild dance, falls down, and is questioned by the police—"the last being an actual event incorporated into the film."[16] So early in Smith's career did the acting-out of a pseudo-exotic transvestism, combined with a manic performance of celebration and a no less manic performance of failure ("launches into a wild dance" *and* "falls down"), and culminating in ritual encounters with the police, establish themselves as the central "business" of Smith's performances.

The small body of writing Smith published is, however transgressive its content, usually grammatically and syntactically conventional, so it may well be worth noting the occasional sentence which does not conform to standard, as in the following passage from his 1962–1963 essay "The Perfect Filmic Appositeness of Maria Montez": "(Before a mirror is a place) is a place where it is possible to clown, to pose, to act out fantasies, to not be seen while one gives (Movie sets are sheltered, exclusive places where nobody who doesn't belong can go)."[17] The repetition here, and the sentence's incoherent-looking movement into and out of parentheses, may seem meaningless—may, even if noticed, be easily ignored, subliminally registered as a typesetting error or at best a compositional complexity not worth puzzling out. Consider, however, that something worth noticing may be going on. This sentence, convoluted and incomplete as it in some ways is, may be taken to be a particularly compelling statement of Smith's idea, the subject of the essay, of the "perfect appositeness" of performances like Maria Montez's and his own to what he sees as the most powerful artistic and political potentials of film. The "place" being somewhat obscurely situated in this difficult sentence is one "before a mirror," where one can see oneself without being seen by anyone else—a place somehow analogous with (or "perfectly apposite" to) the "sheltered, exclusive" movie set of Smith's fantasies, "where nobody who doesn't belong can go." One way of reading this is to imagine that these two "apposite" spaces, the one as small as a mirror and the other as large as a movie set, define the liminal horizons of the closet as Smith sees them. ("What's larger than a mirror but smaller than a movie set? The closet.") A better question may be: Is a closet as big as Universal Studios in the '40s (home of the closed set of Smith's Montez fantasies) still a closet? Can the closet be made to cease being one if/when its bounds are extended beyond a certain point? If so, what is that point? If the closet is the place one visits or inhabits in order not "to . . . be seen while one gives," as Smith puts it, how can what is, in the space of the closet, intransitivized into objectless "giving" be retransitivized—into giving what? in? out? "head"? "the finger"? pleasure? performances? For Smith, the camera is only a more complex kind of mirror, and if the mirror is sometimes the only piece of furniture in a closet, the mirror-extended-as-camera can function as an opening onto two-way streets, onto transitivity of all kinds of officially discouraged or prohibited or persecuted varieties.

The apparent wide-openness of the circuits of pleasure which energized Maria Montez's performances for herself as well as for her fans made her an exemplary figure for Smith and other gay filmmakers and filmgoers of the '60s. Ever her own greatest fan, Montez's most oft-quoted utterance, made to an interviewer in the late '40s, goes, "When I see myself on the screen, I look so beautiful I want to scream with joy." For me, as I suspect for many other gay men who have relished it, the charm of that remark lies not just in what a naive interpreter might call the "childlike" openness of Montez's admiration of her larger-than-life screen image, but in its intensity—signaled by the inflection upward into the hysterical register at the sentence's end: "I want to scream with joy." And one may at least partially attribute the remark's longtime currency among the many gay men for whom American popular film of the '40s and '50s—especially through its female stars—had been formative to the succinct way it brings "screen" and "scream" together. In her adoring self-critique, Montez demonstrates what Smith might call the relation of "perfect appositeness," the lexical as well as psychological near-mirroring, of "screen" and "scream." Smith discovers something similar in his discussion of the related political spaces of "mirror" and "movie set"; his own politics of performance exploits the appositeness of "self-indulgent" fantasy ("screen," mirror) and disruptive public enactment ("scream," movie set). Not the least of the cultural constructs shattered by the impulse to "scream with joy" at the sight of the adorable (self)-image on the movie screen on the part of male fans of Montez or Lana Turner or Jayne Mansfield is their masculine gender identity. For how many gay men of my own and the previous generation were our earliest intimations that there might be a gap between our received gender identity and our subjective or "felt" one the consequence not of noticing our own erotic attraction to another boy or man but of enthusiastically enjoying and identifying with the performative excesses of Maria Montez rather than Jon Hall, or Lana Turner rather than Burt Lancaster, or Jayne Mansfield rather than Mickey Hargitay?

Smith, working in conjunction with Jacobs, had by 1963 articulated a full range of tentative cinematic alter egos for exploring the positions one might occupy in relation to the closet, the mirror, and the movie screen. Besides Smith's own *Flaming Creatures,* Smith and Jacobs's two most compelling collaborations, *Blonde Cobra* and *Little Stabs at Happiness*, also premiered that year. In the first of these, Smith, the Blonde Cobra of the title (a gesture of homage to the Brunette Cobra, Montez, as well as to the Blonde Venus of Dietrich and Sternberg) plays a character called Jack Smith as well as an imperious woman named Madame Nescience. In the film's central episode, the latter dreams that she is a Sadean mother superior putting down an outbreak of mass lesbian sexual activity in the girls' dormitory.

Elsewhere in the film, besides lamenting his generally degenerescent condition ("Leprosy is eating a hole in me, my teeth are falling out, my hair has turned to sauerkraut"), Smith narrates a story apparently about his childhood:

> There was once a little boy, a little tweensy, microscopic little boy. . . . And . . . the little boy would . . . look for his Mother, but she was never there, and so he would finally pass out and just fall onto the floor and fall asleep just weary with loneliness and longing and frustration and frustrated longings, until, until when the shadows were lengthening and the sun was drooping he would hear the front door open and, and he would rush out into the hallway and there, and there was his Mother . . . and she always had little white bags from the ten-cent store and they always had certain kinds of chocolates in them, the brown, the droplet kind . . . and he would eat it and she would give him some but not much, just a little because she would save most of it for herself and ah so ah well ah and then, she'd go away again. Mother Mother Mother Mother Mother Mother and then, and there was a little boy that lived upstairs you see it was a two family apartment and ah and—a two family house! and then one day the little boy found the other little boy that lived upstairs the family who lived upstairs in the upstairs floor and the little boy who was less than seven, the lonely little boy, the lonely little boy was less than seven, I know that because we didn't leave Columbus until I was seven, I know it, I was under seven and I took a match and I lit it and I pulled out the other little boy's penis and burnt his penis with a match![18]

Reversing the narrative logic of the two "Scheherazade" stories recounted earlier, in which "orgy" is interrupted by "slaughter" and sexual "games" are violently broken up by an angry and vengeful parent or spouse, the mother of Smith's "lonely little boy" is represented as absent and withholding. This alternative version of the story culminates in an act that fuses the two principal roles and the two halves of the "Scheherazade-party" story, the "little boy" being both the initiator of a transgressive sexual game and the figure who puts an end (in this case an immediate end) to the game—with an act of violence against (in this case one of) its players. The whole story of "the lonely little boy" organizes itself along the manic lines of wild activity eventuating in failure (i.e., falling) and arrest that, as I have discussed, are the design of Smith and Jacobs's brief early collaboration, *Little Cobra Dance*. The little boy is said to be accustomed to "scamper[ing]" from room to room of the empty house looking for his mother, until he "would finally pass out and just fall onto the floor." There he sleeps until he is in turn awakened by the sound of his mother's arriving home, when he "rush[es] out and dart[s] out" to greet her. What is "arrested" at the end of this episode is both childhood sexuality and male-male sexual play, and what the subject, "the lonely little boy," is shown substituting for it is sadistic violence.

As an isolated anecdote, as a familiar kind of "confessional" story of childhood cruelty made "funny" by distance and by its belated avowal of antisocial behavior, as a shaggy-dog story with the unprepared-for punchline "and I pulled out the other little boy's penis and burnt [it] with a match"—as all of these formulations, the "lonely little boy" episode of *Blonde Cobra* may seem to conform in several ways to common conventions of largely straight male-identified styles of humor ("I was a wild and mean little boy, and here's a story to prove it"). But it figures as more than that in Smith's performance, and it does so by means of its engagement with other aspects of his work—and of this film performance in particular—that are different from and in some ways radically opposed to common conventions of straight male comic performance—whether we think of these performances as being carried out by professionals in clubs or on television or in films, or by nonprofessionals in the course of ordinary social life.

The Madame Nescience episode that immediately follows the "lonely little boy" part of *Blonde Cobra* is similarly potentially repugnant to many viewers, insofar as it fits into a familiar transvestite enactment of hostility toward women, toward women in positions of authority particularly, and toward lesbians and lesbian sexuality. Considered as an isolated episode, after all, Madame Nescience presents the viewer with a familiar butt of sexist comedy, the repressed and lascivious nun, here shown indulging in sadistic (homo)sexuality as she, in conformity with the "despotic" and homophobic "Scheherazade-party" scenario, acts out a repressive "slaughter" of her lesbian "daughters." The rest of the film, however, provides a context in which one can think "otherwise" of Smith's Madame Nescience performance. For example, following as it does on the "lonely little boy" narrative, Madame Nescience's imaginary appearance and behavior may be read as the return of the repressed mother in that episode. And if she still seems a figure of hostile male projection when seen as a displaced version of the rejecting and withholding mother of the "lonely little boy," she may seem considerably less so if her dream of disciplinary behavior toward her "daughters"— lining them up and paddling their bare bottoms with a "silver cross"—is related to the film's ultimate image. As Smith intones a line from Baudelaire—"Life swarms with innocent monsters"—the film shows him bending forward to expose his own bared buttocks with a butcher knife thrust between them, actually held high up between his thighs but placed to look as though penetrating his anus. "Ooooooooh," Smith cries in voice-over, "Sex is a pain in the ass. Sex IS a pain in the ass."

The image of the butcher knife thrust "up the ass" of the mock-lamenting Blonde Cobra is only secondarily an image of male-male rape or of homophobic and sadistic contempt for gay male desire for anal connection. In the economy of the film as a whole it is primarily a comic undoing of the "lonely little boy's" burning the penis of the "other little boy" in the film's first episode and of Madame Nescience's spanking her lesbian "daughters'" bottoms with a silver cross in its central episode. Horrible as it may sound, the film's climactic image of the Cobra figure's stabbed anus is, as it actually appears in the film, more an emblematic or visual metaphysical conceit than any kind of really graphic representation of physical violation. This ostensible wound sheds no blood, nor does the viewer see the knife inserted; it will be obvious to all but the most gullible viewer from the moment of the image's appearance that what one is seeing is in a significant sense not at all a realistically simulated stabbing—no fancy special effects here—but a child's trick of concealing a knife blade in a fold of the body, combined with perhaps the clown's oldest trick for mildly shocking and amusing his audience, exposing his bottom.

Depression, outbursts of mania, fits of hysterical anxiety, of antisocial behavior, hostility, thoughts and memories of sadistic and masochistic desires and behavior, and fantasies of the same, moods of intensely narcissistic self-indulgence (not unrelated to what Leo Bersani has called the "grave doubt resulting from homosexual desire: *the doubt about which self to adore*")[19] alternating with moods of bitter despair and self-destructive impulses: the emotional weather of Smith's performances is the emotional weather of the closet. This is not to say that gay men have any kind of monopoly on these states of mind and behavior. To do so would simply be to reinscribe the homophobic discourses which for a long time deemed (in some quarters still deem) gays "disturbed" or psychically and emotionally inadequate or damaged, and blamed our sexual and social existences as gay people for the alleged damage rather than looking to the twin institutions of homophobia and the closet, which "disturb" and damage gay and straight people both, in different ways and in differing degrees.

What Jack Smith did in his film performances and "live" performance pieces during twenty historically crucial years was to keep projecting gay subjective awareness of the political and psychological realities of the closet onto the "screen" of fantasy for collective, rather than private, recognition, inspection, and analysis. Incapacity and breakdown ceased to be alternative performative modes (the ritualistic "fallings" and failures of his previous work) for him, and he made the endless deferral of performance the hallmark of his work in the '70s. Audiences arriving at his loft for a midnight performance would regularly witness his fumblings with slides and slide projector for two and a half hours. Smith would then announce that owing to technical problems there would be no (further) performance that night.

Smith performed infrequently after the late '70s. When I belatedly saw him in performance in a festival of punk art in the early '80s in a storefront off Times Square, he characteristically appeared late, tinkered for a long time with props and a slide projector that was never activated, and then reclined on a couch to smoke a hookah. All the while an attractive young man and woman, both garbed in "harem pajamas," read aloud in its entirety a biography of Yvonne de Carlo (star of *Song of Schéhérazade*, 1947). Beyond his silent but eloquent presence onstage, Smith restricted his contributions to the rest of the performance to a few momentary interruptions of the boy and girl odalisques, to make minute adjustments to their costumes or poses, or to correct their occasional mispronunciations of words.

Later that year I saw yet another big filmic "Scheherazade party," Pasolini's *Arabian Nights*, one of his three late productions of classic literary cluster-narratives: Scheherazade's, the *Canterbury Tales*, and *The Decameron*. Pasolini subsequently repudiated the trilogy for its "liberal," optimistic "sexual plural-ism," putting in its place his last completed project, the harrowing film fantasy of sexual captivity and torture under fascism called *Salò*. Although I admire some of Pasolini's films, his "Scheherazade party," the *Arabian Nights*, rehearses many of the same repugnant clichés that underlay Diaghilev's. In Pasolini's "Ar-aby," as in so many earlier orientalizing versions of it, sex rather than survival seems to be the first priority of its denizens, and everyone except the few requi-site wise old men is young, extraordinarily sexually attractive, and always avail-able. Falling chronologically between Diaghilev's and Pasolini's *de luxe* productions, Smith's various versions of "Scheherazade" seem by contrast with these others to harbor real deconstructive potential in relation to the underlying sexual-political and nationalist-political agendas of almost all his big-budget pre-decessors and successors.

In the numerous political fables of the "harem" Smith directed and/or per-formed in, he privileges fantasies neither of Western nor male supremacy—as so many other orientalist fantasies do—but of what he calls "moldiness." As Ma-dame Nescience lies on her couch, she is said to be "dreaming of old musty memories, memories that she thought that she had forgot[ten] or so she thought but you see they came up in a funky mass of ah exuding effluviums from the musty past . . . covered with moss and funk" (Smith and Jacobs 2). Smith calls her dream, and by extension the whole episode in which she figures, "La rêve de la purité de Madame Nescience." The manifest content of this "dream of purity," as we have seen, was one of the vigorous suppression of lesbianism in a convent by a mother superior who brings a suspicious degree of enthusiasm to the task. But it is not with her repressive and luridly charged "purity" that I want to close this discussion of Smith's performances, with which purity has indeed had little to do, but rather with an insistence on the paradoxically "moldy," "swampy" (to use his terms) clarity with which his work pungently represents the kind of un-conscious processes that have, over the past couple of decades, fueled innumer-able small- and large-scale eruptions of queer rebellion against the institutions of the closet. On these conditions, Smith's flaming performances and others like them have had wonderfully incendiary effects.

NOTES ⸺ ⸺ ⸺ ⸺ ⸺ ⸺ ⸺

1. My discussion of the Ballets Russes *Schéhérazade* is indebted to Richard Buckle's account of the planning and performance of the ballet in his biography *Nijinsky* (New York: Simon and Schuster, 1971), esp. 137–142. I thank Jonathan Goldberg and Eve Kosofsky Sedgwick for their encouragement and valuable suggestions for improving earlier versions of this chapter, and the conveners of the conference on "The Closet" at Scripps College (December 1988) for the initial impetus for undertaking the project of which this article is a part.

2. Philip Kolb, ed., *Lettres à Reynaldo Hahn* (Paris, 1956), 188; quoted in Buckle 141–142.

3. Wollen's article has been of crucial importance to me in thinking about the kinds of continuities in gay male performance in the twentieth century that I am considering in this project; see his "Fashion/Orientalism/The Body," *New Formations*, no. 1 (Spring 1987): 5–33. Dale Harris takes a more conventionally connoisseurial approach to the subject of the cultural impact of Ballets Russes orientalism in his "Diaghilev's Ballets Russes and the Vogue for Orientalism," in *The Art of Enchantment: Diaghilev's Ballets Russes, 1909–1929*, comp. Nancy Van Norman Baer, catalogue of an exhibition held at the Fine Arts Museum of San Francisco, 1988, pp. 84–95. For accounts of the institution of the harem that tend to deconstruct Western orientalizing fantasies of it, see Malek Alloula, *The Colonial Harem*, trans. Myrna Godzich and Wlad Godzich (Minneapolis: University of Minnesota Press, 1986); and Huda Shaarawi, *Harem Years: The Memoirs of an Egyptian Feminist*, trans. and ed. Margot Badran (London: Virago Press, 1986).

4. The 1911 avant-garde's subversion of prevailing religious and sexual certainties was registered in, among other ways, the ban that the then archbishop of Paris placed on the performance of *The Martyrdom of Saint Sebastian*. Of the many reasons he might have put forward for this ban, he announced two: (1) d'Annunzio's identification of the saint with the pagan god Adonis, and (2) the fact that a male Christian saint was to be played by a Jewish woman. Despite the official condemnation, "the show went on," to only middling success; see Alfred Frankenstein's liner notes for Leonard Bernstein's recording of the *Martyrdom* on Columbia Masterworks discs M2L 353/M2S 753.

5. Bram Dijkstra, *Idols of Perversity: Fantasies of Feminine Evil in Fin-de-Siècle Culture* (New York: Oxford University Press, 1988), 53.

6. Besides marking his performance in *Schéhérazade*, the year 1910 also marks the beginning of Nijinsky's most productive period as a choreographer; it was then that he began to formulate the projects which would issue in 1912–1913 in his three great inaugural modernist ballets, *L'après-midi d'un faune, Jeux,* and *Le sacre du printemps*. For a recent assessment of Nijinsky's achievements as a choreographer, see Lynn Garafola, "Vaslav Nijinsky," *Raritan* 8.1 (Summer 1988): 1–27.

7. Joan Acocella writes briefly but perceptively of the way Nijinsky was cast throughout his career in roles in which he was either "something other than human: a puppet, a god, a faun, the specter of a rose," or, if human, not so in any ordinary sense, but always in either a reduced or excessive way: "a slave, an androgyne, or some other object of sexual connoisseurship." See her article "Vaslav Nijinsky," in *The Art of Enchantment*, 110.

8. For a history of gay and lesbian political organizing and resistance in the three decades before Stonewall, see John D'Emilio, *Sexual Politics, Sexual Communities: The Making of a Homosexual Minority in the United States, 1940–1970* (Chicago: University of Chicago Press, 1983). Eve Kosofsky Sedgwick's *Epistemology of the Closet* (Berkeley: University of California Press, 1990) provides a searching theoretical exploration of the ways in which an endemic crisis of homo/heterosexual definition has structured/fractured Western culture in the twentieth century.

9. Everyone interested in Jack Smith's work in film and performance is indebted to Stefan Brecht and J. Hoberman for their efforts in preserving at least some aspects of Smith's extremely fugitive performance art. Brecht gives a number of informative accounts of Smith's work from 1961 to 1977 in his valuable study *Queer Theatre* (Frankfurt: Suhrkamp, 1978), 10–27 and 157–177. Hoberman surveys Smith's performances during the same period in his article "The Theatre of Jack Smith," *Drama Review* 23.1 (March 1979): 3–12. For further information about Smith and his performances, see Jonas Mekas's July 1970 *Village Voice* article, "Jack Smith, or the End of Civilization," reprinted in Mekas's *Movie Journal: The Rise of a New American Cinema, 1959–1971* (New York: Collier Books, 1972), 388–397. Film scholar Karel Rowe, who worked briefly as Smith's assistant during the summer of 1972, provides useful information about Smith's film performances as well as a Smith filmography in his book *The Baudelairean Cinema: A Trend within the American Avant-Garde* (Ann Arbor: UMI Research Press, 1982). Joan Adler, in a piece entitled "On Location," gives an impressionistic account of the making of *Normal Love*, the unfinished film project Smith undertook after *Flaming Creatures*, in Stephen Dwoskin's *Film Is: The International Free Cinema* (Woodstock, N.Y.: Overlook Press, 1975), 11–21.

10. For most of the time the film has existed, it has been even more difficult to see *Flaming Creatures* than is usual for an "underground" work. Never available for screening beyond a very small circuit of alternative venues, the film seems to have been withdrawn from circulation by Smith by the early 1970s in angry reaction to what he considered its misreception on the part of everyone from the New York Police Department to Susan Sontag. Smith was antagonistic to written analyses of his work; his most frequently quoted utterance has been, "Film critics are writers and they are hostile and uneasy in the presence of a visual phenomenon" (quoted, for example, in Rowe xiii). Given Smith's passionate commitment to his film's being *seen* rather than being made to serve as grist for the mill of what he saw as pseudo-controversy, it is more than ironic, it is deeply unfortunate that *Flaming Creatures* has, owing to its general unavailability, "lived on" to the extent that it has largely in the form of written descriptions of it. On the subject of the general suppression of many of the most radical examples of "underground" films of the 1960s, see David E. James's eloquent prefatory statement to his recent history of noncommercial American film of that decade, *Allegories of Cinema: American Film in the Sixties* (Princeton: Princeton University Press, 1979), ix. Among published descriptions of *Flaming Creatures*, the following are particularly useful: P. Adams Sitney, *Visionary Film: The American Avant-Garde, 1943–1978*, 2d ed. (New York: Oxford University Press, 1979), 354–357; Rowe 49–50.

11. For every person who actually saw Smith's film, perhaps a hundred know it only from Sontag's description of it. Sontag's often-cited essay "Notes on Camp" appeared (in *Partisan Review*) the same year as the *Flaming Creatures* review, and from the vantage point of twenty-five years after their first appearance, one may well be struck rereading her essays by the extreme degree to which they depoliticize the sexual and artistic practices that are their subjects. For example, Sontag praises *Flaming Creatures* for its "joy and innocence" ("*Flaming Creatures* is that rare modern work of art: it is about joy and innocence"), and while I can see speaking of it as a *joyous* film, the other half of the formulation makes one want to paraphrase Mae West: "*innocence* had nothing to do with it."

Sontag says *Flaming Creatures* "is about joy and innocence" in her essay "Jack Smith's *Flaming Creatures*," reprinted in *Against Interpretation* (New York: Farrar, Straus, and Giroux, 1966), 229. Possible political meanings and consequences get thoroughly elided from Sontag's influential account of Smith's film, which, according to her, simply eschews moralizing in order to occupy a purely aesthetic "space": "The space in which *Flaming Creatures* moves is not the space of moral ideas, which is where American critics have traditionally located art. What I am urging is that there is not only moral space, by whose laws *Flaming Creatures* would indeed come off badly; there is also aesthetic space, the space of pleasure. Here Smith's film moves and has its being" ("Jack Smith's *Flaming Creatures*" 231). Sontag similarly writes in "Notes on Camp": "Jews pinned their hopes for integrating into modern society on promoting the moral sense. Homosexuals have pinned their integration into society on promoting the aesthetic sense. Camp is a solvent of morality. It neutralizes moral indignation, sponsors playfulness" ("Notes on Camp," in *Against Interpretation* 290). The problem with such extreme and extremely reductive hypostatizations is that moral and aesthetic practices cannot be rendered stable, plainly disjunct "spaces" or "senses"; categories and categorical dyads such as Jewish moral seriousness versus gay "playfulness" fall explanatorily flat, especially in view of the subsequent history of these two groups in the quarter century since Sontag's essay, during which time many of her New York Jewish liberal intellectual confrères of the mid- to late '60s have turned neoconservative and gays have been engaged in a series of political struggles that have for the most part been anything but "playful."

12. Rowe describes his travails in attempting to show *Flaming Creatures*, in

Baudelairean Cinema xi-xii; Hoberman discusses the prosecution of *Flaming Creatures* and other underground films of the period (chiefly Jean Genet's *Un chant d'amour* and Kenneth Anger's *Scorpio Rising*) in his and Jonathan Rosenbaum's *Midnight Movies* (New York: Harper and Row, 1983), 59–61.

13. Gerard Malanga, "Interview with Jack Smith," *Film Culture*, no. 45 (1967):15.

14. Romola Nijinsky, ed., *The Diary of Vaslav Nijinsky* (Berkeley: University of California Press, 1968). See, for example, pp. 29, 51, 120, 175.

15. Maria Montez's other greatest admirer is Myra Breckinridge, who comes to inhabit Montez's body in the penultimate chapters of Gore Vidal's *Myron* (New York: Random House, 1974).

16. Quoted in Rowe's filmography of Ken Jacobs in *Baudelairean Cinema* 125–126.

17. Jack Smith, "The Perfect Filmic Appositeness of Maria Montez," *Film Culture*, no. 27 (Winter 1962–1963): 30.

18. Jack Smith and Ken Jacobs, "Soundtrack of *Blonde Cobra*," *Film Culture*, no. 29 (Summer 1963):2.

19. Leo Bersani, *A Future for Astyanax: Character and Desire in Literature* (Boston: Little, Brown, 1976), 306–307.

READING DANCE IN TEXTS

Unrest and Uncle Tom: Bill T. Jones/ Arnie Zane Dance Company's Last Supper at Uncle Tom's Cabin/ The Promised Land

Jacqueline Shea Murphy

In the aftermath of the Rodney King beating trial, television news reports showed five-second clips of the same scenes, over and over. These scenes—the video of police repeatedly beating King, the four African American men pulling a white truck driver from his truck and beating him, and the Korean shopkeepers guarding their stores with guns—constructed a story about a country racked with racial tensions and incredible, senseless violence. The narrative that reporters and editors attached to these images emphasized their escalating violence, the way the beating of King and the beating of the truck driver and the smashing and burning of shops and buildings led into one another. The narrative linking of these outbursts helped explain the events to television viewers: many said that while the spiraling destruction was horrible, they understood the rioters' actions, whether or not they approved of them. It seemed clear, these viewers implied, that the only way to be seen or heard, to become a reported part of the story, was to produce a violent outburst worthy of the news.

Alongside their reporting on the racial violence in South Central Los Angeles, the media turned to rap and hip-hop performers whose music deals with racial fury and police violence to explain the events in L.A. and to articulate what lies behind racial tension in America. *Newsweek,* picking up on the relation between rap and the riots, produced a cover story titled "Rap and Race."[1] This media juncture, with stories about violence set next to a heightened attentiveness to rappers, stirred controversies. Chuck D. of Public Enemy, in a statement that itself became a news staple, said that rap is the CNN of the African American community. His claim could be understood as explaining the way rap not only disseminates "newsworthy" information of concern to African Americans (as Cable News does for and about a different audience), but also provides a *way* of sharing information that builds and supports a community: rap grips its listeners and communicates through rhythm, rhyme, energy, and performance skills. It provides for a kind of communion between performer and audience and among audience members, one that compels listeners not only because of the escalating chain of violence it reports, but also and mostly because of the stories it tells and the way it tells them. It is perhaps not surprising, though, that to many the violence presented in rap and hip-hop recordings and videos can only be read as it would be on CNN—as violence, and as incitement to further incident. When then–Vice President Dan Quayle called for Ice-T's "Cop Killer" to be banned because of the fury it unleashed at police ("Die, Die, Die Pig, Die") and then–presidential candidate Bill Clinton took Sister Souljah to task for saying it shouldn't surprise anyone that blacks will kill whites—which he took as an incitement to violence and not a description—they were reading the songs and comments for the five-second clip, for the violent climax they assumed to be the point and purpose of what was being articulated.[2] Violent climax is what they, and many Americans, have been trained to watch for and respond to, what we've been told over and over again makes a story a story, to the point where we start to see it as necessary if one wants to be heard, to the point where we read it as the main point of whatever *is* being said.

This kind of controversy raises a number of questions about ways of reading performance and violence, and particularly about ways of reading performance and violence in African American contexts. The link between performance, violence, and African Americans has a long history in America, dating from contemporary debates about rap, through nineteenth-century blackface minstrel and Jim Crow shows, back to African performance on board Middle Passage slave ships bound for America.[3] The term "Jim Crow" itself provides a clear instance of how tightly intertwined African American performance and violent oppression have been in this country. "Jim Crow" originally named a minstrel song-and-dance act that today one understands to have stereotyped, parodied, and degraded African Americans; the term became synonomous, late in this century, with a system of (sometimes violently enforced) racial segregation. African American performance, in the end, has never been free of the conditions of oppression that slave catchers inscribed it with when they first lured Africans on board slave ships by asking them to sing and dance.[4] These practices transformed African dance, a sophisticated and affirmative art form, into a tool for subjugation. The connection between dance and violent control continued in slaving practices: once on board ships, shackled slaves were exercised daily in a practice referred to as "dancing the slaves"—designed to keep them healthy, and to keep them from "fatal melancholy." Katrina Hazzard-Gordon writes how "usually several crew members paraded on deck with whips and cat-o-nine-tails, forcing the men slaves to jump in their irons, often until their ankles bled."[5] "Dancing the slaves" served the dual purpose of entertaining the whites and increasing the slaves' value. Hazzard-Gordon quotes one ship's officer as commenting: "We had tambourines aboard, which some of the younger darkies fought for regularly, and every evening we enjoyed the novelty of African war songs and ring dances, fore and aft, with the satisfaction of knowing that these pleasant exercises were keeping our stock in good condition and, of course, enhancing our prospects of making a profitable voyage."[6] This use of dance was continued on the plantation, where slave owners encouraged and forced their slaves to sing and dance for similar reasons.[7] Dance, then, which may at first look like the opposite of violence, has instead historically elided with it: even as dance provided a space within slave culture for shared African values, this space existed in the context of oppression from white slave owners.

In his 1990 epic dance theater piece, *Last Supper at Uncle Tom's Cabin/The Promised Land,* Bill T. Jones inhabits and explodes these relations between African American performance, slavery, and political identity. Jones, a renowned, contemporary, African American, gay, HIV-positive dancer/choreographer, restages some of the complicated historical interconnections between race, violence, gender, sentimentalism, and Christianity which circulate through Harriet Beecher Stowe's *Uncle Tom's Cabin.* This restaging starts with the "Middle Passage" opening of the performance piece, where, after the darkened theater has echoed with different voices reading the chapter titles to Stowe's book, the stage lights to a row of dancers, stomping, raising and lowering oars;[8] it continues through to the piece's controversial ending, where dozens of naked bodies face the audience full on. Throughout, Jones forces a relentless questioning of what racial and sexual violence does, what it is for, how it operates, and how dancing bodies are and have been connected to it.

This chapter examines ways that Jones's *Last Supper*—produced in the months immediately following the AIDS-related death of his longtime (European American, half-Jewish) lover and partner Arnie Zane—links dance performance with questions of racial and sexual violence. I argue that the piece shows how dance, in the 1990s, can negotiate a theoretical position for identity that is both performed—constructed through repetition, moving and changing as the dancer moves through different roles and performances—and also clearly centered on a particular, undeniably biological body.[9] I also examine the structure of *Last Supper at Uncle Tom's Cabin/The Promised Land,* and of postmodern dance in general—performance whose meaning is largely embodied in its relation with an audience and its dependence on bodies, rather than in the plot climax or story it tells. I argue that this structure allows a way of representing conflict and violence without narratively and politically requiring it for there to be a dance to perform.

In this way, the piece represents violence, but does not endorse it, much as it both stages and deconstructs identities.

DANCE IN *UNCLE TOM'S CABIN*

Stowe's 1852 tour de force, *Uncle Tom's Cabin*, provides Jones (as well as several other contemporary choreographers) with an apt framework for these questions of racial and sexual identity, and particularly with a way of dramatizing a connection between dance and the violence of slavery that informs African American experience.[10] The book simultaneously inhabits a prominent position in the history of violent conflict in the United States (Abraham Lincoln is infamously reported to have remarked, upon meeting Stowe, that the book sparked the Civil War); in U.S. stage history (where thousands of stage productions earned it billing as the "World's Greatest Hit"); and in the history of African American politics and identity (from the Civil War to the twentieth-century transformation of the novel's title into a term naming spineless, obsequious blacks who appease white culture through their victimized Uncle Tom behavior).[11]

The connection between performance and oppression that Stowe's *Uncle Tom's Cabin* articulates, though, stems not only from the story's illustrious and often offensive stage history. The text of the book itself in subtle and central ways connects African American performance and slavery. A performance by a little slave boy dancing on cue for white men who are negotiating a slave transaction, for example, sets the novel's plot in motion. Little Harry comes into the room where his kindly master, Mr. Shelby, is talking with Haley, a slave trader to whom Mr. Shelby is in debt. Shelby cajoles the boy into dancing the "Jim Crow":

> "Come here, Jim Crow," said he. The child came up, and the master patted the curly head, and chucked him under the chin.
> "Now, Jim, show this gentleman how you can dance and sing." The boy commenced one of those wild, grotesque songs common among the negroes, in a rich, clear voice, accompanying his singing with many comic evolutions of the hands, feet, and whole body, all in perfect time to the music.[12]

Harry's performance charms the trader, who insists Shelby sell the boy—and with this Stowe's story begins. Harry's performance, with all of its racial complexities (he, a light-skinned slave, while ostensibly mimicking another, darker slave, is actually copying the minstrel performance techniques of whites in blackface), shows song-and-dance to be a loaded act in Stowe's highly theatrical novel and its treatment of slavery.[13] Harry's enticement to dance (Shelby and Haley throw him raisins and orange sections) and his subsequent sale, for example, replay the technique by which European American slave catchers lured Africans on board ship by offering them rewards to perform their tribal dances. Likewise, Harry's dance as sign of his value and worth echoes the slave ship practice of "dancing the slaves." And by naming Harry "Jim Crow," Stowe's depiction further embodies the way dance continued to serve as a sign of the position of Africans in America even after slave ships reached shore.[14] Nineteenth-century Jim Crow blackface minstrel acts like the one Harry mimics, as critic Eric Lott has demonstrated, arose from and embodied a "racial unconscious" on the part of whites, an unconscious that worked overtime to police and affirm whites' precarious sense of their own whiteness and subsequent hegemony (Lott 23–24). The slave trader Haley, a brutish, coarse, and profane would-be gentleman, achieved just such an identity through witnessing Harry.

In addition to enacting the ways that African American dance has been related to the identity, and oppression, of slaves, Stowe's depictions of Jim Crow dancing also engage contemporary theoretical questions about "race" and "blackness" as justifications for slavery.[15] The more famous depiction of "black dance" in *Uncle Tom's Cabin*—that of the heathen Topsy, "one of the blackest of her race" (Stowe 351)—allows perhaps most clearly for a reading of Jim Crow dancing as something that clever and cunning blacks do to appease their white audiences. When St. Clare first brings Topsy to his cousin Miss Ophelia, he explains his interest in her:

> "I thought she was rather a funny specimen in the Jim Crow line. Here, Topsy," he added, giving a whistle, as a man would to call the attention of a dog, "give us a song, now, and show us some of your dancing."
> The black, glassy eyes glittered with a kind of wicked drollery, and the thing struck up, in a clear shrill voice, an odd negro melody, to which she kept time with her hands and feet, spinning round, clapping her hands, knocking her knees together, in a wild, fantastic sort of time, and producing in her throat all those odd guttural sounds which distinguish the native music of her race. (352)

When Topsy is done, she stands "with her hands folded, and a most sanctimonious expression of meekness and solemnity over her face" (352); Stowe's depiction is obviously troublesome for its own stereotyping, yet it also shows how clearly Topsy has been playing the part of the heathen, dancing Negro as a way of toying with those who have power over her—how both the stance of the black dancing and of the meek, solemn, sactimonious girl are roles she adopts to fit whatever tricksterlike purpose she is up to.

In general, *Uncle Tom's Cabin* can hardly be considered as critical of essential notions of identity. Stowe's story's depictions of gender, in particular, insist on a maternal sentiment and sphere too strongly for a deconstructive reading of the feminine domestic space at the heart of her novel to hold for long. Likewise, Stowe's depiction of African Americans can be (and, of course, has been) read as reinforcing essential and sterotypical ideas about race. Her description of Harry dancing to "one of those wild, grotesque songs common among the negroes" and of the stereotypical "rich, clear voice" and "perfect time" of the African American performer itself stereotypes blacks as "naturally" musical and rhythmic. Other aspects of her novel, too, lead to a reading of her portrayal of race as a fixed category (such as the seemingly necessary return to Africa of Eliza, George, and company at the end of the book).

Yet dance in the novel—particularly the "Jim Crow" acts in it—also, in some ways, shows the faultiness of justifying slavery on racial grounds, and thereby leaves room in the text for contemporary understandings of "race" as ideology and not as fact. Little Harry, like Topsy, dramatizes ways that race is an act. Harry, with his dimples and giggles and curls and other signs of gentle breeding, is clearly *not* the slave he is depicting. Much like the "mulatto" figure critic Hazel Carby has identified as a late nineteenth-century literary device enabling and expressing racial relations,[16] the figure of light-skinned Harry turning on and off a "negro slave" dance at will serves as a way of interrogating the ideology of "race," and thus the racial justification of slavery. This dance in the book hardly deconstructs the power relations at hand; the slave trader and owner are still, in this dynamic, making the slave dance as they like. Nevertheless, Harry is not the reified black person he dramatizes. Dance, in this way, intimates codes through which the enslaved body is constricted.

Along with the intimation that race is an act that can be danced, the book also hints that dance performance can be at least part of the solution to slavery. In Stowe's book, making slaves dance the Jim Crow is one of the slaveholding system's vulgar tools for keeping slaves down and for increasing their value as exchangeable commodities. Yet Stowe's stated purpose in writing the book is to do away with slavery. It is perhaps not surprising, then, that one of Stowe's envisionings seems to be for the slaves in the book to be able to dance differently—to dance not like vulgar and degraded Africans, but rather like refined Europeans. This is, in fact, what St. Clare's slaves (at least the light-skinned ones), whom he treats kindly and indulgently, aspire to do. Augustine St. Clare's rather dandyish personal servant Adolph, who we're told was in the habit of adopting his master's name and "the style under which he moved," wants to appropriate not only St. Clare's toilet water and clothes, but also the dance forms and dance floors of men of upper-class, European American New Orleans. He flirts in the kitchen with one of the family's servants by asking:

> "Pray, Miss Benoir, may I be allowed to ask if those drops are for the ball, to-morrow night? They are certainly bewitching!"
>
> "I wonder, now, Mr. St. Clare, what the impudence of you men will come to!" said Jane, tossing her pretty head til the ear-drops twinkled again. "I shan't dance with you for a whole evening, if you go to asking me any more questions." (321)

On the one hand, Stowe's description can be seen as gently chiding Adolph and company for their airs and pretentions in wanting to ballroom dance and otherwise mimic the indulgent behavior of their genteel masters. And even if she could be read as granting these light-skinned, well-bred men and women this indulgence, her vision is certainly not that of a ballroom where slaves and masters would share the same dance floor. Still, Stowe aligns Adolph and Jane's desire to ballroom dance with other desires that she sees as commendable and human, and which are understood as inalienable to European Americans: the desire to love and be loved, to raise families and maintain family ties without threat of separation, to care for and protect one's children. Here, she uses Adolph's class-privileged desire to go to the ball as a way of calling into question the notion that genteel and cultured behaviors, desires, or attributes are intrinsically "white" and instead suggests that any person of requisite character should be able to partake of (what she believes are) the advantages of refined, European culture.

Stowe reinforces this idea—that moving slaves to a more genteel dance floor will help emancipate them—by describing her novel, with its many scenes and entrances and exits, as, itself, a ballet. Stowe ends the chapter "Topsy," in which Topsy enters the scene doing the Jim Crow, by writing: "Topsy, to do her justice, was good-natured and liberal, and only spiteful in self-defense. She is fairly introduced into our *corps de ballet,* and will figure, from time to time, with other performers" (370). Stowe thus turns Topsy from a Jim Crow dancer into a performer in the ballet of the book. The tentativeness of Stowe's description here illustrates some of the problems in reading dance in Stowe as a space for performing race; there is no expectation that Topsy, one of "the blackest of her race," will herself become a prima ballerina—she'll only make occasional appearances in the ballet of the book. Nonetheless, Stowe's description reinforces the notion that one way of getting slaves to figure in mid-nineteenth-century America—and what she, in writing the book, wants to do—is to position them on the ballroom floor or in the ballet.

The obvious problem with this metaphoric envisioning of a way out of slavery is that it calls for slaves to wipe out distinctly African aspects of their culture and instead conform to Euro-phile standards of conduct. Stowe's book has, of course, been long and fiercely criticized for suggesting just this; conforming readily and submissively to European American culture is a large part of what it means to be an Uncle Tom in twentieth-century America. This problem translates, in theoretical terms, into an illustration of the criticism some recent critics have had with poststructuralist theories of identity, where (the criticism goes) the deconstruction of categories such as "race" or "gender" ends up, once again, denying those who have been oppressed (people of color, women) a subject position or identity. In other words, even if parts of Stowe's novel were read as deconstructing race and showing it to be not intrinsic but performed, the book ends up, at best, prescribing the performance of whiteness as a solution to the oppression of African Americans.

"TOM SHOWS" AND AFRICAN AMERICAN DANCE

The illustrious theater history of *Uncle Tom's Cabin* further reinforces the connections Stowe dramatizes between dance and the disciplining of African Americans—from dance's role in capturing and subjugating Africans, to demands that African Americans dance like Europeans. *Uncle Tom's Cabin* was a stage phenomenon, running (at various places, and often in many places at once) without interruption from September 1852 into 1930—more than seventy-seven years. By the turn of the century, at least twelve *Uncle Tom* scripts were in circulation and roughly five hundred "Tom troupes" were traveling the country performing the story. At the beginning of the twentieth century, the motion picture industry took up the story as one of its first subjects: Thomas Edison Company's twenty-one-minute 1903 silent film "Uncle Tom's Cabin, or Slavery Days" was one of the earliest American movies. It is, of course, difficult to know how dance was presented in these many theater versions of the book, but from the reviews, posters, and film productions it seems that writers, directors, and performers attempted to inscribe and parody African American movement as a sign of fixed racial identity. Some of the more insidious versions of Stowe's text twisted her plot and purpose by providing a happy ending and sometimes even a justification of slavery: in the P. T. Barnum version, for example, Tom is rescued by George Shelby; in *Happy Uncle Tom,* Tom is not murdered by Simon Legree but lives on as a contented slave.[17] In many of these versions and perversions of Stowe's text, dance became a way of performing race: European American actors in blackface put on stereotypically "black" dance movement to convey their character. Just as Stowe's purpose in portraying the horrors of slavery was perverted into portrayals of "happy Uncle Tom," her complicated depiction of Harry and Topsy being made to "jump Jim Crow" for their masters—and thus being forced into a degraded position and made into an exchangeable commodity—was read straight, for the stereotypes it foregrounded. Topsy, whose blackface paint wasn't any darker than that of the others, would flail absurdly on stage as a clear indication to the audience of her status as "one of the blackest of her race." (In the 1903 silent film version, for example, Topsy is played by a fully grown woman who enters the stage and starts tap dancing, with wildly flapping arms, while Miss Ophelia watches and fans herself frantically.) Background scenes of "blacks" dancing merrily were likewise used to set the plantation scene and indicate the players as slaves, and often to portray the stereotype of the "happy darky" that some of the more insidious stage versions sought to reinforce. The cover to the text of a 1928 "Tom show," *Eva the Fifth,* for example, is split in half with a tree, with stereotypically drawn slaves grinning and dancing merrily on one side and an Eliza being chased by dogs on the other; outside the frame, over twice as large as the figures in it, a man with a long, curling whip looms menacingly (see fig. 7); the cover embodies a connection between dance and the disciplining of

FIG. 7. Book cover for "Fly by Night; a comedy of a Tom show in three acts," by Kenyon Nicholson and John Golden. Published in 1928 under the title *Eva the Fifth*. First New York Production under this title at the Little Theater, August 28, 1928. Billy Rose Theatre Collection, New York Public Library for the Performing Arts, Astor, Lenox and Tilden Foundations.

"darkies" as slaves. Topsy and her dancing, in particular, seem to have resonated with audiences: on the stage, her position and role are consistently foregrounded more prominently than they are in the novel. Several posters for stage versions of the book, for example, choose to portray Topsy dancing as a way of representing the play as a whole (see figs. 8, 9, and 10). In general, then, these productions seem to have mirrored the troublesome, racist aspects of Stowe's descriptions, and of the (lack of) position available to African Americans who did not in some way "pass" as white.

Theater and film versions of *Uncle Tom's Cabin* formed a major chapter in the history of African American dance, and the attitudes about African Americans

FIG. 8. Topsy dancing; late nineteenth-century poster for a stage adaptation of *Uncle Tom's Cabin*. Granger Collection, New York.

FIG. 9. "Two Topsys"—Peck and Fursman's Mammoth Spectacular Uncle Tom's Cabin Co. poster. Billy Rose Theatre Collection, New York Public Library for the Performing Arts, Astor, Lenox and Tilden Foundations.

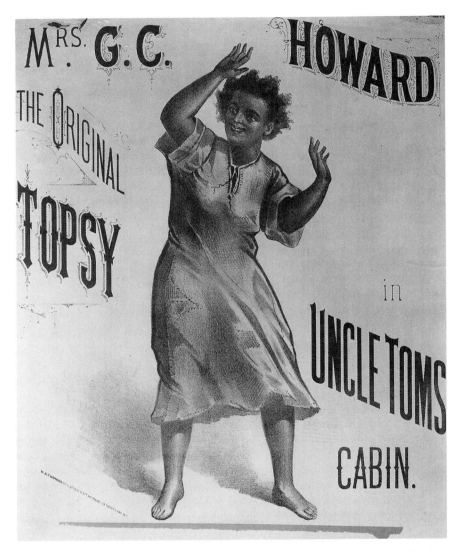

FIG. 10. "Mrs. G. C. Howard, the Original Topsy," poster. Billy Rose Theatre Collection, New York Public Library for the Performing Arts, Astor, Lenox and Tilden Foundations.

and dance that they reinforced in turn echoed through the development of American theater dance. By the early part of this century, "black dance" had virtually no space on the American theater dance stage.[18] When Katherine Dunham, who formed and ran the Ballet Negre in Chicago in the 1920s, tried to teach African dance to her students, she found, as one critic writes, that "black parents did not want their daughters to learn 'primitive dances'; they wanted them to learn ballet, so they would be graceful and 'refined' " (Haskins 95). Long after Dunham had found a successful market and an enthusiastic audience for her African-based dances—and after other African American dancers and choreographers had made major contributions to the American theater dance tradition—dance critics and historians continued to ignore Africans and African American culture. The development of modern dance, for example, is most frequently traced through such dancers as Loie Fuller, Martha Graham, Ruth St. Denis and Ted Shawn, and Isadora Duncan, through Doris Humphrey, Jose Limon, through Merce Cunningham, Paul Taylor, and Twyla Tharp—to list just a few major innovators commonly mentioned in chronicles of American theater dance. The work of African American dancers and choreographers, and the use of African-derived movements and rhythms by various choreographers are rarely mentioned.[19] These include, according to dance scholar Brenda Dixon-Stockwell, "the use of clusters of movement rather than linear exposition" and of dance that is "characterized in movement by the equivalent of polyrhythms, call-and-response, and multiple meter."[20] Recently, with the development of critical theories in multicultural and performance studies, general (i.e., European American) interest in these works has increased and has motivated multicultural programming agendas. This, combined with the impact of the performances, has resulted in the emerging prominence of African American choreographers and dance companies (such as Alvin Ailey's American Dance Theater, Dance Theater of Harlem, Bill T. Jones/Arnie Zane Dance Company, Urban Bush Women, and Garth Fagan). This in turn has provoked wider-spread understanding of the history of the contributions of African Americans to American theater dance, and increasing inclusion of the work of such dancers and choreographers as Katherine Dunham, Pearl Primus, Eleo Pomare, Donald McKayle, and Talley Beatty (and numerous others) in dance histories.

In various ways, then, American theater dance traditions have embodied the representations of dance in Stowe's novel. Her representations of African Americans' singing "wild, grotesque songs" while dancing "in a wild, fantastic sort of time" made their way into "Uncle Tom" minstrel traditions mocking African movement styles. The book's suggestion that an end to slavery and racial oppression is connected to an end to the need to dance in a way "common among the negroes," and the subsequent implication that African culture should be erased, or at least kept in Africa, echoes in the way concert dance traditions denied African culture—as when ballet was privileged over African-derived dance and African-derived techniques were attributed to European American choreographers.

LAST SUPPER AT UNCLE TOM'S CABIN/
THE PROMISED LAND

So how does Bill T. Jones's dance piece fit into this history? How does it utilize and remake—within black choreography and within postmodern dance—what a

"Tom show" is? What does this treatment do to the connections between dance, identity, and oppression which *Uncle Tom's Cabin* sets up? As numerous critics have noted, Stowe's more overt strategy for ending slavery involves not dance but rather urging all to adhere to a sentimental sphere, with its center in private, domestic space, in the attributes of women, in identity with Jesus and with re-demptive death.[21] In what follows, I look at how Jones combines this Christian sentimentalism—in, for one, the "Last Supper" and "Promised Land" references of his title—with *Uncle Tom's Cabin*'s connection between dance and politics; I argue that these connections comprise a political strategy applicable to issues of race, gender, and sexuality in the 1990s. This move to re-dance the sentimental at the end of the twentieth century, in turn, also provides a way of including recog-nition and consideration of the physical body in modern theoretical inquiries— inquires that have, as dance theorists in particular have recently begun to insist, long dismissed the body as a concept.[22]

Last Supper at Uncle Tom's Cabin/The Promised Land enacts these connec-tions between dance and politics by tapping, first, into the racially deconstructive dance moments in Stowe. In the first of the piece's four sections, in particular, Jones plays with the ways that dance movement has been problematically linked to racial identity, especially in the Uncle Tom tradition. He stages a ShrinkLit-style dance version of the Uncle Tom plot in which the characters match the vaudeville feel of the opening set framing the piece—a checkered, cartoony cabin, with a white-haired lady carrying an oversized book hovering near it—in their own movement. Parodying dance in the novel and in its stage history, and the way it has been attached to racial identity, Harry and Topsy flail in exagger-ated Jim Crow form, while Eva, Miss Ophelia, and St. Clare prance in delicate balletic entrechats back and forth across the stage. Many (though not all) of the dancers wear masks—either blackface or whiteface masks—to signify the race of the character danced; occasionally (though not necessarily) the race of the mask doesn't match that of the dancer (see fig. 11). Aunt Chloe, for example, is danced by Lawrence Goldhuber, a hefty white man with a pillow stuffed under his shirt; Simon Legree is danced by R. Justice Allen, an African American man in a whiteface mask.

The technique of parody and play with African American dance traditions, and with the implied relation of movement to race, here seems analogous to the vernacular theories of African American literature heralded by Henry Louis Gates and Houston Baker. Jones picks up, exaggerates, "signifies on," the history of black dance in the American stage tradition. In keeping with this technique, the section also registers its place in a tradition of African American dance by including echoes of Donald McKayle's 1959 classic *Rainbow 'Round My Shoul-der*, a work inspired by the music and rhythms of Southern black chain gangs. In Jones's piece, following the narration of Tom's sale and the suffering he wit-nesses on his transport down the river, the dancers move together, arms crossed, in chain gang formation, mirroring part of McKayle's work.

FIG. 11. Scene from "The Cabin," section one of *Last Supper at Uncle Tom's Cabin/The Promised Land*. Photo copyright © Carol Rosegg/Martha Swope Associates

The play in this first section deals not only with danced representations of race, but also, as the Aunt Chloe caricature makes clear, with the performance of gender. In the second section, "Eliza on the Ice," Jones more directly addresses the category of "woman" and notions of "femininity." "Eliza on the Ice" opens with a row of snarling male dancers playing hypermasculine dogs doing football-type exercises (see fig. 12); it then presents five Elizas, hounded throughout by the dogs, acting out contemporary gender and sex roles. The section most obviously explores the positions of women as, always and still, "between two shores," as Eliza was. The first four dancers reflect this exploration of what it means to be a woman from particular racial/ethnic/individual positions: an African American woman, Andrea Woods, depicts the pain and dilemma of a "historic" Eliza; then Heidi Latsky, a small Jewish woman, dances a solo in which she speaks of being in an abusive heterosexual relationship; the piece then turns to Betsy McCracken, dancing an Eliza who controls men, and to Maya Saffrin, playing a "beautiful woman" Eliza who is passed from man to man.[23] The exploration of these femininities seems fairly straightforward; each registers a troublesome position to which women, historically and culturally, have been relegated. Just before the section ends, though, a fifth Eliza enters the stage, this one danced

FIG. 12. The dogs in "Eliza on the Ice," section two of *Last Supper at Uncle Tom's Cabin/ The Promised Land*. Photo copyright © Carol Rosegg/Martha Swope Associates

by Gregg Hubbard, an African American man dressed in a miniskirt and high heels. On the quiet, darkened stage, this Eliza walks slowly and then repeats the movements of the female dancers—sometimes exaggeratedly, adjusting the skirt, swinging the hips, making the audience laugh. Here, then, an understanding of the difficult subject position of women—and a nineteenth-century sentimental herald-ing of "women"—is shifted to allow, within the same scene, for a questioning of the attachability of gender/sexual positions to particular biological bodies.

Stowe's heralding of "feminine sentiment" in *Uncle Tom's Cabin* is thus moved into an arena that opens the stage, and the book, to the position of not just "woman" but also the construction of gender, and more specifically, in Jones's context, the position of gay men and their bodies in this sentimental economy. Even within this depiction, though, lies another layer of questioning. Ironically merged with this fifth Eliza's dramatization of a gay man's precarious cultural position is, I think, a trickster-ish parody of the gay man as spectacle. Jones stages this first overt treatment of homosexuality in the performance as not only a man in a miniskirt, on the ice, between two shores; he also, through this depic-tion, plays with the ways that homosexuality is defined and constituted as campy performance. Unlike the earlier appearances of cross-dressing (where the gender play is somewhat hard to discern, as when Goldhuber appears as Aunt Chloe), this first overt, public treatment of unstable gender positioning is staged through the campy, drag queen clichés of the fifth Eliza's hip-swinging act. This depiction itself plays with, as Eve Kosofsky Sedgwick puts it, an "appropriation by the larger culture of male homosexuality as spectacle."[24] In doing this Jones makes his subject, in part, the act of public staging itself, challenging the "fundamentally private" values of nineteenth-century sentimentalism by forcing a recognition of gendered identity as constructed in and by and for the viewing, laughing public.

The doubleness here—the simultaneous staging and showing to be staged which dance performance enables—is furthered in the way the next section, "The Supper," both presents and confronts Christianity. "The Supper" opens with Bill T. Jones's mother Estelle Jones on stage praying and Jones next to her, beginning, slowly, to dance; as she begins to sing the spiritual "Wade in the Water," his movement picks up until he is dancing full out. In this section Jones concurrently presents and questions, via his dancing, the Christian religious faith he grew up with (he has explained that, in the black church, dancing to prayers is "like a kind of sacrilege").[25] The religion still registers, but the dance performance forces Jones's moving body to be taken into its picture. A more overt engagement with Christian religious topoi—and literal deconstruction of them— becomes apparent when the curtain next opens to a tableau vivant reenactment of Leonardo da Vinci's *Last Supper,* which holds for a minute before it, as archetypal religious depiction, dissolves into the dance of the section (see fig. 13).

FIG. 13. Leonardo tableau, moments after dissolution, from "The Supper," section three of *Last Supper at Uncle Tom's Cabin/The Promised Land*. Photo copyright © Carol Rosegg/ Martha Swope Associates

"Faith," the prologue to the final section "The Promised Land," foregrounds the way that this ambivalent representation of Christianity arises in part through its complicated relation to homosexuality. The original title to the dance piece, "Last Supper at Uncle Tom's Cabin with 52 Handsome Male Nudes" (based on a bawdy deck of cards given to Arnie Zane), provides a hint that the performance will address a connection between gay male aesthetics and identity, and the role of Christian tropes in *Uncle Tom's Cabin*. "Faith" then takes up the issue, dramatizing Christianity's complicated relation to homosexuality. It plays, for example, with questions such as those Sedgwick has raised about the relation of Christianity to Jesus, whose unclothed body, "often in extremis and/or in ecstasy, [is] prescriptively meant to be gazed at and adored." Jesus, as various critics have noted, invites the erotic attachment of viewers, whatever their gender identity.[26] In "Faith," a minister from the community—different ministers participated across the country as the company was on tour—comes on stage to tell the story of Job, and Jones dances to this sermon also. This time, though, as he dances, his shirt is ripped off of his back and shredded, and he continues to dance, shirtless, an embodiment of both Job, whose faith is being tested, and of the gay male body on display in the face of religious doctrine that shuns it, yet meant it to be "gazed at and adored." Jones then joins the minister on stage for an impromptu conversation, where he asks the minister such questions as What is faith? Is anger evil? Is homosexuality evil? Is Christianity an Uncle Tom religion? Is Job's faith really possible for real people?

It is through Jones's grappling with these questions, and particularly with the story of Job and its suggestion that, if only one had faith enough, all would be restored in the end, that *Last Supper at Uncle Tom's Cabin/The Promised Land* resurrects its central, absent body. Thematizing the missing body of Arnie Zane could be seen as—and in some ways, is—ironic commentary on the sentimental trope of tragic early death that is at the core of the Christian tradition, of *Uncle Tom's Cabin,* and also of contemporary media representations of gay men.[27] The melodrama of little Eva's death (in the first section, she gets carried off stage with angels; Tom, after he's been beaten to death, tiptoes after her) is in some ways refigured not only in the scenario of Jesus's Last Supper, but also in the death of Zane at the heart of the piece; everyone knows that the context of AIDS is part of the dance. In this final section, though, the treatment of tragic early death is turned from being a parodic and performative comment on this sentimental trope (though the parody remains as well), into a staging of, literally, a not-dead male body on display with its private parts made public. Part way through "The Promised Land" (which is what the last part of the original title, "52 Handsome Male Nudes," evolved into), Arthur Aviles, a dancer with a body type somewhat similar to Zane's, dances on stage naked. Little by little, he is joined in his nakedness by the other dancers, who include not only the company members but also forty people from whichever community the company is performing in, until at the end, all completely naked, they turn and stand together to face the audience. The layers of parody and play have been left backstage, and what confronts the audience here are naked bodies. Along with the multiple layers of performativity that this piece presents—the theories of racial and sexual identity as performatively produced that it acts out, in other words—it also performs an awareness of particular, physical, vulnerable bodies, rendered more palpably vulnerable by being a mix of aging, fat, and inept bodies as well as those that are strong, young, and lean.[28]

Just as Jones's dance relates the performativity of racial, gender, and sexual identities to physical, dancing bodies, it also, and similarly, presents ways that contemporary, postmodern dance performance—and the postmodern audiences trained to watch it—can start to take apart the central role violence now has as a tool for political reform. That that performance, in and of itself, is a central concern of *Last Supper at Uncle Tom's Cabin/The Promised Land* becomes clear by the end of the first segment of the piece. After Tom is murdered and tiptoes off stage, all raise their fists, shout "freedom," and the frame freezes. Then, while lights flash, the entire plot is rewound, quickly and silently, through Tom's murder, back to the scene where Tom refuses to whip a fellow slave, and the narrator asks, "What is there for those who are left behind?" This video-style replay that ends the section, combined with the raised fists and the question, suggests that the piece will address ways that contemporary media and performance can themselves play a political role in late twentieth-century, racially frought America. The end of the "Supper" section dramatizes the suggestion: here, the dancers re-form the Leonardo tableau and freeze-frame there momentarily while company guest artist R. Justice Allen comes forward and starts to rap an intense, angry, autobiographical piece. "Sumthin ta Think About (They call me Justice)," tells a story about his life as a "young, gifted and black" man who was sent to Vietnam, came back and became hooked on heroin, killed someone in a stickup, and was then sent to Attica for fifteen years. The dancers start to move as he describes the forces that led him to be "consumed by the streets" and the fury and racism of his prison experience:

> Out of sight, out of mind, A forgotten man
> victimized, and taunted by the Ku Klux Klan
> herded, and prodded from block to block
> I was just another nigger in a cracker box

At the end of the rap piece, though, it has become clear that Justice's response to this violence, which he both experienced and contributed to, is not to condemn, justify or continue it, but instead to perform it:

> A new day dawned the day I got out
> I had no fears, I had no doubts
> my house is glass so I throw no stones
> now I'm rockin' 'round the world with Bill T. Jones

This final reference to the rap song itself, to the *Last Supper at Uncle Tom's Cabin/The Promised Land* piece, and to the act of performance as a whole points up the ways performance in and of the piece are functioning as a response to the social, economic, and racial violence of which R. Justice Allen's narration speaks. The replacement of violence with performance here is literalized—Allen is spending his time in the rehearsal studio and on the stage, and not on the streets; more significantly, though, it stages what the piece as a whole is doing in the way it performs past the violence it describes.

That the piece suggests performance as political tool for African Americans is made even more explicit by the way the dance ends by presenting itself, and the fact of its own performance, as a third position in the popular polarity pitting Martin Luther King–style religious, nonviolent devotion against Malcolm X–identified racial reform "by any means necessary." In "The Promised Land," Jones both stages and disrupts this dichotomy. The dance of the section begins while excerpts from Martin Luther King's "I Have a Dream" speech are broadcast backward ("Last at free are we! Almighty God thank!"). King's position is, in other words, both presented and (quite literally) turned around through the particularities of Jones's performance of it. From here, Jones stages an enactment of (Malcolm X–aligned) violent revolt: the dance moves from King's speech into the climactic murder scene from LeRoi Jones's (aka Amiri Baraka's) one-act race drama, *Dutchman*. In the scene, a white woman subway rider stabs the young black man she has been flirting with, and whom she has been taunting with racial stereotypes (calling him an Uncle Tom who would "let the white man hump his ol'mama, and he jes' shuffle off in the woods and hide his gentle gray head"). The Bill T. Jones dance piece, though, doesn't end with the murder that Baraka's drama does, where the audience leaves with the impression that violence is an indisputable and perhaps even necessary fact of interracial contact. Instead, it moves immediately into the final scene of "The Promised Land," where the increasingly naked bodies of varied shapes, sizes, colors, and contours move in and out of formations, leaning on each other at times and at times pushing each other away, and finally turning naked together to face the audience. Bill T. Jones is clearly putting forth this final image of stark, naked bodies, and not the narrative violence propelling and concluding the "Dutchman" excerpt, as his response to the issues his piece confronts.

The structure and genre of contemporary postmodern dance are particularly conducive to this kind of performance refiguring, where violence is acknowledged but not depended on. Audiences approaching contemporary dance performances are not expecting well-developed plots complete with climax and resolution; they aren't watching for linear development, for a narrative that builds, climaxes, and then resolves, but rather for the overall sense the piece is communicating, for the emotional and kinesthetic connection they find in it.[29] The Uncle Tom "plot" is over in the first act, "The Cabin," with over three quarters of the piece left to go. Few viewers, I think, would expect the narrative violence of

Stowe's book to be taken up and furthered. Nor would they read the violence included in the last three sections (say, the Eliza who speaks of being in an abusive relationship; the murder related in the rap piece) as they saw, for example, the violence in Los Angeles—as necessary parts of an escalating chain of violence set in motion by the offenses of a slave system and a white writer's text, although they might well see a relation between the violence and these systems and texts. Audience interest in the dance does not hinge on these elements, but the dance nonetheless enables them to be voiced and embodied. The dance piece, in short, takes a history of violence—of slavery, of Uncle Tom's murder, of racism, of the often-offensive stage history of *Uncle Tom's Cabin,* of AIDS, of loss—and deconstructs it, and then performs the incorporation of this deconstruction by live, vulnerable, naked bodies. The nonnarrative form of this performance resonates with non-Eurocentric dance forms, such as the clusters of movement and polyrhythms that characterize African dance; the nonnarrative approach, in turn, further reinforces Jones's ability to perform a solution in between King and Malcolm X. The dance takes Stowe's "ballet" and turns it into the best kind of postmodern critique—reflexive, complex, and embodied in ways that bring together concerns regarding racial and gender oppression.

Last Supper at Uncle Tom's Cabin/The Promised Land, in this way, provides more than a way of registering the difficult positions of those who have been historically and culturally oppressed, and simultaneously the instability of their gender and racial identities. It also dramatizes a way of recognizing, commenting on, and representing violence without further requiring it. The dance itself becomes a tool—for neither an Uncle Tom narrative of victimization nor a narrative built on violent conflict, but rather for expressing and confronting oppression.

NOTES　　　　　— — — — — — —

I am grateful to the many people who shared their responses to *Last Supper at Uncle Tom's Cabin/The Promised Land* and to versions of this chapter, and who generously passed reviews, videos, and articles along to me. Special thanks to Bruce Burgett, Susan L. Foster, and Randy Martin for comments on later versions of this chapter, and to Rob Zeiger for ever-astute editing advice.

1.　John Leland, "Rap and Race," *Newsweek,* June 29, 1992, pp. 47–52.
2.　Clinton quoted Sister Souljah (Lisa Williamson) as saying, "If black people

kill black people every day, why not take a week and kill white people?" Sister Souljah said her comments were misinterpreted and were not meant as a call to violence: "I was just telling the writer that . . . if a person would kill their own brother, or a baby in a drive-by, or a grandmother, what would make white people think that [he] wouldn't kill them too?" (Leland, 47, n. 1).

3. Critic Eric Lott, for example, has recently argued that the nineteenth-century minstrel song-and-dance act was part of a tradition that dedicated itself, both consciously and unconsciously, to staging or constructing racial boundaries. See Lott, "Love and Theft: The Racial Unconscious of Blackface Minstrelsy," *Representations* 39 (Summer 1992):23–50; see also idem, " 'The Seeming Counterfeit': Racial Politics and Early Blackface Minstrelsy," *American Quarterly* 43.2 (June 1991).

4. Dance historians have noted how the supposed interest of whites in African and Caribbean dance was used to trick slaves into capture: "Not infrequently it was through dance that many slaves were first enticed on board; rewards were offered to perform their tribal dances as entertainment, then, when the dancing was over, they were taken below, given intoxicating drinks, and when they awoke from an alcoholic stupor found themselves far out to sea." See Edward Thorpe, *Black Dance* (Woodstock, N.Y.: Overlook Press, 1990), 10.

5. Katrina Hazzard-Gordon, *Jookin': The Rise and Fall of Social Dance Formations in African-American Culture* (Philadelphia: Temple University Press, 1990), 8. She cites another report of how "Those with swollen or diseased limbs were not exempt from partaking of this joyous pastime, though the shackles often peeled the skin off their legs" (8). Quoted in Hazzard-Gordon from Edmund B. D'Auvergne, *Human Livestocka* (London: Grayson and Grayson, 1933), 69–70.

6. Hazzard-Gordon 9, quoting from George Francis Dow, *Slave Ships and Slaving* (Westport, Conn.: Negro Universities Press), 50.

7. For a fuller discussion of this ambivalence, see Frederick Douglass's discussion of the practice and product of slaves' enforced singing, in Douglass, *Narrative of the Life of Frederick Douglass, An American Slave* (New York: Signet Classics, 1968), 30–32; and idem, *My Bondage and My Freedom* (New York: Dover, 1969), 97–100.

8. Thanks to Randy Martin for pointing out this reading of the opening to me.

9. Questions of "performance" are frequently raised, in current theoretical circles, to address questions of identity—whether racial, gendered, and sexual positions are biologically based or instead performed through the repeated putting on of a racial, gendered, or sexual position. See Judith Butler, *Gender Trouble, Feminism and the Subversion of Identity* (New York: Routledge, 1990); and Diana Fuss, *Essentially Speaking: Feminism, Nature and Difference* (New York: Routledge, 1989). For more on the relationship between philosophical and theatrical conceptions of the "act," see Judith Butler, "Performative Acts and Gender Constitution: An Essay in Phenomenology and Feminist Theory," in *Performing Feminisms: Feminist Critical Theory and Theatre,* ed. Sue-Ellen Case (Baltimore: Johns Hopkins University Press, 1990).

10. In 1990 and 1991 alone, at least three high-profile contemporary dance and theater troupes staged highly playful, critical, and adaptive versions of the "Uncle Tom" text. The San Francisco Mime Troupe and Lorraine Hansberry Theater opened an adaptation by African American playwright Robert Alexander in November 1990, rerun in 1992 as "I Ain't Yo Uncle"; Seattle's Empty Space Theatre and the Alice B. Theatre, a gay and lesbian troupe, staged *Unkle Tomm's Kabin: A Deconstruction of the Novel by Harriet Beecher Stowe* in early 1991. See Misha Berson, "Cabin Fever: Stowe's Once-Taboo Anti-Slavery Classic Takes on a New Urgency in the '90s," *American Theatre,* May 1991, pp. 16–23, 71–73.

11. The most exhaustive treatment of the stage history of *Uncle Tom's Cabin* is Harry Birdoff, *The World's Greatest Hit—Uncle Tom's Cabin* (New York: S. F. Vanni, 1947).

12. Harriet Beecher Stowe, *Uncle Tom's Cabin or, Life among the Lowly* (New York: Penguin Books, 1986), 44.

13. Despite the connections between staged song-and-dance performance and the construction, and embodiment, of African American cultural identities which a history of minstrel performance supports and *Uncle Tom's Cabin* plays with, literary critics concerned with analyzing performance aspects of African American traditions have, somewhat oddly, left the dance part of performance out of their theorizing. Houston Baker's work has used black vernacular music—the blues—to explore African American texts and literary tropes; the work of Henry Louis Gates, Jr., has likewise focused attention on how the vernacular tropes of "Signifyin(g)" are written into African American literature and criticism, and on how these "speakerly" texts perform blackness. See Henry Louis Gates, Jr., *The Signifying Monkey: A Theory of Afro-American Literary Theory* (New York: Oxford University Press, 1988); and Kimberly W. Benston, "Performing Blackness: Re/Placing Afro-American Poetry," in *Afro-American Literary Study in the 1990s,* ed. Houston Baker and Patricia Redmond (Chicago: University of Chicago Press, 1989). In these approaches, though, the emphasis has been on the inscription of voice and the vernacular; the body, and ways that it too signifies, has not been the focus of discussion.

14. Minstrel and Jim Crow performances flourished during the first half of the nineteenth century, starting in the 1820s and developing, by the 1840s, from a single act into entire shows in which white actors in blackface performed skits, songs, and dances. See James Haskins, *Black Dance in America: A History through Its People* (New York: Thomas Y. Crowell, 1990), 15–16; and Robert C. Toll, *Blacking Up: The Minstrel Show in Nineteenth-Century America* (New York: Oxford University Press, 1974).

15. Historian Barbara Fields (among others) has argued that "race" is neither a biological fact nor an idea but rather an ideology invoked and insisted upon by colonial European Americans some time *after* the enslavement of Africans became widespread, in order to justify the practice. See Barbara Fields, "Slavery, Race and Ideology in the United States of America," *New Left Review* 181 (May/

June 1990): 95–118. For a more theoretical discussion of "race" as a cultural construct, see Henry Louis Gates, Jr., ed., *"Race," Writing, and Difference* (Chicago: University of Chicago Press, 1986). See especially the discussion between Gates (in his introduction, "Writing 'Race' and the Difference It Makes," 1–20) and Tzvetan Todorov (in his essay " 'Race,' Writing, and Culture," 370–380) in this volume.

16. See Hazel V. Carby, " 'On the Threshold of Woman's Era': Lynching, Empire, and Sexuality in Black Feminist Theory," in Gates, *"Race," Writing, and Difference*, 313–314.

17. For an exhausive discussion of the novel's theater and film history, see Birdoff. See also Eric J. Sundquist, "Introduction," in *New Essays on Uncle Tom's Cabin* (New York: Cambridge University Press, 1986), 4–5; and Berson 18–21.

18. It is beyond the scope of this chapter to rehearse the complexities of the current debate on the term *black dance*. The following quote, from Zita Allen, "What Is Black Dance?" should give an idea of the complexity of the issue. She writes: "What is 'Black Dance?' Is it Alvin Ailey's racially-mixed company in his soul-stirring masterpiece 'Revelations,' but not American Ballet Theatre's performance of his more abstract ballet 'The River'? Is it Dance Theatre of Harlem's percussive, pelvic thrusts in Geoffrey Holder's 'Dougla,' or its distinguished adaptation of the Romantic ballet 'Giselle,' or the company's crisp neo-classicism in George Balanchine's 'Concerto Barocco'? Is it Charles Moore's brilliant re-creation of Asadata Dafora's 'Ostrich,' Pearl Primus' classic version of the 'Fanga,' or any other stylized reproduction of authentic African dances? Is it works whose themes reflect the unique Afro-American experience, like Donald McKayle's 'Games,' Talley Beatty's 'Road of the Phoebe Snow,' or Eleo Pomare's 'Blues for the Jungle,' but not more abstract ballets by these same choreographers? Is it choreographer Blondell Cummings' own 'Chicken Soup' but none of her work with white choreographer Meredith Monk? Does the label apply to works by Bill T. Jones, Ralph Lemon, Bebe Miller, and other experimentalists who emphasize form more than content and make no thematic reference to the broad-based Afro-American experience? Is it Katherine Dunham's theatricalized version of Afro-Caribbean ritual, 'Shango,' or the original Trinidadian cult dances which inspired it? Is it white choreographer Helen Tamiris' 'Negro Spirituals'?" Allen, "What Is Black Dance?" in *The Black Tradition in American Modern Dance*, comp. Gerald E. Meyers and Stephanie Reinhart, a pamphlet produced for American Dance Festival's 1991–1992 season, p. 22.

19. For a much more extensive discussion of the contributions of African Americans and of an African American aesthetic to American concert dance, and the ways critics and historians have (by and large) failed to credit it, see *Black Choreographers Moving: A National Dialogue*, ed. Julinda Lewis-Ferguson and comp. Halifu Osumare (Berkeley, Calif.: Expansion Arts Services, 1991); and *Black Tradition in American Modern Dance*.

20. See Brenda Dixon-Stockwell, "Black Dance and Dancers and the White Public: A Prolegomenon to Problems of Definition," in *Black Tradition in American Modern Dance*.

21. In a longer version of this essay, I discuss more fully current critical debate about the relationship of sentimentalism to movements for political reform (such as, in Stowe's case, emancipation). For discussion of Stowe and of sentimentalism, see, among others, Ann Douglas, *The Feminization of American Culture* (New York: Avon, 1977); Jane Tompkins, *Sensational Designs: The Cultural Work of American Fiction, 1790–1860* (New York: Oxford University Press, 1985); Richard Brodhead, "Sparing the Rod: Discipline and Fiction in Antebellum America," *Representations* 21 (1988): 67–96; Lauren Berlant, "The Female Woman: Fanny Fern and the Form of Sentiment," *American Literary History* 3.3 (Fall 1991): 436; and Lori Merish, "Women and Consumer Culture in American Literature, 1790–1913," Ph.D. diss., University of California, Berkeley, 1993.

22. For a full and compelling discussion of the ways twentieth-century philosophy has sidestepped the body, see Randy Martin, *Performance as Political Act: The Embodied Self*, Critical Perspectives in Social Theory (New York: Bergin and Garvey, 1990).

23. Jones explained these positions in a PBS Great Performances "Art in America" documentary on *Last Supper at Uncle Tom's Cabin/The Promised Land*, aired in spring 1992.

24. Eve Kosofsky Sedgwick, *Epistemology of the Closet* (Berkeley: University of California Press, 1990), 145. While numerous critics have debated the desirability of attaching a "gay sensibility" to the meaning of camp—arguing that doing so requires, paradoxically, a gay essentialism, the debate itself arises from the fact that camp is, today, most often read and coded gay. See, in particular, Carole-Anne Tyler, "Boys Will Be Girls: The Politics of Gay Drag," 56, in *Inside/out—Lesbian Theories, Gay Theories*, ed. Diana Fuss (New York: Routledge, 1991.

25. Maya Wallach, "Bill T. Jones: In Search of the Promised Land," *Dance Magazine*, October 1991, pp. 56–59.

26. Sedgwick, for one, discusses these links between Christianity and men's desire for the male body. See Sedgwick 140.

27. For more on the media conflation of gay men and early death, see Jeff Nunokawa, "'All the Sad Young Men': AIDS and the Work of Mourning," in Fuss, *Inside/Out*, 311–323. See also Sedgwick 144. For more on the the relation between nineteenth-century sentimentalism and mourning, see Karen Halttunen, "Mourning the Dead: A Study in Sentimental Ritual," in *Confidence Men and Painted Women: A Study of Middle Class Culture in America, 1830–1870* (New Haven: Yale University Press, 1982), 124–152.

28. The way the body has historically and culturally been used as a site of control for both race and gender, and how often this control has been levied through forced, or restricted, sexualities, has been widely discussed. See Karen Sanchez-Eppler, "Bodily Bonds: The Intersecting Rhetorics of Feminism and Abolition," *Representations* 24 (1988): 28–59. Hazel Carby has argued that the figure of the mulatta in late nineteenth-century African American women's fiction represents "the physical consequences of a social system that exercised white supremacy through rape" (313). In *Representations*, Eric Lott writes how at the root of the blackface minstrel texts he examines are "omnipresent nineteenth-century fears of the black penis" (34); he argues that white male spectators' fears of "racial undoing," because of the "phallic competition and imagined homosexual threat" of the represented black males they observed, was what underlay the minstrel show (35).

29.   For a related discussion of the relation between the narrative and nonnarrative features of this dance piece, see Randy Martin, "Overreading 'The Promised Land': Toward a Narrative of Context in Dance," manuscript.

Douglas Fairbanks: Thief of the Ballets Russes

Gaylyn Studlar

Perhaps the American cinema was never so primed for the influence of dance as in those fleeting years between the advent of feature films and the coming of sound. In that decade-plus between 1915 and 1927, the movies embraced both social and high art forms of terpsichore in the wake of America's enthusiastic coming to dance during the "dance mad" teens. While it sometimes has been assumed that dance was not important to American film until the 1930s, the heyday of the sound musical, these earlier years evidenced a textual and extratextual interest in dance drawn from a broad variety of sources, both aesthetic and popular. By the late 1910s, many films included scenes featuring contemporary or historical social dances such as the tango and Castle Walk, the waltz and the minuet. Café society dancers such as Irene Castle and Rudolph Valentino became movie stars, while European ballet dancers, such as Anna Pavlova and Theodore Kosloff, entered the domain of Hollywood.[1]

During these years, the destiny of American film and dance, especially concert dance, was marked by a multifaceted, complexly played-out convergence. Both were preoccupied with finding new ways for the body to move, with developing an expressive vocabulary beyond verbal language, and with creating visual spectacle accompanied by music. Dance and silent film had, from the very debut of the latter, shared the spectacle of the human body in movement; film quickly added live music as a conventionalized element of its appeal. Film's silent mime, like that of dance, moved to music, not only in its presentation mode but also in its creation, as on-set musicians provided music for actors to emote by.

Dance found a secure place in American film as the latter became increasingly sophisticated in narrative form, in production values, and in its exploitation of popular cultural trends that might attract a more high-toned, middle-class audience. Elizabeth Kendall claims that during these years, Hollywood was willing to exploit theatrical dance because some film directors, like many dancers and choreographers, conceived of dance as "distilled action, pure motion." As a result, she suggests, "Movies made dance a presence, a mood, instead of a choreographic art with rules."[2] If dance's formal choreographic presence in film often seemed limited, its influence was still abundantly demonstrable, especially in the movie industry's enthusiasm for the visual styles associated with dance, for dance-inspired costumes, poses and decor, for the stars and themes of dance. By 1926, the presence of dance in America's film capital was so strong that one dance magazine satirically declared Hollywood a heaven of opportunity where "good dancers go when they die."[3]

Ruth St. Denis and Ted Shawn were among those who responded to the opportunities created by the film industry. Their Los Angeles–based Denishawn school trained students, mainly women, who entered the movies as actors, actor-dancers, or choreographers. Those young aspirants to screen stardom who were not dance trained still could look respectably artistic and admirably graceful in the many self-consciously dancelike costumes and poses assumed for promotion photographs. These were often featured in fan magazines, which emerged as a ubiquitous form of film industry promotion that proved particularly enthusiastic in promoting the linkage between film and contemporary forms of dance. Perhaps because of their orientation to women—the same gender-specific audience that was known to fill dance matinées—these magazines often featured photo layouts and articles with exclusive emphasis on dance.[4]

Extending beyond the usual discussion of dance personalities and the highlights of the latest season is a 1924 article in the most erudite of them, *Shadowland*. In it, Albert Lewin asserts that Hollywood actors and directors needed to realize that "their art . . . is closer to the dance than to the drama. . . . Art fails unless it is dynamic." Motion pictures generally had failed to achieve "this dynamic quality," he added, but certain stars managed to possess it: "The success of Douglas Fairbanks is due less to his smile than to his activity. He is always 'on the go.' He does not stand and speak. His movement may be silly but he moves."[5]

Lewin stated the obvious. According to legend, when Fairbanks first came to Hollywood from Broadway, he moved so much that D. W. Griffith thought him best suited for Mack Sennett pie-throwing.[6] To some thoughtful observers like Lewin, Fairbanks probably did seem "silly" in the some three dozen athletic comedies he made between 1915 and 1922, but he quickly became the world's most famous filmic exponent of energetic, vital American masculinity as he literally bounded, jumped, ran, leapt, and scaled his way into manhood. His tremendous box office draw and his unrivaled business savvy combined to make "Dr. Smile," otherwise known as "Mr. Pep" or "Douggie," into one of the most powerfully self-governing stars in Hollywood.

In 1919, Fairbanks became one of the founders of United Artists, a radical new enterprise for movie production and distribution that dared to assign all rights and privileges to the film artists rather than to studio moguls. Fairbanks's ability to write his own scenarios, choose his own technical collaborators, and control every aspect of his productions meant that he could become the major creative force behind (and in) a film that stands as one of the most sophisticated convergences of pre-talkies cinema with dance as a *gesamtkunstwerk*.[7] This film, *The Thief of Bagdad* (1924), is driven by dance aesthetics at every level in spite of not containing one conventional dance scene.

To suggest that someone like Fairbanks, apparently so professionally removed from dance, should be the guiding hand behind such a filmic mediation of "high art" dance might seem farfetched. But not if one considers the self-conciousness with which Fairbanks increasingly approached film as art during the 1920s.[8] Nor is it without precedent if one recalls, as Alexandre Benois noted in *Reminiscences,* that the Ballets Russes was "originally conceived not by the professionals of the dance, but by a circle of artists linked together by the idea of Art as an entity . . . there was nothing specific or professional in their dreams. On the contrary, there was a burning craving for Art in general" (371). Ballets Russes productions, according to Benois, "were not ballets in the former, narrow sense of the word: rather, a new form of spectacle based on a rejuvenation of the traditions of the St. Petersburg Ballet" (364).

One might see a similar "craving for Art" as well as the search for a "new form of spectacle" in *The Thief of Bagdad* as part of Fairbanks's and Hollywood's attempts in the 1920s to cultivate new forms of cinematic spectacle that would enhance American film's status as art and capitalize on middle-class interest in other cultural forms. While his son has remarked on the influence of the Ballets Russes in Fairbanks's conceptualization of *The Thief of Bagdad,*[9] the film's representational indebtedness to dance as a *gesamtkunstwerk* has been overlooked. This is not surprising since the intersection of dance and cinema is one of the most profoundly neglected arenas of film scholarship.[10] Additionally, those few (male) scholars who have been interested in Fairbanks's career often seem perplexed by *The Thief of Bagdad* and its place in the oeuvre of one of the era's icons of all-American masculinity. They seem mystified by its odd, artsy nature, which is frequently attributed, in an offhand fashion, to the influence of German Expressionism.[11]

No doubt partially inspired by a short-lived cycle of imported German costume epics,[12] *The Thief of Bagdad* is set apart from these films as well as other American films utilizing orientalized settings by its treatment of scenic decor as a "dance space" and by the Léon Bakst–influenced style of its production design, with sets by William Cameron Menzies and costumes by Mitchell Leisen. It is also distinguished by the quality of figure movement and, more specifically, by its treatment of the male body in motion. Thus the film appears as a self-consciously artful mediation of trends found in the Ballets Russes's scenic and costume design, setting, and figure movement. However, the effect of such artful borrowing is not without its textual stresses. As a result, Mary Pickford's retrospective statement, "Watching him move [in *The Thief of Bagdad*] was like watching the greatest of Russian dancers," assumes more filmically significant and culturally troublesome implications than might first be apparent.[13]

Within the specific sociohistorical context that framed the meaning of *The*

Thief of Bagdad's representations of performative masculinity, the decorative, sensual body associated with orientalism in fashion and in the visual arts was virtually inseparable from the revolutionary influence of the Ballets Russes, these "last orientalists" who were also, paradoxically, the "first modernists."[14] In discussing the beginnings of modernism, Peter Wollen has suggested that Henri Matisse, courturier Paul Poiret, and scenic designer Léon Bakst each "created a scenography of the Orient that enabled them to redefine the image of the body, especially, but not exclusively, the female body" (5). Bakst's designs for the Ballets Russes visually redefined the male body as a highly stylized spectacle in motion which was striking in its ambiguous inscription of sexual difference. But radical too, Wollen suggests, was the Ballets Russes's gender inversion of sexual power in which it is the phallicized woman who is desiring and the feminized male who is desired and sexually objectified (20–21).

The collapse of conventional gender codification in Ballets Russes productions was accomplished through this narrative inversion of desire, but also through costuming and elemental performative means—the androgynous grace, energy, and movement of male dancers. The atmospheric spectacle of Bakst's designs was incomplete without the virtuoso display of astonishing physicality achieved through Michel Fokine's choreography, the latter soon inseparable in the public consciousness from the perception that Russian dance, was, at its very origins, oriental.[15] Exemplified by *Schéhérazade,* the retextualization of the body through the fantastic iconography and moral disorder of the East allowed the male body to speak in terms that many associated with the feminine: grace, gestural nuance, physical submission, and a polymorphously suggestive exhibitionism. This "feminization" was particularly evident in the dancing of Vaslav Nijinsky, who was credited (rightly or not) with restoring the male dancer to the center of ballet. While collaborators such as Fokine and Benois remarked on the necessity of Nijinsky's femininity to his portrayals,[16] American commentators were particularly hostile toward the world's premier danseur. Occasionally, other danseurs were praised if, by comparison with him, they managed, like Mikhail Mordkin, to appear "more virile and quite as much at home in the air."[17] Nevertheless, to mention Mordkin or any other danseur meant that the issue of masculinity required discussion, and Nijinsky's "effeminate quality," remarked upon in numerous reviews, was regarded by many Americans as "almost inseparable from the male Ballet dancer."[18]

By offering up an eroticized and androgynous male body, dance appeared as a threat to an athletic, physically based notion of American masculinity known as the cult of the body. Several historians have suggested that this cult, emergent at the turn of the century, privileged an ideal of masculinity centered around the efficacy of the body. It addressed the perceived difficulty American middle-class men were having validating their masculinity through work as more and more of them were confined to industrialized, bureaucratic, and sedentary jobs.[19] Americans began to embrace the idea that not only must a subject must be in motion to

have being, but that American character, masculine in its essence, was fundamentally shaped through action defined as bodily movement.[20]

In the 1890s, bodybuilding, football, boxing, and the hero worship of the
lower-class athlete emerged as a part of a discourse on masculinity aimed at
revalidating male identity in the face of a perceived "feminization" of American
culture and the loss of traditional institutional supports for defining masculinity.
A new emphasis on physical prowess in leisure sports served as a means for
revalidating a masculinity that yearned for the boyish energy, instinctive de-
cisiveness, and physical superiority that middle-class men were afraid had been
lost in the modern world. The muscular male body in movement, especially in
movement across the American landscape, became the middle-class ideal of robust manliness which had to be carefully constructed to ward off the enfeebling
influence of women in an "overcivilized" world as well as the myriad temptations
of an urban, industrialized society that might cause boyhood's instinctual energy
to deteriorate into immoral chaos.[21]

Dancing men were particularly dangerous because they seemed to suggest that
the admirably fit male body in motion was not enough to guarantee proper masculine character. While the graces of social dancing might make a man mildly
suspect, such prominent male dancers as Ted Shawn, Nijinsky, and, later,
Rudolph Valentino, transgressively undercut the foundation of the cult of the
body since they were obviously muscular and athletic yet, at the same time,
regarded as effeminate if not queer.[22] In spite of their interest in dance, Americans
were mistrustful at best, scornful more typically, of danseurs, foreign or home-
grown. "Apollo-like" Ted Shawn, the most self-consciously American and "virile" of concert dancers, stirred up controversy about the relationship between
dance and masculinity in virtually every venue in which he appeared. In an ironically toned article, a Los Angeles paper remarked: "Mr. Shawn has been rather
disgusted at certain critics who appear to regard a man who dances as necessarily
effeminate. Such foolishness! He is merely a well-balanced and splendidly
formed man."[23] Shawn publicly asserted endless variations on the theme that
"there is a great difference between having some of the feminine qualities and in
being effeminate,"[24] but that distinction seemed lost on most Americans; there
was a lingering tendency to believe, as one critic noted, that "dancing is female
and frippery" (Caspery 60).

Douglas Fairbanks also was a "well-balanced and splendidly formed man,"
and other than Theodore Roosevelt, he was probably the best known embodiment
and public proponent of the cult of the body's ideal of masculinity. In such films
as *The Lamb, Double Trouble,* and *The Mollycoddle,* Fairbanks's character
would often begin as an effete, overcivilized "mollycoddle," or, as in *The Mark
of Zorro,* he would pretend to be one to further his heroic aims. Even though his
films might gently satirize the cultish extremism of male pursuit of the "strenuous
life," in the end, a robust Rooseveltian physicality would be reaffirmed.[25] Off
screen too, Fairbanks promulgated the virtues of manliness achieved through

physical transformation and constant motion. In numerous magazine articles and a series of ghostwritten books for boys, Fairbanks became one of the most vociferous public advocates of male "character building" as he determinedly linked physical reform, dynamic exuberance, and goodness.[26]

If the dancing male body revealed contradictions and tensions in the ideals of contemporary American masculinity, it is astonishing that in *The Thief of Bagdad,* Fairbanks imitates the look, even some of the modernist dance technique of the Ballets Russes, and places this specularized male body within a unified decorative environment appropriate to dance. The film creates an environment in which, as was said of Bakst, "everything is animated by the spirit of the enchanted world before us."[27] Exploiting the sensuous textures of a fantastic oriental heterocosm, *The Thief of Bagdad* offers a visionary world dependent, first of all, on architecture. Like Bakst's production designs, the scenic design of Menzies is triumphantly artificial and theatrical and meets the fundamental requirement of being "an open, deep, picture space, sufficiently ample to hold the magical world of the ballet" (Gregor 107).

The scenic opulence of Bakst's set and costume designs for *Schéhérazade* was the object of effusive critical hyperbole. *The Thief of Bagdad* cannot, by virtue of the limitations of film technology, exploit a Bakstian palette of vivid colors, but with the monochrome resources of film tinting, it manages to evoke some of the atmosphere characteristic of Bakst. The monumentally sized sets, especially the interior of the caliph's Bagdad palace, are designed like a typical Bakst theatrical dance space, with an emphasis on the open grandeur of space matched with gleaming expanses of floors, on curved and entrance-framing staircases without visible means of support, on superimposed planes and foreshortened perspective, and on a fantastic distortion of detail that hints of Russian folk influence (or German Expressionism). Immensely oversized decorative objects such as vases and jars bring the scale of the environment into perpetual question to add to the impression of a dream mise-en-scène that could never be mistaken for waking reality. Even the bed of the caliph's daughter, plunked down in the midst of the palace's open space, evokes the arrangements of Bakst and his use of fabrics to evoke the mystery of the harem (see fig. 14).

The Ballets Russes's controversial productions used Bakst's evocative designs as the backdrop for direct and shocking expressions of an already established Western fantasy revolving around the Orient as the locus of a decadent passion.[28] Aptly described by Jean Cocteau as an "exotic fairy-story of the irresponsible and the irreparable," *Schéhérazade* was not unique in suggesting that the imaginary Orient privileged in Western narratives was, at its core, a vision of eroticism associated with voyeuristic fascination and interracial desire.[29] *Schéhérazade*'s "orgy of mad caresses" in its infamous harem scene suggested that all manner of transgressive desire might be acted out in such a fantastic world (Cocteau 32), even as it also confirmed—with the sultan's violent retribution for his wife's

FIG. 14. The scenic opulence of Bakst orientalism. Douglas Fairbanks, Anna May Wong, and Julanne Johnston in *The Thief of Bagdad*. Photo: Jerry Ohlinger's, New York

infidelity—the already circulating stereotype of the Orient as a site of despotic violence.

Although *The Thief of Bagdad* is subtitled *An Arabian Nights Fantasy*, the film studiously avoids the pessimism and brutal sensuality associated with the Ballets Russes's modernist imagining of the Orient as a place where "eternal agony was the price of the happiness of the poignant fleeting moment."[30] In this respect, the film becomes the equivalent of a pink tea, that American social ritual of utter respectability (and predictability) which Serge Diaghilev, when faced by the specter of American censorship, declared that *Schéhérazade* could never be.[31] *The Thief of Bagdad* tells the story of Amhed (Fairbanks), whose carefree life of crime is interrupted by his glimpse of a princess (Julanne Johnston). At first, Ahmed plans on drugging and kidnapping her in fulfillment of his motto: "What I want—I take." When three exotic princes from the East arrive to court her, Ahmed masquerades as yet another princely suitor. The princess quickly falls in love with Ahmed, and he is too ashamed to carry out his plan. He has a spiritual conversion sparked by her utter chasteness: As he tells her, "When I held you in my arms, the very world did change. The evil in me died." After being expelled as an imposter, Ahmed turns to a holy man, who tells him that his nobler aspirations will be rewarded if he learns that "Happiness must be earned," a motto seen written across the night sky in the film's opening. Ahmed sets out on a perilous journey to procure the rarest treasure that will win him the princess's hand in marriage. On his return to Bagdad, he thwarts the nefarious plot of the Prince of the Mongols (So-Jin) to take over the city and kill the Caliph of Bagdad (Brandon Hurst). In the end, Ahmed is accepted as true royalty because of his deeds. He and the princess ride away on a flying carpet. He has learned the truth in the maxim reiterated yet again in the final intertitle: "Happiness must be earned."

The Thief of Bagdad's story line offers a variation on the familiar Rooseveltian/Fairbanksian transformation of a mollycoddle into a man. What requires transformation within this context is not the overly civilized male subject who must reawaken his manly instincts by building his physique and his nerve for challenging experience, but the boyish criminal, the juvenile delinquent. Ahmed does not lack for physical vitality but is governed by the instincts of childhood. Those instincts were believed rooted in the natural lawlessness of the savage (see fig. 15). In the words of J. Adams Puffer in *The Boy and His Gang,* a boy is "essentially a savage, with the interests of a savage, the body of a savage, and to

FIG. 15. "What I want—I take." Ahmed, the thief (Douglas Fairbanks), a joyous figure with culturally troublesome implications. Production still from *The Thief of Bagdad* (1924). Photo: Jerry's Ohlinger's, New York

no small extent, the soul of one."[32] Just as the advocates of the cult of the body feared feminization, they also feared that boys who grew up unsupervised by men would never achieve a true manliness that wedded physical perfection with spirituality defined through action.[33]

The Thief of Bagdad utilizes its hero to suggest a spiritual transformation that adheres to the principles of the cult of the body as a search for moral meaning through validating and revitalizing experience. Fairbanks articulates this viewpoint in a statement attributed to him in the souvenir program for the film's Liberty Theatre debut:

> It [the film] is a tribute to the fineness that I believe underlies the workaday philosophy of men; a recognition of the inner forces that belie the sordidness of life. . . . The brave deeds, the longing for better things, the striving for finer thoughts, the mental pictures of obstacles overcome and successes won are nearer to our real selves than our daily grind of earthly struggle.[34]

In spite of its narrative strategies for reaffirming these conventional bourgeois ideals of American manhood, *The Thief of Bagdad* offers a stylized filmic pantomime that threatens at almost every moment to become a dance-drama centered around an exhibitionistic male performer potentially compromised in his manhood by every visual element of the production: setting, costume, and movement. It is the orientalized and feminized male body of the Ballets Russes danseur which Fairbanks emulates in *The Thief of Bagdad*. Fairbanks, like Mordkin, acquires his masculinity, in important part, through sheer comparison, in this case, to every other orientalized man in the film. In particular, he is continually contrasted with the feminized royal suitors. While the Prince of the Indies is compromised by his inactivity and passivity, the Mongol Prince, whose first appearance elicits gasps of fear from the princess, hides his cadaverous face behind an ever fluttering, feminizing fan. The rotund, babyish Prince of Persia is even portrayed by a short, corpulent actress (Matilde Comont).

In their decadent re-gendering of desire, the Ballets Russes's "oriental" dance-dramas (especially *Cléopâtre, Schéhérazade, Le dieu bleu,* and *Thamar*) exploited the sexually ambiguous quality of Bakst's costume designs. While his designs often emphasized the display of a voluptuous female body (as, memorably, in the odalisques of *Schéhérazade*), they androgynized, if not outright feminized, youthful male dance roles. See-through gauze pantaloons, iridescent halter-tops, colorful turbans, robes of intense color juxtapositions with oversize patterns were given shape in sensuously textured materials that frankly displayed the male body as a decorative object rather than as the functional subject.

Fairbanks's costumes imitate some of those Bakst designed for *Schéhérazade*'s Golden Slave (see fig. 16).[35] Ahmed (Fairbanks) is introduced sleeping, face down, with his arm languidly extended over the edge of a stone water fountain that is his perch. He is naked from the waist up, darkly bronzed and perfectly muscled. The wind softly blows his pantaloons. Their boldly patterned gauze

Fɪɢ. 16. The Golden Slave. Nijinsky in *Schéhérazade*. Dance Collection, New York Public Library for the Performing Arts, Astor, Lenox and Tilden Foundations.

legs flow from a tight little girdle. As a citizen bends to drink from the fountain, Fairbanks imperceptibly steals the man's purse. In the ensuing melee caused by his thievery, Ahmed pauses to extend his leg in a remarkably poised *attitude* position, then gracefully runs away, pausing to take yet another of the many plastic poses that seem in direct imitation of Nijinsky in *Schéhérazade.*

This moment establishes the kinesic strategy for the film: dance arises out of everyday movement—in extensions of Fairbanks's limbs, in the rhythm of his pantomime, the alignment of his body, and in the agile *en l'air* quality of dance that infuses the leaps across space which were already an established Fairbanks trademark. This is particularly well illustrated by a scene in which the thief, attempting to purloin jewels from the palace treasure room, overhears lute music coming from the palace harem. He gracefully leaps up onto an open staircase. Mesmerized by the music, he slowly ascends the stairs: each step is punctuated by a leg extension. Finally, he pauses to listen. His hands extend in a sharply angled pose reminiscent of Nijinsky in *L'après-midi d'un faune.* He assumes the "friezelike design," profiled stance, and alteration of movement and plastic pose that recall Nijinsky's choreography for the ballet.[36]

Fairbanks's movements often have the look of postclassical ballet technique: in the thief's extensions of his arms and legs while while begging, in his stylized physical reactions to the dramatic flogging of another thief, and in his acrobatic propulsions across the peculiar landscapes of Bagdad. Perhaps significant in supporting this dancelike quality of movement was the film's musical accompaniment. An original score composed by Mortimer Wilson was praised for synchronizing the actor's movement to music in a more sophisticated way than the usual "running comment on the text of the picture" provided by much silent film music.[37] This too may have added to the dancerly impression conveyed by Fairbanks's movement, as well as that of other characters, for almost all of the featured actors in *The Thief of Bagdad* leave naturalistic action behind. When in danger of capture by the Mongol Prince, the princess twirls out of harm's way like an Isadorable. A trio of fat eunuchs, in amazingly exaggerated costumes, form a comic corps de ballet for Fairbanks as he steals into the palace.

At decisive moments, however, Fairbanks tends to revert to movement that can only be described as all-American stomping; fluid, measured dance style flies out the window as surely as his magic carpet. This kind of regression to the conventional occurs at other levels as well, such as at the end of the scene in which he views the sleeping princess. This scene demonstrates how the film's reliance on dance spectacle is counterbalanced by elements that work to reassert conservative moral and physical ideals identified with contemporary American character building. Ahmed's venture into the palace harem initially aligns him with the voyeuristic and forbidden sexual desires emphasized in the Ballets Russes's "unexpurgated" treatment of typical Western fantasies centered on the Orient. The thief's guilty pleasure in viewing the sleeping princess is marked by an extended sequence that shows him progressing from a boyish gaze, to one of curiosity blended with shrugging dismissal, and finally, to one of fetishistic fascination. Ahmed steals down the stairs and approaches the bed of the caliph's daughter. He lifts one of her discarded satin shoes in his hand. In Nijinsky's *L'après-midi d'un faune,* a parallel moment occurs in which the faun secures a scarf left behind by a wood nymph. The faun's fetishistic fascination logically develops into a masturbatory final spasm performed over the scarf. This shocking gesture, says Lynn Garafola, "amounted to a declaration of war against the received conventions of ballet" (8). In contrast, Fairbanks's fetishistic moment with the shoe becomes a mere prelude to romantic reverence. He drops it as his attention is quickly transferred to the princess when her arm brushes against his as she sleeps. Even though Fairbanks might have had a modernist, "pagan body" that, in the words of Booth Tarkington, "yields instantly to any heathen or gypsy impulse," Tarkington was also not far wrong when he described the actor as a "faun who had been to Sunday school."[38] The possibilities of sexual and racial liminality cultivated by the Ballets Russes are neatly turned aside. Instead, the film signals that the lily-white princess who elicits love rather than lust and the bronzed male star masquerading as an alms-begging Arab will achieve a romantic union that triumphs over the hero's moral failings and the nefarious machinations of the stereotypical Oriental Other.

If dance was instrumental in confronting post-Victorian America with a "confused realm of beauty and moral uncertainty" (Kendall 119), Fairbanks takes the Ballets Russes's visual evocation of the Orient as a site of perverse fantasy and utilizes it in the service of a moralistic fairy tale of antimodernist innocence to match the assumed sensibilities of his American audience. *The Thief of Bagdad* draws on transgressive aspects of the spectacle of the Ballets Russes, but sets about taming the very elements of contemporary dance which made the latter both so fascinating and so problematic to Americans. Moral and masculine certainty, even the certainty of the American work ethic, are rearticulated out of the potential disorder of oriental fantasy aligned with a dance aesthetic dominated by sensual scenic opulence and the virtuosic display of the male body.

Although Fairbanks attempts to use his body as an expressive dancing instrument, the all-important therapeutic values of morally-directed male energy and exuberant activity are reasserted in narrative terms that signal the overwhelming need to reinscribe filmic masculinity in culturally comfortable, sexually unambiguous terms.[39] Nevertheless, reviewers, while praising the film's visual artistry, wondered how *The Thief of Bagdad* would be received by Fairbanks's fans. One suggested: "there are intervals when he is not the Fairbanks as we have come to recognize him," and concluded: "in all likelihood most of them [the audience] would prefer him in such a role as he portrayed in *The Mark of Zorro*. . . . Will it be a financial success? We offer no predictions."[40] Such reactions may attest to the difficulty of converting a dance spectacle linked to transgressive masculinity into a triumph of star-centered cinematic spectacle reasserting the gender and racial norms of Hollywood film in the 1920s. Sensual oriental opulence and the transformative power of dance as offered by the Ballets Russes threaten moral and masculine certainty. It is no surprise, then, that the film is obsessively framed and reframed by that quintessential character-building maxim, "Happiness must be earned." Purloining dance to serve defensive masculine ideals, *The Thief of Bagdad* rather desperately strives to become, in Fairbanks's own words, "the story of every man's inner self."[41]

NOTES

I thank Melissa Miller of the Theatre Arts Collection and the staff of the Rare Book and Manuscript Collection of the Harry Ransom Humanities Research Center, the University of Texas at Austin, for their help in locating Ballets Russes materials. I am indebted also to Matthew Bernstein for editorial advice and to Janet Lorenz of the Margaret Herrick Library of the Academy of Motion Picture Arts and Sciences for her hospitality and her help in locating film-related sources.

1. Pavlova made her screen debut in the 1916 feature *The Dumb Girl of Portici* (directed by Lois Weber and Phillips Smalley), adapted from the opera *La muette de portici*. Ads touted her as "the most wonderful, emotional actress of the decade," and the Universal film as "A weird-wild-wonderful spectacle." *Motion Picture World* 28 (April 1, 1916): 4–5. Kosloff appeared in feature roles in a number of films in the late 1910s and early 1920s, including Cecil B. DeMille's *Why Change Your Wife?* and *The Woman God Forgot.* For a discussion of the contextualizing influence of dance in the construction and reception of Valentino, see Gaylyn Studlar, "Valentino, 'Optic Intoxication,' and Dance Madness," in *Screening the Male*, ed. Steven Cohan and Ina Rae Hark (London: Routledge, 1993), 23–45.

2. Elizabeth Kendall, *Where She Danced* (New York: Knopf, 1979), 136. Michael Morris details some of Kosloff's various activities, including serving as a technical adviser to teach film stars how to move, in Morris, *Madame Valentino* (New York: Abbeville Press, 1991).

3. "A Dance Mappe of These U.S.: Culture Made Pleasant," *The Dance* 6 (October 1926): 25. By 1920, the dance schools in Hollywood included Denishawn, the Celeste School of Ernest Belcher, and Theodore Kosloff's.

4. Typical is "Figures of the Dance," which offers pictures and commentary on, among others, Irene Castle ("We personally have never gotten enough of her" the caption declares), Ruth St. Denis, Kosloff in clown costume, a Fokine-choreographed *Russian Toys* ballet, Doris Niles of the ballet corps of New York City's Capitol motion picture theater and other "delightful exemplars of Terpsichore" from vaudeville. *Motion Picture Classic* 15.6 (February 1923): 50–51. For a discussion of fan magazines' orientation toward women, see Gaylyn Studlar, "The Perils of Pleasure? Fan Magazines as Women's Commodified Culture in the 1920s," *Wide Angle* 31.1 (1991): 6–23. On women's attraction to dance during this era and on the Denishawn influence, see Kendall.

   5.   Albert Lewin, "Dynamic Motion Pictures," *Shadowland* 9.2 (October 1923): 46.

   6.   For the often-repeated view that Griffith reacted negatively to Fairbanks, see Richard Schickel, *Douglas Fairbanks: The First Celebrity* (London: New Elm Books, 1976), 36–41.

   7.   Relevant is the comment by Alexandre Benois: "The ballet is one of the most consistent and complete expressions of the idea of gesamtkunstwerk." See Benois, *Reminiscences of the Russian Ballet* (London: Wyman, 1941), 370–371.

   8.   Although it may have been a publicity stunt, Anna Pavlova visited the set of *The Thief of Bagdad* during its production, and Fairbanks, supposedly in response to the shocking news that her dance technique had never been recorded on film, made a short film of her dancing. See Schickel 98. As a demonstration of the lengths to which Fairbanks went in his pursuit of artistic filmmaking, he hired Maurice Leloir, illustrator of Alexandre Dumas's novels, to work on designing the costumes and sets for *The Iron Mask* (1929), the actor's last silent film.

   9.   Fairbanks, Jr., refers directly to this in an interview that prefaces the most recent restoration of the film by Kevin Brownlow and the BBC/Thames Television.

   10.   For the rare venture into this arena outside of the context of discussion of the musical, see Marcia Butzel, "Movement as Cinematic Narration: The Concept and Practice of Choreography in Film," Ph.D. diss., University of Iowa, 1985, soon to be published by the University of Illinois Press; also Angela McRobbie, "*Fame, Flashdance,* and Fantasies of Achievement," in *Fabrications,* ed. Jane Gaines and Charlotte Herzog (New York: Routledge, 1990), 39–58; Adrienne McLean, "The Image of the Ballet Artist in Popular Film," *Journal of Popular Culture* 25 (1991): 1–19; and idem, " 'It's Only That I Do What I Love and Love What I Do': *Film Noir* and the Musical Woman," *Cinema Journal* 33.1 (Fall 1993): 3–16.

   11.   See, for example, Alistair Cooke, *Douglas Fairbanks: The Making of a Screen Character* (New York: Museum of Modern Art, 1940), as well as John C. Tibbetts and James M. Welsh, *His Majesty the American: The Cinema of Douglas Fairbanks, Sr.* (South Brunswick, N.J.: A. S. Barnes, 1977); and, for a more sympathetic discussion of the film, see Schickel.

   12.   The influence of German costume spectacle on Fairbanks should not be underestimated, even though he tried to distance himself and his production of *The Thief of Bagdad* from these films. See Douglas Fairbanks, "Let Me Say This

about Films," *Ladies Home Journal* 39 (September 1922): 120. His son has been quoted as saying that his father was "impressed by the better German films . . . [but] did not like them as commerical enterprises and usually opposed suggestions that United Artists distribute them." Quoted in Schickel 80. However, the plot of *The Thief of Bagdad* has similarities to that of Fritz Lang's episodic, quest-structure fantasy, *Der Müde Tod* (*Destiny*, 1921), and Lang's film also anticipates some of *The Thief of Bagdad*'s most spectacular special effects. Also, the oriental setting of Fairbanks's film is anticipated by sequences in Lang's film and also by the Ernst Lubitsch costume epics: *One Arabian Night* and *The Loves of Pharaoh*. These Lubitsch films impressed urban American audiences and critics alike on their U.S. release in 1920–1922, but also ignited anti-German sentiment and a decidedly mixed response in the important market of small-town America. See David B. Pratt, "'Fit Food for Madhouse Inmates': The Box Office Reception of the German Invasion of 1921," *Griffithiana* 48/49 (October 1993): 96–157.

13. Mary Pickford (Fairbanks's second wife), quoted in Scott Eyman, *Mary Pickford: From Here to Hollywood* (Toronto: Harper Collins, 1990), 301.

14. Peter Wollen, "Fashion/Orientalism/The Body," *New Formations* 1.1 (Spring 1987): 5, 7.

15. This popular perception was reinforced by critics. For example, Arsène Alexandre notes in 1913: "They do not understand that the only dancing that is a fine art is of antique tradition and of Oriental origin." See Arsène Alexandre and Jean Cocteau, *The Decorative Art of Leon Bakst*, trans. Harry Melville (1913; reprint, New York: Benjamin Blom, 1971), 7.

16. Fokine remarked of Nijinsky as the Golden Slave, "he [Nijinsky] would have looked ridiculous had he acted in a masculine manner," while Benois described the dancer as "half-cat, half-snake, fiendishly agile, feminine and yet wholly terrifying." See Michel Fokine, quoted in Wollen 20; and Benois 316.

17. Henry T. Finck, "The Ballet Russe, Bakst, and Nijinsky," *The Nation* 101 (April 27, 1916): 464. Also comparing Nijinsky and Mordkin is Vera Caspery, "The Twilight of the Dance Gods: Merely a Theory Regarding Masculine Arms and Feminine Ankles," *The Dance*, May 1926, pp. 395. She notes: "Nijinsky came to these shores. . . . And strong women did not faint when he appeared on the stage, nor flappers cry out when he took his bows. Mordkin creates more of a furor for his virile grace, capturing the imagination and the adoration of his audiences, male and female" (19). Although he danced with the Ballets Russes and also formed his own company, Mordkin was best known as Pavlova's dance partner.

18. *Evening Post,* quoted in Nesta MacDonald, *Diaghilev Observed by Critics in England and the United States, 1911–1929* (New York: Dance Horizons, 1975), 174.

19. Jeffrey Hantover, "The Boy Scouts and the Validation of Masculinity," in *The American Man,* ed. Elizabeth Pleck and Joseph Pleck (Englewood, N.J.: Prentice-Hall, 1980), 285. See also E. Anthony Rotundo, *American Manhood:*

Transformations in Masculinity from the Revolution to the Modern Era (New York: Basic Books, 1993), esp. 247–283.

20. For the influence of specific texts such as J. Bell Pettigrew's *Animal Locomotion* (1888) on early twentieth-century ideals of masculinity, see Donald J. Mrozek, *Sport and American Mentality* (Knoxville: University of Tennessee Press, 1983).

21. Among the many contemporary views on the danger of too much female influence in the lives of boys are G. Stanley Hall, "Feminization in Schools and Home: The Undue Influence of Women Teachers—The Need for Different Training for the Sexes," *World's Work* 16 (1908): 10238; also Carl Werner, *Bringing up the Boy* (New York: Dodd, Mead, 1913).

22. A short story of 1915 relates: "'shades of Terpsichore, he can't even dance. . . . If he wants me to keep on loving him, he'd better not learn.' Then, what woman wants a prancing, mincing, intensely correct husband? She wants a regular man and the sort that falls over everything and is always getting in the way of his own feet." Justus Dickson, "On Awkwardness: Adeline Genee Gives Her Estimate of a Regular Man," *Greenbook* 13.3 (March 1915): 395.

23. Pearl Rall, "New Dance Music Ideal," *Los Angeles California Graphic,* June 9, 1917, n.p., clipping, Denishawn Scrapbook, vol. 5, 1917–1918, New York Public Library, Dance Collection.

24. Van Ryan, "Should Men Be Graceful?" *Physical Culture Magazine*, June 1924, p. 97. Of course homophobia also plays into this equation, as it no doubt did in the case of Nijinsky. For an interesting take on Nijinsky in relation to his projection of masculinity and gayness, see Michael Moon, "Flaming Closets," *October* 51 (1989): 19–54, reprinted in this volume.

25. See Theodore Roosevelt, "The Strenuous Life," in *The Works of Theodore Roosevelt*, memorial ed. (New York: Scribner's, 1924–1926), 260–272.

26. In addition to numerous articles such as "How I Keep Running on 'High,'" *American Magazine* 94 (August 1922): 36–39, there were some dozen books ghostwritten for Fairbanks, including *Youth Points the Way* (New York: D. Appleton, 1924); *Taking Stock of Ourselves* (New York: Britton, 1918); *Making Life Worth While* (New York: Britton, 1918), and *Wedlock in Time* (New York: Britton, 1918). See also David I. MacLeod, *Building Character in the American Boy: The Scouts, YMCA, and Their Forerunners, 1870–1920* (Madison: University of Wisconsin Press, 1983). Character building for boys was not limited to Americans; for one discussion of the British institutionalization of it, see Michael Rosenthal, *The Character Factory* (New York: Pantheon, 1984).

27. Joseph Gregor, *The Russian Theatre* (London: George G. Harrap and Co., 1930), 106.

28. For a broad survey of how Western narrative cinema has represented the Orient as an "otherized territory," see Ella Shohat, "Gender and Culture of Empire: Toward a Feminist Ethnography of the Cinema," *Quarterly Review of Film and Video* 13.1–3 (1991): 45–84.

29. Jean Cocteau, "Notes on the Ballets," in Alexandre and Cocteau, *Decorative Art of Leon Bakst*, 32.

30. Martin Birnbaum, *Léon Bakst: Catalogue of the First American Exhibition of the Original Work of Léon Bakst* (New York: Berlin Photographic Co., 1913), 11.

31. Pink teas were perfectly color-coordinated social events which were the rage among American women of the privileged class. Diaghilev, quoted in McDonald 145.

32. J. Adams Puffer, *The Boy and His Gang* (Boston: Houghton Mifflin, 1912), 78. In an article published a few months following the release of *The Thief of Bagdad*, Fairbanks claimed his childhood was one of mischievous adventure-seeking that would have landed him "within the clutches of Ben Lindsey's Juvenile Court" except for the fact that "Lindsey hadn't started that court yet." See Charles K. Taylor, "The Most Popular Man in the World," *Outlook* 138 (September 24, 1924): 684.

33. For a survey of views on the relationship between morality, spirituality, and physicality during this era, see Mrozek, *Sport and American Mentality*, especially 189–236. An archetypal "cult of the body" view of Christ as "the highest type of a strong, virile man" is offered by R. Warren Conant, *The Virility of Christ: A New View: A Book for Men* (Chicago: n.p., 1915).

34. Quoted from "Prefatory" of souvenir program issued for March 3, 1924, premiere at the Liberty Theatre. *The Thief of Bagdad* clipping file, Margaret Herrick Library, Academy of Motion Picture Arts and Sciences, hereafter cited as MH-AMPAS.

35. Another costume, depicted in preproduction publicity when the film's working title was *Bagdad* and Fairbanks's costar was going to be Evelyn Brent, is also amazing for its dance inspiration. It can be described only as a lamé mini-apron. It bears passing resemblance to a costume worn by Léonide Massine when he essayed the role of Amoun in *Cléopâtre*. [Photo], "Douglas Fairbanks," by C. W. Warrington [clipping, no publication information given], 38, *The Thief of Bagdad* file, MH-AMPAS.

36. Lynn Garafola, "Vaslav Nijinsky," *Raritan* 8.1 (Summer 1988): 2–3.

37. "A Higher Order of Music for the Movies," clipping [no publication information given], *The Thief of Bagdad* clipping file, MH-AMPAS.

38. Tarkington, quoted in Douglas Fairbanks, "Combining Play with Work," *American Magazine*, July 1917, p. 33. In response to the film, Charles K. Taylor wrote: "Douglas Fairbanks' films are clean in the best sense of the word. . . . From the receding sea of sensuousness and sensuality, of cheapness and vulgarity . . . the work of Douglas Fairbanks rises like a mountain peak at the ocean's brim." Taylor, "Ancient Bagdad and a Joyous Thief," *Outlook* 136.16 (April 16, 1924): 643.

39. Fairbanks's films were assumed to appeal to a broad range of viewers, including, importantly, children. See George Creel, "A 'Close-up' of Douglas Fairbanks," *Everybody's* 35.6 (December 1918): 138; and also Taylor 685.

40. Untitled clipping from *Motion Picture News*, March 5, 1924, p. 1554. *The Thief of Bagdad* file, MH-AMPAS. The financial success of the film is disputed. Implying an access to new research on box-office figures, Richard Koszarksi suggests it made money despite its unusually high production costs (over two million dollars, by some reports). Richard Koszarski, *An Evening's Entertainment: The Age of the Silent Feature Picture, 1915–1928* (New York: Scribner's, 1990), 270, 349.

41. Fairbanks quoted in souvenir program, Liberty Theatre, *The Thief of Bagdad* clipping file, MH-AMPAS.

"A World without Collisions": Ballroom Dance in Athol Fugard's "MASTER HAROLD" . . . and the boys

J. Ellen Gainor

In the spring of 1992, theater critic Malcolm L. Johnson wrote of the "recurring motif of dance in works by modern playwrights."[1] Prompted by the recent success of the Broadway production of Brian Friel's *Dancing at Lughnasa,* Johnson also commented on two other contemporary dramas featuring ballroom dance as a central image, A. R. Gurney's *The Snow Ball* and Athol Fugard's *"MASTER HAROLD" . . . and the boys* (4).[2] Johnson attributes the use of dance in these dramas to the playwrights' desire "to go beyond words into a realm of freedom and beauty and exhilaration," and, particularly in the Fugard piece, for characters to "escape into perfection and equality" (4).

This last observation hints at the political implications of the dance theme Johnson sees in Fugard's 1982 play,[3] set in Port Elizabeth, South Africa, in 1950, shortly after the government began to institute "apartheid as a national policy, and the same year as the enactment of the Group Areas Act."[4] Fugard's dramas have come to be identified with the fight against apartheid, and many critics consider *"MASTER HAROLD"* his best work for its skillful blend of artistry and political impact. In *"MASTER HAROLD,"* Fugard employs ballroom dance as a structuring metaphor to shape his play and to convey his political theme. My goal for this chapter is to unpack his use of that image, exploring not only how it ramifies within its dramatic context, but also how Fugard manipulates ballroom dance, particularly in regard to the racial, class, and gender contexts of the South African milieu.

I see this kind of critical analysis emerging from the still-evolving field of cultural studies. Quoting Robert Scholes, David Bathrick explains of this new discourse, "'textual studies must be pushed beyond the discrete boundaries of the page and the book into institutional practices and social practices.'"[5] As I have argued elsewhere, theater and performance are cultural phenomena ideally suited to this kind of theoretical analysis.[6] If we see theater and dance as social practices engaged with their specific cultural contexts, then to study them as texts, bringing to bear the same considerations other scholars might a written text, is a logical and relevant extension of this methodology. According to Joseph Roach:

> Ideology comprises the categories and judgments that connect utterances and practices to dominant structures and powers. Cultural studies reveal the material specificity of such connections. In the theatre, remote abstractions become physical practices. In the theatre, the media of representation—particularly the body—insist on what the late Raymond Williams . . . called "the material character of the production of a cultural order."[7]

In the case of *"MASTER HAROLD,"* the play demands a cultural analysis precisely because it is so rooted in the larger South African context, and because it incorporates popular culture so insistently in the construction of its larger thematic and political thrust.

A hundred-minute tour de force, *"MASTER HAROLD" . . . and the boys* premiered at the Yale Repertory Theatre in the spring of 1982. Following its highly successful run in New Haven, the play moved to Broadway amid great critical acclaim. The regional theater production featured South African actor Zakes Mokae (a longtime Fugard collaborator), Danny Glover, and Željko Ivanek, who was replaced by Lonny Price on Broadway. The drama, Aristotelian in its single setting and limitation of dramatic time, depicts an afternoon in the lives of Sam (Mokae) and Willie (Glover), two middle-aged employees in the St. George's Park Tea Room, owned by the mother of Master Harold (Ivanek). Hally, as he is known, is a disaffected teenager struggling toward maturity. He is hampered by rigid educational and social systems and by his relations with his parents, a passive mother and a physically handicapped father who is also an alcoholic. Hally's closest friendships are with Sam and Willie, who have worked for his mother for many years. On the rainy afternoon during which the play takes place, Hally arrives at the tearoom after school to discover Sam and Willie practicing for an upcoming ballroom dance competition. The play recounts their history together and builds toward a climactic confrontation between Sam and Hally, brought on by the conflicting emotions Hally feels toward his real father and his surrogate father, Sam. Many critics have commented on the highly personal associations of this moment for Fugard, and how it is constructed dramatically as a turning point for the boy who would later become the playwright himself.[8] In this pivotal scene, Hally repeats one of his father's racist jokes, built on a pun about the "unfairness" of "a nigger's arse" (55). To help Hally see the true ugliness of the remark, Sam literalizes his reaction, showing Hally exactly how black his backside really is. Although Sam thinks this self-exposure has taught the youth something about seemingly innocuous racism, Hally instead spits in his face. Only Sam's maturity, dignity, and sympathy keep him from allowing the moment to escalate to further violence.

Fugard contrasts the hate and degradation in the black characters' domestic and political lives to the beauty of the life they create through dance. During the course of the play, Fugard develops the seemingly marginal detail of the ballroom dance competition into a central dramaturgical device that functions on many levels: as a motivation for dialogue and action; as a plot element central to the depiction of Hally's schooling (and, by extension, the emerging national political climate built around the formal system of apartheid); and most memorably, as a political metaphor—an image of a utopian "'world without collisions'" (47), where struggles between peoples and nations miraculously do not occur.

Fugard shares this idealized vision of dance with other ballroom commentators. Albert Wertheim suggests that Fugard may have derived his metaphor from Victor Silvester, an English authority whose influential writings and recordings helped spread ballroom dance throughout the world. In *Dancing for the Millions,* Silvester remarks that the English style of ballroom "is danced in all competitions. It has won universal popularity. Certain bigwigs of world politics placed an Iron Curtain across Europe—but they could not keep the English style out. It is danced in many lands behind the Iron Curtain" (quoted in Wertheim 148). Even more recently, *Dancing USA,* a journal devoted to the "romance of ballroom dance," featured in 1992 a similar set of observations by former champion Neil Clover:

> The process of re-educating a torn civilization will be a slow one. . . . Building dance floors is expensive, but so is the cost of an F-15 Fighter, and far too often our neighbors are only seen through gun sights. Never once in history has political rationalization ever accomplished what a few soft-spoken ballroom dancers did in recent years—penetrated 40 foreign frontiers with genuine . . . common ground—ballroom dance.[9]

Clearly, for these writers, ballroom dance transcends language and cultural barriers, and its practitioners surmount international differences far more effectively than politicians. These beliefs are shared by Sam in the play, who tries to convey to Hally both the beauty of dance and its importance to the lives of the blacks who come to witness and participate in the competitions: "Without the dream we won't know what we're going for" (46). What lies behind such encomiums, however, is an unstated tribute to Western—and in this case, specifically British—cultural dominance. Every country and people that participate in this artistic communion do so because they have embraced British regulations and aesthetic values for ballroom dance, bowing to a form of cultural imperialism built on an illusion of equality and internationalism. Writing of this imperial phenomenon with regard to printed texts, Homi Bhabha asserts: "The immediate vision of the book figures those ideological correlatives of the Western sign— empiricism, idealism, mimeticism, monoculturalism . . .—that sustain a tradition of English 'national' authority."[10]

Although, as Wertheim has pointed out, a knowledge of the close auto-biographical connection of Fugard to this play is unnecessary to appreciate its theatrical power (141), I would argue that it is germane to a critical exploration of the work. Rob Amato has called *"MASTER HAROLD"* "a portrait of the artist as a young man" and argues that one "cannot perceive its depth of analysis and its humanity" without a cognizance of the biographical connections.[11] Although Hally is a teenager in the play, the climactic events dramatized occurred when the author was ten.[12] The other characters are based on real individuals, Sam Semela and Willie Malopo, who "worked for Fugard's mother in a café she ran in Port Elizabeth" (Gussow 47). Fugard uses the same name of a band in which his father played—the Orchestral Jazzonians—for the black band that is to perform at the upcoming ballroom competition in the drama (Gussow 52), and like the Sam in the play, the original Sam Semela was an accomplished dancer who taught ballroom in New Brighton after he left the Fugards' employ (Gussow 93).

In a December 1982 interview with Mel Gussow for the *New Yorker,* Fugard explained that part of his reason for casting Mokae as Sam was the actor's deep understanding of the play's older South African milieu. Fugard recounted Mokae's memories of men like Semela "whose whole life was ballroom dancing" (90). But, as Gussow points out, Fugard was selective about which personal details he chose to use for the play. One strategic difference between himself and the drama's Hally involves dance. While Hally initially scoffs at the two men's devotion to ballroom, never having tried to dance (Fugard 39), Fugard was the Eastern Province Ballroom Junior Dancing Champion three times, and he uses this same region for the competition event in the play (Gussow 55). Thus Fugard's knowledge of the world of amateur ballroom competitions was central to his composition of *"MASTER HAROLD."* For dramatic purposes, however, he transfers the depiction of that world to Sam alone. Thus we must begin to question Fugard's contextualization of ballroom within the play, rendering it an activity practiced by his black characters, and juxtapose this to the specificity of black and white ballroom culture(s) in South Africa, which the universalizing gestures of Silvester and Clover—and perhaps Fugard—tend to elide.

Although the play never acknowledges this distinction, the world of dance Sam and Willie experience could never be exactly the same as that in which Fugard participated as a youth, for the simple reason that such competitions were segregated. And just as the typography of Fugard's title encapsulates the status of the white and black races in South Africa (see n. 2), so history has treated the phenomenon of black ballroom dancers. While there is comparatively more in-formation available about the history of white ballroom dancers in South Africa, no chronicle exists of black participation in what was, and continues to be, a popular activity.[13] During the period of Fugard's involvement in ballroom competitions, for example, the *South African Dancing Times* featured a lengthy section in each issue on ballroom, and it sponsored competitions. However, the entry forms stipulated that "the Competitions are open to any European, irrespective of Association or School of Dancing, in South Africa."[14] Clearly, these contests were not the place for the Sams and Willies. By removing his own biographical context as a white ballroom dancer from the world of the play, Fugard simultaneously eliminates a node for political critique. We might question why ballroom competition does not function within the play as a synechdoche for apartheid.

David Coplan provides some important background to the development of various music, dance, and theatrical forms among blacks in South Africa in his lively and informative study, *In Township Tonight!*[15] Coplan traces the influence of British dance forms on native South Africans to the early eighteenth century, noting that English contributions to "local performance culture" date to "before their takeover of the Cape in 1806." "English country dances became popular with whites at the Cape as early as the 1730s, and slaves enjoyed performing them at 'Rainbow Balls' modelled on the social occasions of the wealthier masters" (11). Focusing primarily on developments in the twentieth century, Coplan demonstrates how various forces in South Africa—religious, economic, and political—conspired to impress on the native population the value of Western over African culture and to instill a competitive spirit among the blacks through artistic performance. Fugard's play reflects these phenomena both in Sam and Willie's devotion to ballroom and in Hally's attitude toward their embracing a British, rather than native, art form. Coplan notes that during the 1920s, ballroom dance emerged as the most popular form of working-class and middle-class entertainment and also became "an important arena for social competition":

> The leading ballroom dancers were Africans in domestic and restaurant service.... A knowledge of Western culture was of great value in domestic service, and many became highly self-educated. . . . Their interest in ballroom dancing was part of a struggle for status through the competitive display of symbols of Westernisation, such as dress, social comportment and cultural skills such as dancing. (129)

Coplan also details the ongoing cultural dominance of whites within this arena, as the competition "judges were almost always white and demonstrations by professional white dancers often began the programme" (129).

Over the next few decades, black ballroom dance championships became institutionalized, often sponsored by social clubs at least in part under white control. Although competitions within the clubs had broadened to include performances based on both African and Western art forms, by the late 1940s working-class Africans began to see these events differently. Quoting new, oppositional voices, Coplan describes the shifting perception of the competitions and demonstrations now as "affair[s] for the 'whites' good boys,' a place where 'the whites tell us how to perform our music.'" He observes, "Certainly, raising 'the standard of performance' meant encouraging conformity to European criteria, not only in ballroom but even in traditional African dancing" (169).

None of these racial and societal tensions emerges explicitly in *"MASTER HAROLD."* For Sam and Willie the ballroom championships only hold the promise of participation in an idealized realm of beauty and harmony; we hear nothing of their value as economic status enhancers nor of the pressures of cultural domination, despite the characters' correspondence with the historical, professional profile Coplan establishes. Perhaps even more interesting is the unproblematized participation of the characters in a state-sponsored competitive structure that not only separates South Africans racially, but is divisive within the communities themselves.

Rather, Fugard uses the opening scene in the play primarily to establish the personal relationship between Sam and Willie. Sam quickly emerges as the dominant character, whom Willie respects for his superior knowledge in many arenas, including ballroom dance and relations with women. Willie asks for advice on his quickstep, which he is practicing with some difficulty. Here, and throughout the play, Fugard's own knowledge of ballroom guides his creation of dialogue and action for these two characters. Through descriptions of the standard dances: waltz, slow fox-trot, and quickstep (he leaves out tango and the Viennese waltz), as well as through the physical depictions of Sam's and Willie's practice with imaginary partners—visually humorous, and technically accurate—Fugard generates a detailed and realistic sense of the characters' involvement with their art (4–7).[16] Sam's admonitions to Willie include the need to relax his shoulders, stand straight, avoid the appearance of stiffness, glide through the steps to make them smooth, and give the appearance of enjoyment (4–5).

Fugard also immediately begins to use this ballroom practice as the foundation for his thematic concerns, particularly the opposition between real-world conflict and the utopian harmony that ballroom is to represent. In its most simplified form, the metaphor connects the rigor of ballroom practice and the necessity of mastering technique for ballroom competition with the patience necessary for an eventual triumph in the arena of global unity. He introduces this concept first in terms of personal relationships. When Willie complains because his partner does not come to rehearse, Sam suggests that the explanation lies in Willie's brutality: "Beating her up every time she makes a mistake in the waltz? (*Shaking his head*) No, Willie! That takes the pleasure out of ballroom dancing" (7). Albert Wertheim parallels the problems of female dance partners to the "white treatment of non-whites" (149), but his equation of racial and gender oppression is theoretically problematic—many critics in the fields of both gender and race studies oppose the paralleling of these forms of oppression, stressing the importance of their distinctions rather than their similarities—despite Fugard's own more explicit connection of the two in such other works as *Boesman and Lena*. As Homi Bhabha asserts,

> the construction of the colonial subject in discourse, and the exercise of colonial power through discourse demands an articulation of forms of difference—racial and sexual. Such an articulation becomes crucial if it is held that the body is always simultaneously inscribed in both the economy of pleasure and desire and the economy of discourse, domination, and power.[17]

By contrast, Fugard here seems to be setting up interpersonal relations as a microcosm of the kind of world tensions he sees as pandemic, specifically not using ballroom as the explicit means of conveying opposition to the current political regime based on racial oppression.

Perhaps the most profound irony that begins to emerge with the deconstruction of the images of ballroom practice and competition resides in Fugard's avoidance of ballroom as itself a metaphor for repression and control. Given ballroom's detailed codes for technique and choreography that cannot be transgressed without severe penalty in competition, Fugard might have constructed this entire image as oppressive rather than liberating. The dancer might then emerge as a puppet of the state, and the black dancer in particular as part of a hierarchy of domination, controlled by imperially determined codes dictating subservience to state order refracted through black dance culture.

Fugard presents a different slant on the specific issue of race, however. Sam explains that ballroom must not look as difficult as it is:

> Sam: . . . The secret is to make it look easy. Ballroom must look happy, Willie, not like hard work. It must . . . Ja! . . . it must look like romance. . . . A handsome man in tails, and in his arms, smiling at him, a beautiful lady in evening dress!
> Willie: Fred Astaire, Ginger Rogers.
> Sam: You got it. (5)

As David Coplan explains, "the rapid development of the recording and cinema industries during the 1920s and 1930s brought American performance culture to many countries, including South Africa" (120). Coplan details the influence of American popular culture on the development of native dance and music in particular,[18] and thus it is not surprising that such filmic icons of romantic ballroom dance as Astaire and Rogers serve as models for emulation. What is potentially disturbing for contemporary audiences, of course, is the realization of what that idolatry signifies: the desire to emulate two white American performers through an imperially introduced art form built on the pretense of romance and, even more importantly, on images of race and class privilege these characters can never attain under apartheid. This scene perfectly exemplifies the colonial phenomenon Bhabha, invoking Frantz Fanon, has described as "camouflage, mimicry, black skin/white masks" ("Signs" 181).

Willie has had to rent the costumes for the competition for himself and his partner: two pairs of shoes, tuxedo, and gown, probably at considerable cost, given his inability even to afford both a jukebox song to practice by and bus fare home (Fugard 6). Audiences must wonder, even within the somewhat nostalgic environment invoked by the portrayal of the playwright's youth, how Fugard wanted them to understand this dance world. Are they to perceive it as a notable emblem of the inequalities rampant in South Africa—an exemplar of Western cultural domination? If so, Fugard gives no textual indication of this irony. This omission is particularly telling given his development of the other main metaphor in the play, the kite episode, which is also part of the shared experience of Sam and Hally. As a younger boy, Hally once had to ask Sam to help him carry his drunken father home from a bar. In order to alleviate the boy's sense of shame and failure, Sam built him a kite, which he helped the boy fly, despite Hally's conviction that it, too, would fail him. The twist in the story, related late in the play, is that Sam could not stay to share Hally's pleasure, since he had to leave the boy resting on a "whites only" bench in the park. The surrogate father is forbidden from fully developing a relation with the boy, solely because of race. Fugard drives home his theme clearly here, whereas the ballroom image is left unexamined, even though it holds possibly greater potential for political impact with regard to race and class. This failure to explore a powerful image fully exemplifies a dramaturgical problem in Fugard's work which Dennis Walder has identified: "It is his greatest strength as a dramatist to move us deeply by his account of the South African experience; it is his greatest weakness that he is unable to analyse that experience, or be clear about its social and historical implications" (120–121).

Fugard seems to have a different goal for his ballroom theme, which emerges in connection with our exposure to Hally's education in the rigid public school system. Throughout the play, Hally and Sam's education of each other is contrasted to the official education Hally is receiving. While the school system seems to rely on violence to instill its lessons—Hally describes receiving six strokes to his backside as a punishment (14)—Sam sees brutality as antithetical to learning, exemplified by his chastising Willie for his striking his dance partner when she made a mistake (7). Here again, Fugard chooses a universalizing trajectory for the extrapolation from ballroom instruction, rather than one which would specifically correlate dance pedagogy with state oppression.

During the afternoon in the tearoom, Hally shares anecdotes about his teachers with Sam and Willie, and tries to complete an assignment, a five-hundred-word essay "describing an annual event of cultural or historical significance" (35). Hally explains to Sam, "You know what he wants, don't you? One of their useless old ceremonies. The commemoration of the landing of the 1820 Settlers, or if it's going to be culture, Carols by Candlelight every Christmas" (35). Clearly, such exercises are designed to foster the internalization of specific types of national myths and to promote attitudes in keeping with the political goals of the minority government. However, after seeing Sam and Willie rehearse, hearing them talk about their dancing, and determining that ballroom could safely be categorized as "high" culture (he has earlier remarked, "There's a limit, Sam. Don't confuse art and entertainment" [40]), it occurs to Hally that he might write about the upcoming competition.

Fugard interjects one possible note of political critique here, through Hally's description of his teacher's probable response to his subject:

> Old Doc Bromely—he's my English teacher—is going to argue with me, of course. He doesn't like natives. But I'll point out to him that in strict anthropological terms the culture of a primitive black society includes its dancing and singing. To put my thesis in a nutshell: The war-dance has been replaced by the waltz. But it still amounts to the same thing: the release of primitive emotions through movement. (43)

Although we see Hally waver throughout the play between the racist view of blacks represented by his teachers and father, and a more egalitarian humanist position depicted through the genuine friendship he shares with Sam and Willie, it may be that the attitude he plans to present in the essay he describes is calculated. While his view appears to be in keeping with the intellectual pretentiousness he has been displaying all afternoon with regard to his education, it may instead be a pose taken to mollify his teacher, whose own prejudices would render him skeptical about the suitability of the topic. The authorial position Hally proposes, blatantly insulting to Sam and Willie, seems to recapitulate the outdated tenets of an imperialist cultural anthropology that theorized its own culture as the ideal toward which more "primitive" cultures were evolving. As Bhabha explains:

> It is crucial to remember that the colonial construction of the cultural (the site of the civilizing mission) through the process of disavowal is authoritative to the extent to which it is structured around the ambivalence of splitting, denial, repetition—strategies of defence that mobilize culture as an open-textured, warlike strategy whose aim "is rather a continued agony than a total disappearance of the pre-existing culture." ("Signs" 175)

Edward Said has observed the repetition of similar tropes within much imperialist discourse: "What are striking in these discourses are the rhetorical figures one keeps encountering . . . the notions about bringing civilization to primitive or barbaric peoples."[19] This notable moment in the drama certainly leaves room for the audience to question the views expressed by Hally. The dialogue simply moves forward, however, with Sam and Willie enthusiastically launching into a narration of the excitement and beauty of the competitive dancing.

Here again, Fugard's knowledge of competitions helps him provide realistic details, such as the number of finalist couples (six), the atmosphere at the event, and the manner of judging (43–46). However, in order to develop ballroom into his main political metaphor, he fudges the realities of competition a bit. Hally asks if the dancers are ever penalized for errors: "Say you stumble or bump into somebody . . . do they take off any points?" (45). While the question is reasonable—and in fact collisions do occur, particularly in the quickstep—Sam laughs at the idea, denying its possibility to foster the utopian vision of the competition as idealized world image:

> There's no collisions out there, Hally. Nobody trips or stumbles or bumps into anybody else. That's what that moment is all about. To be one of those finalists on that dance floor is like . . . like being in a dream about a world in which accidents don't happen. . . . And it's beautiful because that is what we want life to be like. But instead, like you said, Hally, we're bumping into each other all the time. Look at the three of us this afternoon. . . . None of us knows the steps and there's no music playing. And it doesn't stop with us. The whole world is doing it all the time. Open a newspaper and what do you read? America has bumped into Russia, England is bumping into India, rich man bumps into poor man. Those are big collisions, Hally. . . . People get hurt in all that bumping, and we're sick and tired of it now. It's been going on for too long. Are we never going to get it right? . . . Learn to dance life like champions instead of always being just a bunch of beginners at it? (45–46)

Malcolm Johnson reads this passage as "a metaphor for an ordered, civilized, non-apartheid world," and Sam and Willie's dancing as "a declaration of personal freedom" (4). It is interesting that, despite the absence of any reference to race or to his native country in Sam's speech, a critic would imbue the dialogue and action with political connotations specific to Fugard's homeland. Hally interprets Sam's vision geopolitically, at first thinking the subtitle of his essay should be "Global Politics on the Dance Floor," but then deciding on the more general "Ballroom Dancing as a Political Vision" (47). This scene exemplifies how Fugard's drama can work on both a specific level integral to his South African context and a universalized, human level available to all audiences. He clearly is leaving the interpretation of this section open to both possibilities, although the more certain option is the general, in which his own country's politics may be implied as sharing elements with the examples he does specify, replete with their imperial and class connotations.

Critics have wondered whether it is this scene, the final scene, or qualities of the play overall which led to its initial banning by the government in South Africa. In the play's closing moments, after Hally projects his anger at his father —a crippled man who epitomizes the reality of a world that cannot dance[20]— onto Sam through the racial insult, leaving the potential for the continuation of their friendship ambiguous, Sam and Willie remain alone onstage, struggling to regain their equanimity. Willie suggests they practice dancing together: a slow fox-trot which, as the predecessor to the quickstep in ballroom pedagogy, symbolizes their determination to regroup and get the "steps" right for the future (Wertheim 155).[21] Trying to encourage Sam, Willie invokes his friend's vision: "How did you say it, Boet Sam? Let's dream. . . . You lead. I follow" (60). Giving in to impulse, Willie declares, "To hell with it! I walk home" and deposits

FIG. 17. Willie (Danny Glover) and Sam (Zakes Mokae) practice ballroom dancing in the final scene of the play. Photo courtesy of Gerry Goodstein and the Yale Repertory Theatre, by permission of the photographer.

his only coin in the jukebox to play Sarah Vaughan (60). As the curtain closes, the two men dance together, creating an image of their bond and the beauty of ballroom, finally depicted through a real partnership.[22]

On December 5, 1982, the *New York Times* reported that Fugard's play had been banned by the Directorate of Publications in Johannesburg, and the following week provided more details, to the effect that the work had been found to be "'indecent, obscene, immoral and offensive to public morals.'"[23] Rob Amato proposed one explanation for the censorship, which had been temporarily lifted on December 9: "The play is banned as an 'undesirable' publication. The censors state that this is because it contains obscene language and not because of its political content. . . . Those who agree . . . to read for the censors use obscenity of language as cover for their act of suppression, which is of course intensely political" (198–199).[24] Another possibility resides in the final action of the play, Sam and Willie's dance, which could be read as a symbol of racial bonding and a call to unite for blacks' political goals, acts clearly antithetical to the interests of the government's white-minority rulers.[25] It is particularly significant that this moment is essentially unscripted, that its power resides exclusively in performance, where the black actors/dancers demonstrate the efficacy of motion coordinated in space and time. There is no other human activity that conveys this union so clearly as ballroom: the effect is only possible when two partners work together, their movement perfectly synchronized, to create the visual image of fusion. Dennis Walder believes "Fugard's work also contains a potential for subversion, a potential which . . . is the hallmark of great art" (10). This final silhouette may carry with it the suggestion of colonial mimicry—of resistance—through the jarringly antiromantic semiotics of Sam and Willie's positionality with regard to race, class (using costuming as marker), and gender.

Yet as Amato reports, there is also criticism of Fugard in South Africa for not sufficiently and directly attacking the apartheid system:

> He cannot actually transcend his class position as a white South African artist paid by local and overseas liberal theatres and their audiences. He cannot understand the true nature of the experience, or the struggle, of the majority in South Africa and has, in his plays of sole authorship, presented black characters as capable only of stoical perseverance. (203)

This comment certainly resonates with the final image of Sam and Willie. Fugard leaves their vision of "'a world without collisions'" bathed in the "soft, romantic colors" (60) of the jukebox glow, diffusing the power and horror of the moment when Sam shows Hally the blackness of his bare skin and Hally spits in his face. Sam and Willie have not realized the full political implications of the dance they love, beautiful but charged with repression. The dream they dance can never fulfill their ideal until it becomes truly their own.

NOTES

I am grateful to David Faulkner for his editorial assistance with this essay. This piece is dedicated to the memory of the late Neil Clover.

1. Malcolm L. Johnson, "Dance," *Hartford Courant,* May 24, 1992, p. G1. I am grateful to Robert Wildman, former press director at the Yale Repertory Theatre, for bringing this essay to my attention.

2. For the world premiere of this play at the Yale Repertory Theatre in 1982, Fugard was extremely concerned about the typography of the title of this work. The use of capitals and quotation marks for *"MASTER HAROLD,"* and the ellipses and use of lowercase for *. . . and the boys* all serve to highlight with irony

the atmosphere of apartheid in the play, which gives apparent societal dominance to a youth while relegating grown men to lesser status, virtual afterthoughts. As press director for this production, I learned the significance of the title as well as its importance to the playwright, who also directed the premiere. Although many critics use conventional typography to refer to the play, I follow Fugard's wishes in this chapter.

3. Athol Fugard, *"MASTER HAROLD"* . . . *and the boys* (New York: Penguin, 1982), 3–4.

4. Albert Wertheim, "Ballroom Dancing, Kites and Politics: Athol Fugard's *Master Harold and the Boys*," *South Pacific Association Newsletter* 30 (April 1990): 146. The Group Areas Act forced blacks to live in segregated communities, often at great distances from the whites' homes and businesses where they worked.

5. David Bathrick, "Cultural Studies," in *Introduction to Scholarship in Modern Languages and Literatures*, ed. Joseph Gibaldi (New York: MLA, 1992), 322.

6. J. Ellen Gainor, "Playing Politics: The Provincetown Players and Greenwich Village Bohemia," American Society for Theatre Research meeting, Seattle, November 1991.

7. Joseph R. Roach, "Theatre History and the Ideology of the Aesthetic," *Theatre Journal* 41.2 (May 1989): 157.

8. See, for example, Dennis Walder, *Athol Fugard* (London: Macmillan, 1984), 10.

9. Neil Clover, "The Importance of Ballroom Dance," *Dancing USA* 10.1 (January/February 1992): 19.

10. Homi K. Bhabha, "Signs Taken for Wonders: Questions of Ambivalence and Authority under a Tree outside Delhi, May 1817," in *"Race," Writing, and Difference*, ed. Henry Louis Gates, Jr. (Chicago: University of Chicago Press, 1986), 166.

11. Rob Amato, "Fugard's Confessional Analysis: *'MASTER HAROLD'* . . . *and the boys*," in *Momentum: On Recent South African Writing*, ed. M. J. Daymond, J. V. Jacobs, and Margaret Lenta (Pietermaritzburg, South Africa: University of Natal Press, 1984), 200.

12. Mel Gussow, "Profiles: Witness," *New Yorker*, December 20, 1982, p. 47.

13. I am grateful to Peter Larlham, Temple Hauptfleisch, and David Coplan for consulting with me on this topic. While each of these scholars acknowledged the need for documentation of the history of black ballroom dance, they also confirmed my sense of the nonexistence of this work to date. David Coplan provided a starting point for future scholarship in this area, citing such African newspapers as *Bantu World* and *Umteteli Wa Bantu* and *Drum* magazine, as primary sources. However, a knowledge of both the Xhosa and Zulu languages would be necessary for an in-depth investigation of the field.

14. *South African Dancing Times* 11.7 (January 1947): 22.

15. David Coplan, *In Township Tonight! South Africa's Black City Music and Theatre* (London: Longman, 1985).

16. The technique of the men's practicing with imaginary partners is particularly effective, for at the same time that it is accurate—dancers learn their parts separately and then coordinate them with their partners—it is dramaturgically effective, given the absence of other characters, as well as entertaining for the audience, who are to be mildly amused by Willie and impressed with Sam.

17. Homi K. Bhabha, "The Other Question: Difference, Discrimination and the Discourse of Colonialism," in *Literature, Politics and Theory: Papers from the Essex Conference, 1976–84*, ed. Francis Barker et al. (London: Methuen, 1986), 150.

18. See, for example, Coplan's description of jive dancing (152–153).

19. Edward Said, *Culture and Imperialism* (New York: Knopf, 1993), xi.

20. Sheila Roberts, "'No Lessons Learnt': Reading the Texts of Fugard's *A Lesson from Aloes* and *Master Harold . . . and the Boys*," *English in Africa* 9.2 (October 1982): 31.

21. In current ballroom instruction, this progression from fox-trot to quickstep is not always practiced. In fact, quickstep is sometimes taught early in ballroom training.

22. While for American and perhaps other audiences, this moment might suggest a homoerotic subtext, within the South African context this would not be the case, as male-male physical contact does not carry this connotation. I am grateful to Peter Larlham for pointing out this cross-cultural issue.

23. "South Africa Bans Script of a Broadway Play," *New York Times,* December 5, 1982, p. 8:1. "South Africa Temporarily Lifts Ban on 'Master Harold' Play," *New York Times,* December 10, 1982, p. 14:1.

24. Amato further explains that the censors were apparently initially unaware of the fact that they were banning a Fugard work, a detail he finds remarkable, given the publicity the world premiere of the play in the United States had received in the South African press.

25. I am grateful to Michael Cadden for this reading.

DANCE IN THEORIES OF WRITING

Choreographies

JACQUES DERRIDA
and CHRISTIE V. McDONALD

McDonald: Emma Goldman, a maverick feminist from the late nineteenth century, once said of the feminist movement: "If I can't dance I don't want to be part of your revolution." Jacques Derrida, you have written about the question of woman and what it is that constitutes 'the feminine.' In *Spurs/Eperons*, a text devoted to Nietzsche, style and woman, you wrote that "that which will not be pinned down by truth [truth?] is, in truth, *feminine*." And you warned that such a proposition "should not . . . be hastily mistaken for a woman's femininity, for female sexuality, or for any other of those essentializing fetishes which might still tantalize the dogmatic philosopher, the impotent artist or the inexperienced seducer who has not yet escaped his foolish hopes of capture."[1]

What seems to be at play as you take up Heidegger's reading of Nietzsche is whether or not sexual difference is a "regional question in a larger order which would subordinate it first to the domain of general ontology, subsequently to that of a fundamental ontology and finally to the question of the truth [whose?] of being itself." You thereby question the status of the argument and at the same time the question itself. In this instance, if the question of sexual difference is not a regional one (in the sense of subsidiary), if indeed "it may no longer even be a question," as you suggest, how would you describe 'woman's place'?

Derrida: Will I be able to write improvising my responses as I go along? It would be more worthwhile, wouldn't it? Too premeditated an interview would be without interest here. I do not see the particular finality of such an endeavor, its proper end. It would be interminable, or, rather, with respect to these questions— which are much too difficult—I would never have even dared to begin. There are other texts, other occasions for such very calculated premeditation. Let us play surprise. It will be our tribute to the dance [in French the word dance, *la danse*, is a feminine noun requiring the use of a feminine pronoun, *elle*]: it should happen only once, neither grow heavy nor ever plunge too deep; above all, it should not lag or trail behind its time. We will therefore not leave time to come back to what is behind us, nor to look attentively. We will only take a glimpse. [In French, to take a glimpse is to look into the spaces between things, *entrevoir,* that is, inter-view.]

It was a good idea to begin with a quotation, one by a feminist from the end of the nineteenth century maverick enough to ask of the feminist movement its questions and conditions. Already, already a sign of life, a sign of the dance.

One can question the repetition. Was the matrix of what was to be the future of feminism already there at the end of the last century? You smile, no doubt, as I do, at the mention of this word. [The word matrix in English, like *matrice* in French, comes from the Latin *matrix* meaning womb. In both languages it has taken on, among others, the following two meanings: (1) a situation or surrounding substance within which something originates, develops, or is contained; (2) in printing, a metal plate used for casting typefaces.] Let us make use of this figure from anatomy or printing a bit longer to ask whether a program, or locus of begetting, was not already in place in the nineteenth century for all those configurations to which the feminist struggle of the second half of the twentieth century was to commit itself and then to develop. I refer here to their being in place at all levels—those of sociopolitical demands, alliances with other forces, the alternatives of compromise or various political radicalisms, the strategies of discourses, various forms of writing, theory or literature, and so forth. One is often tempted to think of this program—and to arrive by way of conclusion at the stasis of a simple combinatory scheme—in terms of all that is interminable and exhausting in it. Yes, it is exhausting (because it always draws on the same fund of possibilities) and tedious because of the ensuing repetition.

This is only one of the paradoxes. The development of the present struggle (or struggles) is extraordinary not only in its quantitative extension within Europe—because of its progress and the masses that have been slowly aroused—but also, and this is a much more important phenomenon I believe, outside of Europe. And such progress brings with it new types of historical research, other forms of reading, the discovery of new bodies of material that have gone unrecognized or misunderstood up until now; that is to say, they have been excessively [*violemment*] concealed or marginalized. The history of different "feminisms" has often been, of course, a past "passed-over-in-silence." Now here is the paradox: having made possible the reawakening of this silent past, having reappropriated a history previously stifled, feminist movements will perhaps have to renounce an all too easy kind of progressivism in the evaluation of this history. Such progressivism is often taken as their axiomatic base: the inevitable or rather essential presupposition (*dans les luttes,* as we say in French) of what one might call the ideological consensus of feminists, perhaps also their "dogmatics" or what your "maverick feminist" suspects to be their sluggishness. It is the image of a continuously accelerated "liberation" at once punctuated by determinable stages and commanded by an ultimately thinkable *telos,* a truth of sexual difference and femininity, etc. And if there is no doubt that this theater, upon which the progress of feminist struggles is staged, exists, it is a relatively short and very recent sequence within "extreme-Western" history. Certainly, it is not timely politically, nor in any case is it possible, to neglect or renounce such a view of "liberation." However, to credit this representation of progress and entrust everything to it would be to surrender to a sinister mystification: everything would collapse, flow, founder in this same homogenized, sterilized river of the history of mankind [man's kind in the locution *l'histoire des hommes*]. This history carries along with it the age-old dream of reappropriation, "liberation," autonomy, mastery, in short the *cortège* of metaphysics and the *tekhnè.* The indications of this repetition are more and more numerous. The specular reversal of masculine "subjectivity," even in its most self-critical form—that is, where it is nervously jealous both of itself and of its "proper" objects—probably represents only one necessary phase. Yet it still belongs to the same program, a program whose exhaustion we were just talking about. It is true that this is valid for the whole of our culture, our scholastics, and the trouble may be found everywhere that this program is in command, or almost everywhere.

I have not begun as yet to answer your question, but, if you will forgive me, I am going to try to approach it slowly. It was necessary to recall the fact that this "silent past" (as that which was passed-over-in-silence) could still reserve some surprises, like the dance of your "maverick feminist."

McDonald: Yes, and in that respect, recognition of the paradox suggests that while nineteenth-century and late twentieth-century feminism do resemble each other, it is less because of their historical matrix than because of those characteristics which define them. True, the program was in place.[2] The resurgence in the United States during the 1960s of anarchistlike attitudes, particularly within the feminist movement, attests to that. But Goldman was not before or behind the times. An admirer of Nietzsche as "rebel and innovator," she proclaimed that "revolution is but thought carried into action." She was an activist unable to support those forms of organized feminism which focused on merely contesting the institutionalizing of inequalities for women. Her stance was more radical— one that called for the restructuring of society as a whole. If she refused the vote, for example, it was because she deemed that behind standard forms of political action there lay coercion. As an anarchist-feminist she had no truck with statism.

Derrida: Perhaps woman does not have a history, not so much because of any notion of the "Eternal Feminine" but because all alone she can resist and step back from a certain history (precisely in order to dance) in which revolution, or at least the "concept" of revolution, is generally inscribed. That history is one of continuous progress, despite the revolutionary break—oriented in the case of the women's movement toward the reappropriation of woman's own essence, her own specific difference, oriented in short toward a notion of woman's "truth." Your "maverick feminist" showed herself ready to break with the most authorized, the most dogmatic form of consensus, one that claims (and this is the most serious aspect of it) to speak out in the name of revolution and history. Perhaps she was thinking of a completely other history: a history of paradoxical laws and nondialectical discontinuities, a history of absolutely heterogeneous pockets, irreducible particularities, of unheard of and incalculable sexual differences; a history of women who have—centuries ago—"gone farther" by stepping back with their lone dance, or who are today inventing sexual idioms at a distance from the main forum of feminist activity with a kind of reserve that does not necessarily prevent them from subscribing to the movement and even, occasionally, from becoming a militant for it.

But I am speculating. It would be better to come back to your question. Having passed through several detours or stages you wonder how I would describe what is called "woman's place"; the expression recalls, if I am not mistaken, "in the home" or "in the kitchen." Frankly, I do not know. I believe that I would not describe that place. In fact, I would be wary of such a description. Do you not fear that having once become committed to the path of this topography, we would inevitably find ourselves back "at home" or "in the kitchen"? Or under house arrest, *assignation à résidence* as they say in French penitentiary language, which would amount to the same thing? Why must there be a place for woman? And why only one, a single, completely essential place?

This is a question that you could translate ironically by saying that in my view there is no one place for woman. That was indeed clearly set forth during the 1974 Cerisy Colloquium devoted to Nietzsche in the lecture to which you referred entitled *Spurs/Eperons*. It is without a doubt risky to say that there is no place for woman, but this idea is not antifeminist, far from it; true, it is not feminist either. But it appears to me to be faithful in its way both to a certain assertion of women and to what is most affirmative and "dancing," as the maverick feminist says, in the displacement of women. Can one not say, in Nietzsche's language, that there is a "reactive" feminism, and that a certain historical necessity often puts this form of feminism in power in today's organized struggles? It is this kind of "reactive" feminism that Nietzsche mocks, and not woman or women. Perhaps one should not so much combat it head on—other interests would be at stake in such a move—as prevent its occupying the entire terrain. And why for that matter should one rush into answering a *topological* question (what is *the* place of *woman* [quelle est *la* place de *la* femme])? Or an *economical* question (because it all comes back to *l'oikos* as home, *maison, chez-soi* [at home in this sense also means in French within the self], the law of the proper place, etc. in the preoccupation with a woman's place)? Why should a new "idea" of woman or a new step taken by her necessarily be subjected to the urgency of this topo-economical concern (essential, it is true, and ineradicably philosophical)? This step only constitutes a step on the condition that it challenge a certain idea of the *locus* [*lieu*] and the place [*place*] (the entire history of the West and of its metaphysics) and that it dance otherwise. This is very rare, if it is not impossible, and presents itself only in the form of the most unforeseeable and most innocent of chances. The most innocent of dances would thwart the *assignation à résidence,* escape those residences under surveillance; the dance changes place and above all changes *places.* In its wake they can no longer be recognized. The joyous disturbance of certain women's movements, and of some women in particular, has actually brought with it the chance for a certain risky turbulence in the assigning of places within our small European space. (I am not speaking of a more ample upheaval en route to worldwide application.) Is one then going to start all over again making maps, topographics, etc.? distributing sexual identity cards?

The most serious part of the difficulty is the necessity to bring the dance and its tempo into tune with the "revolution." The lack of place for [*l'atopie*] or the madness of the dance—this bit of luck can also compromise the political chances of feminism and serve as an alibi for deserting organized, patient, laborious "feminist" struggles when brought into contact with all the forms of resistance that a dance movement cannot dispel, even though the dance is not synonymous with either powerlessness or fragility. I will not insist on this point, but you can surely see the kind of impossible and necessary compromise I am alluding to: an incessant, daily negotiation—individual or not—sometimes microscopic, sometime punctuated by a pokerlike gamble; always deprived of insurance, whether it be in private life or within institutions. Each man and each woman must commit his or her own singularity, the untranslatable factor of his or her life and death.

Nietzsche makes a scene before women, feminists in particular—a spectacle which is overdetermined, divided, apparently contradictory. This is just what has interested me; this scene has interested me because of all the paradigms that it exhibits and multiplies, and insofar as it often struggles, sometimes dances, always takes chances in a historical space whose essential traits, those of the matrix, have perhaps not changed since then in Europe (I mean specifically in Europe, and that perhaps makes all the difference although we cannot separate worldwide feminism from a certain fundamental Europeanization of world culture; this is an enormous problem that I must leave aside here). In *Spurs/Eperons* I have tried to formalize the movements and typical moments of the scene that Nietzsche creates throughout a very broad and diverse body of texts. I have done this up to a certain limit, one that I also indicate, where the decision to formalize fails for reasons that are absolutely structural. Since these typical features are and must be unstable, sometimes contradictory, and finally "undecidable," any break in the movement of the reading would settle in a countermeaning, in *the meaning* which becomes countermeaning. This countermeaning can be more or less naive or complacent. One could cite countless examples of it. In the most perfunctory of cases, the simplification reverts to the isolation of Nietzsche's violently anti-feminist statements (directed first against reactive, specular feminism as a figure both of the dogmatic philosopher and a certain relationship of man to truth), pulling them out (and possibly attributing them to me, though that is of little importance) of the movement and system that I try to reconstitute. Some have reacted at times even more perfunctorily, unable to see beyond the end of phallic forms projecting into the text; beginning with style, the spur or the umbrella, they take no account of what I have said about the difference between style and writing or the bisexual complication of those and other forms. Generally speaking, this cannot be considered reading, and I will go so far as to say that it is *to not read* the syntax and punctuation of a given sentence when one arrests the text in a certain position, thus settling on a thesis, meaning or truth. This mistake of hermeneutics, this mistaking of hermeneutics—it is this that the final message [*envoi*] of "I forgot my umbrella" should challenge. But let us leave that. The truth value (that is, Woman as the major allegory of truth in Western discourse) and its correlative, Femininity (the essence or truth of Woman), are there to assuage such hermeneutic anxiety. These are the places one should acknowledge, at least, that is, if one is interested in doing so; they are the foundations or anchorings of Western rationality (of what I have called "phallogocentrism" [as the complicity of Western metaphysics with a notion of male firstness]). Such recognition should not make of either the truth value or femininity an object of knowledge (at stake are the norms of knowledge and knowledge as norm); still less should it make of them a place to inhabit, a home. It should rather permit the invention of an other inscription, one very old and very new, a displacement of bodies and places that is quite different.

You recalled the expression "essentializing fetishes" (truth, femininity, the essentiality of woman or feminine sexuality as fetishes). It is difficult to improvise briefly here. But I point out that one can avoid a trap by being precise about the concept of fetishism and the context to which one refers, even if only to displace it. (On this point, I take the liberty of alluding to the discussions of fetishism and feminine sexuality in *Spurs, Glas* or *La carte postale,* specifically in *Le facteur de la vérité.*) Another trap is more political and can only be avoided by taking account of the *real* conditions in which women's struggles develop on all fronts (economic, ideological, political). These conditions often require the preservation (within longer or shorter phases) of metaphysical presuppositions that one must (and knows already that one must) question in a later phase—or an other place—because they belong to the dominant system that one is deconstructing on a *practical level.* This multiplicity of places, moments, forms, and forces does not always mean giving way either to empiricism or to contradiction. How can one breathe without such punctuation and without the multiplicities of rhythm and steps? How can one dance, your "maverick feminist" might say?

McDonald: This raises an important question that should not be overlooked, although we haven't the space to develop it to any extent here: the complicated relationship of a practical politics to the kinds of analysis that we have been considering (specifically the "deconstructive" analysis implicit in your discussion). That this relationship cannot simply be translated into an opposition between the empirical and the nonempirical has been touched on in an entirely different context.³ Just how one is to deal with the interrelationship of these forces and necessities in the context of feminine struggles should be more fully explored on some other occasion. But let's go on to Heidegger's ontology.

Derrida: To answer your question about Heidegger, and without being able to review here the itinerary of a reading in *Spurs/Eperons* clearly divided into two moments, I must limit myself to a piece of information, or rather to an open question. The question proceeds, so to speak, from the end; it proceeds from the point where the thought of the gift [*le don*]⁴ and that of "propriation" disturbs without simply reversing the order of ontology, the authority of the question "what is it," the subordination of regional ontologies to one fundamental ontology. I am moving much too rapidly, but how can I do otherwise here? From this point, which is not a point, one wonders whether this extremely difficult, perhaps impossible idea of the gift can still maintain an essential relationship to sexual difference. One wonders whether sexual difference, femininity, for example— however irreducible it may be—does not remain derived from and subordinated to either the question of destination or the thought of the gift (I say "thought" because one cannot say philosophy, theory, logic, structure, scene, or anything else; when one can no longer use any word of this sort, when one can say almost nothing else, one says "thought," but one could show that this too is excessive). I do not know. Must one think "difference" "before" sexual difference or taking off "from" it? Has this question, if not a meaning (we are at the origin of meaning here, and the origin cannot "have meaning") at least something of a chance of opening up anything at all, however im-pertinent it may appear?

QUESTION II

McDonald: You put into question the characteristic form of women's protest, namely, the subordination of woman to man. I attempt here to describe the direction of your argument, as I understand it, and then comment on it.

The new sense of writing (*écriture*) with which one associates the term deconstruction has emerged from the close readings that you have given to texts as divergent as those of Plato, Rousseau, Mallarmé and others. It is one in which traditional binary pairing (as in the opposition of spirit to matter or man to woman) no longer functions by the privilege given to the first term over the second. In a series of interviews published under the title *Positions* in 1972, you spoke of a two-phase program (phase being understood as a structural rather than a chronological term) necessary for the act of deconstruction.

In the first phase a reversal was to take place in which the opposed terms would be inverted. Thus woman, as a previously subordinate term, might become the dominant one in relation to man. Yet because such a scheme of reversal could only repeat the traditional scheme (in which the hierarchy of duality is always reconstituted), it alone could not effect any significant change. Change would only occur through the 'second' and more radical phase of deconstruction in which a 'new' concept could be forged simultaneously. The motif of *différance,* as neither a simple 'concept' nor a mere 'word,' has brought us the now familiar constellation of attendant terms: trace, supplement, pharmakon, and others. Among the others, two are marked sexually and in their most widely recognized sense pertain to the woman's body: *hymen* (the logic of which is developed in *La double séance*) and *double invagination* (a leitmotif in *Living On/Borderlines*).

Take only the term hymen in which there is a confusion or continuation of the term coitus, and from which it gets its double meaning: (1) "a membranous fold of tissue partly or completely occluding the vaginal external orifice" [from the Greek for *membrane*], and (2) marriage [from Greek mythology; the god of marriage]. In the first sense the hymen is that which protects virginity and is in front of the uterus. That is, it lies between the inside and the outside of the woman, between desire and its fulfillment. So that although (male) desire dreams of violently piercing or breaking the hymen (consummation in the second sense of the term), if that happens there is no hymen.

It seems to me that while the extensive play on etymologies (in which unconscious motivations are traced through the transformations and historical excesses of usage) effects a displacement of these terms, it also poses a problem for those who would seek to define what is specifically feminine. That comes about not so much because these terms are either under- or overvalued as parts belonging to woman's body. It is rather that, in the economy of a movement of writing that is always elusive, one can never decide properly whether the particular term implies complicity with or a break from existent ideology. Perhaps this is because, as Adam says of Eve in Mark Twain's satire, *The Diary of Adam and Eve,* not only does the "new creature name . . . everything" because "it looks like the thing," but—and this is the crux of the matter—"her mind is disordered [or, if you like, Nietzschean]—everything shows it."

In this regard there comes to mind a footnote to p. 207 of *La double séance,* concerning the displacement of writing, its transformation and generalization. The example cited is that of a surgeon who, upon learning of Freud's own difficulty in admitting to the possibility of masculine hysteria, exclaims to him: "But, my dear colleague, how can you state such absurdities? *Hysteron* means uterus. How therefore could a man be a hysteric?"

How can we change the representation of woman? Can we move from the rib where woman is wife ("She was called Woman because she was taken from man"—Genesis 2:23) to the womb where she is mother ("man is born of woman"—Job 14:13) without essential loss? Do we have in your view the beginning of phase two, a 'new' concept of woman?

Derrida: No, I do not believe that we have one, if indeed it is possible to *have* such a thing or if such a thing could exist or show promise of existing.

Personally, I am not sure that I feel the lack of it. Before having one that is new, are we certain of having had an old one? It is the word "concept" or "conception" that I would in turn question in its relationship to any essence which is rigorously or properly identifiable. This would bring us back to the preceding questions. The concept of the concept, along with the entire system that attends it, belongs to a prescriptive order. It is that order that a problematics of woman and a problematics of difference, as sexual difference, should disrupt along the way. Moreover, I am not sure that "phase two" marks a split with "phase one," a split whose form would be a cut along an indivisible line. The relationship between these two phases doubtless has another structure. I spoke of two distinct phases for the sake of clarity, but the relationship of one phase to another is marked less by conceptual determinations (that is, where a new concept follows an archaic one) than by a transformation or general deformation of logic; such transformations or deformations mark the "logical" element or environment itself by moving, for example, beyond the "positional" (difference determined as opposition, whether or not dialectically). This movement is of great consequence for the discussion here, even if my formulation is apparently abstract and disembodied. One could, I think, demonstrate this: when sexual difference is determined by *opposition* in the dialectical sense (according to the Hegelian movement of speculative dialectics which remains so powerful even beyond Hegel's text), one appears to set off "the war between the sexes"; but one precipitates the end, with victory going to the masculine sex. The determination of sexual difference in opposition is destined, designed, in truth, for truth; it is so in order to erase sexual difference. The dialectical opposition neutralizes or supersedes [Hegel's term *Aufhebung* carries with it both the sense of conserving and negating. No adequate translation of the term in English has yet been found] the difference. However, according to a surreptitious operation that must be flushed out, one insures phallocentric mastery under the cover of neutralization every time. These are now well-known paradoxes. And such phallocentrism adorns itself now and then, here and there, with an appendix: a certain kind of feminism. In the same manner, phallocentrism and homosexuality can go, so to speak, hand in hand, and I take these terms, whether it is a question of feminine or masculine homosexuality, in a very broad and radical sense.

And what if the "wife" or the "mother"—whom you seem sure of being able to dissociate—were figures for this homosexual dialectics? I am referring now to your question on the "representation" of woman and such "loss" as might occur in the passage from man's rib to the womb of woman, the passage from the spouse, you say, to the mother. Why is it necessary to choose, and why only these two possibilities, these two "places," assuming that one can really dissociate them?

McDonald: The irony of my initial use of the cliché "woman's place," which in the old saw is followed by "in the home" or "in the kitchen," leaves the whole wide world for other places for the same intent. As for the "place" of women in

Genesis, and Job, as rib (spouse) or womb (mother), these are more basic functional differences. Nevertheless, within these two traditional roles, to choose one implies loss of the other. You are correct in observing that such a choice is not necessary; there could be juxtaposition, substitution, or other possible combinations. But these biblical texts are not frivolous in seeing the functional distinction which also has distinguished "woman's place" in Western culture.

Derrida: Since you quote Genesis, I would like to evoke the marvelous reading that Emmanuel Levinas has proposed of it without being clear as to whether he assumes it as his own or what the actual status of the "commentary" that he devotes to it is.[5] There would, of course, be a certain *secondariness* of woman, Ischa. The man, Isch, would come first; he would be number one; he would be at the beginning. Secondariness, however, would not be that of woman or femininity, but the *division* between masculine and feminine. It is not feminine sexuality that would be second but only the relationship to sexual difference. At the origin, on this side of and therefore beyond any sexual mark, there was humanity in general, and this is what is important. Thus the possibility of ethics could be saved, if one takes ethics to mean that relationship to the other as other which accounts for no other determination or sexual characteristic in particular. What kind of an ethics would there be if belonging to one sex or another became its law or privilege? What if the universality of moral laws were modeled on or limited according to the sexes? What if their universality were not unconditional, without sexual condition in particular?

Whatever the force, seductiveness or necessity of this reading, does it not risk restoring—in the name of ethics as that which is irreproachable—a classical interpretation, and thereby enriching what I would call its panoply in a manner surely as subtle as it is sublime? Once again, the classical interpretation gives a masculine sexual marking to what is presented either as a neutral originariness or, at least, as prior and superior to all sexual markings. Levinas indeed senses the risk factor involved in the erasure of sexual difference. He therefore maintains sexual difference: the human in general remains a sexual being. But he can only do so, it would seem, by placing (differentiated) sexuality beneath humanity which sustains itself at the level of the Spirit. That is, he simultaneously places, and this is what is important, masculinity [*le masculin*] in command and at the beginning (the *arkhé*), on a par with the Spirit. This gesture carries with it the most self-interested of contradictions; it has repeated itself, let us say, since "Adam and Eve," and persists —in analogous form—into "modernity," despite all the differences of style and treatment. Isn't that a feature of the "matrix," as we were saying before? or the "*patrix*" if you prefer, but it amounts to the same thing, does it not? Whatever the complexity of the itinerary and whatever the knots of rhetoric, don't you think that the movement of Freudian thought repeats this "logic"? Is it not also the risk that Heidegger runs? One should perhaps say, rather, the risk that is *avoided* because phallogocentrism is insurance against the return of what certainly has been feared as the most agonizing risk of all. Since I have named Heidegger in a context where the reference is quite rare and may even appear strange, I would like to dwell on this for a moment, if you don't mind, concerned that I will be both too lengthy and too brief.

Heidegger seems almost never to speak about sexuality or sexual difference. And he seems almost never to speak about psychoanalysis, give or take an occasional negative allusion. This is nether negligence nor omission. The pauses coming from his silence on these questions punctuate or create the spacing out of a powerful discourse. And one of the strengths of this discourse may be stated (though I am going much too quickly and schematizing excessively) like this: it begins by denying itself all accepted forms of security, all the sedimented presuppositions of classical ontology, anthropology, the natural or human sciences, until it falls back this side of such values as the opposition between subject/object, conscious/unconscious, mind/body, and many others as well. The existential analytic of the *Dasein* opens the road, so to speak, leading to the question of being; the *Dasein* is neither the human being (a thought recalled earlier by Levinas) nor the subject, neither consciousness nor the self [*le moi*] (whether conscious or unconscious). These are all determinations that are derived from and occur after the *Dasein*. Now—and here is what I wanted to get to after this inadmissible acceleration—in a course given in 1928, Heidegger justifies to some degree the silence of *Sein und Zeit* on the question of sexuality (*Gesamtausgabe*, band 26, no. 10, pp. 171ff.). In a paragraph from the course devoted to the "Problem of the *Sein und Zeit*," Heidegger reminds us that the analytic of the *Dasein* is neither an anthropology, an ethics, nor a metaphysics. With respect to any definition, position or evaluation of these fields, the *Dasein* is *neuter*. Heidegger insists upon and makes clear this original and essential "neutrality" of the *Dasein*: "This neutrality means also that the *Dasein* is neither of the two sexes. But this asexuality [*Geschlechtlosigkeit*] is not the indifference of empty invalidity, the annulling negativity of an indifferent ontic nothingness. In its neutrality, the *Dasein* is not the indifferent no-one-and-everyone [*Niemand und Jeder*], but it is originary positivity and the power of being or of the essence, *Mächtigkeit des Wesen*." One would have to read the analysis that follows very closely; I will try to do that another time in relation to some of his later texts. The analysis emphasizes the positive character, as it were, of this originary and powerful asexual neutrality which is not the *neither-nor* (*Weder-noch*) of ontic abstraction. It is originary and ontological. More precisely, the asexuality does not signify in this instance the absence of sexuality—one could call it the instinct, desire, or even the libido— but the absence of any mark belonging to one of the two sexes. Not that the *Dasein* does not ontically or in fact belong to a sex; not that it is deprived of sexuality; but the *Dasein* as *Dasein* does not carry with it the mark of this opposition (or alternative) between the two sexes. Insofar as these marks are opposable and binary, they are not existential structures. Nor do they allude in this respect to any primitive or subsequent bisexuality. Such an allusion would fall once again into anatomical, biological, or anthropological determinations. And the *Dasein*, in the structures and "power" that are originary to it, would come "prior" to these determinations. I am putting quotation marks around the word "prior" because it has no literal, chronological, historical, or logical meaning. Now, as of 1928, the analytic of the *Dasein* was the thought of ontological difference and the repetition of the question of being; it opened up a problematics that subjected all the concepts of traditional Western philosophy to a radical elucidation and interpretation. This gives an idea of what stakes were involved in a neutralization that fell back this side of both sexual difference and its binary marking, if not this side of sexuality itself. This would be the title of the enormous problem that in this context I must limit myself to merely naming: ontological difference and sexual difference.

And since your question evoked the "motif of difference," I would say that it has moved, by displacement, in the vicinity of this very obscure area. What is also being sought in this zone is the passage between ontological difference and sexual difference; it is a passage that may no longer be thought, punctuated, or opened up according to those polarities to which we have been referring for some time (originary/derived, ontological/ontic, ontology/anthropology, the thought of being/metaphysics or ethics, etc.). The constellation of terms that you have cited could *perhaps* be considered (for nothing is ever taken for granted or guaranteed in these matters) a kind of transformation or deformation of space; such a transformation would tend to extend beyond these poles and reinscribe them within it. Some of these terms, "hymen" or "invagination," you were saying, "pertain in their most widely recognized sense to the woman's body." Are you sure? I am grateful for your having used such a careful formulation. That these words signify "in their most widely recognized sense" had, of course, not escaped me, and the emphasis that I have put on resexualizing a philosophical or theoretical discourse, which has been too "neutralizing" in this respect, was dictated by those very reservations that I just mentioned concerning the strategy of neutralization (whether or not it is deliberate). Such re-sexualizing must be done without facileness of any kind and, above all, without regression in relation to what might justify, as we saw, the procedures—or necessary steps—of Levinas or Heidegger, for example. That being said, "hymen" and "invagination," at least in the context into which these words have been swept, no longer simply designate figures for the feminine body. They no longer do so, that is, assuming that one knows for certain what a feminine or masculine body is, and assuming that anatomy is in this instance the final recourse. What remains undecidable concerns not only but also the line of cleavage between the two sexes. As you recalled, such a movement reverts neither to words nor to concepts. And what remains of language within it cannot be abstracted from the "performativity" (which marks and is marked) that concerns us here, beginning—for the examples that you have chosen—with the texts of Mallarmé and Blanchot, and with the labor of reading or writing which evoked them and which they in turn evoked. One could say quite accurately that the hymen *does not exist*. Anything constituting the value of existence is foreign to the "hymen." And if there were hymen—I am not saying if the hymen existed—property value would be no more appropriate to it for reasons that I have stressed in the texts to which you refer. How can one then attribute the *existence* of the hymen *properly* to woman? Not that it is any more the distinguishing feature of man or, for that matter, of the human creature. I would say the same for the term "invagination" which has, moreover, always been reinscribed in a chiasmus, one doubly folded, redoubled and inversed,[6] etc. From then on, is it not difficult to recognize in the movement of this term a "representation of woman"? Furthermore, I do not know if it is to a change in representation that we should entrust the future. As with all the questions that we are presently discussing, this one, and above all when it is put as a question of representation, seems at once too old and as yet to be born: a kind of old parchment crossed every which way, overloaded with hieroglyphs and still as virgin as the origin, like the early morning in the East from whence it comes. And you know that the word for parchment does not come from any "road" leading from Pergamus in Asia. I do not know how you will translate this last sentence.

McDonald: It is a problem. In modern English usage the word for parchment no longer carries with it the sense of the French *parchemin,* on or by the road, as the Middle English *perchement* or *parchemin* did. The *American Heritage Dictionary* traces the etymology thus: "Parthian (leather) from *pergamina,* parchment, from Greek *pergamene,* from *Pergamenos,* or *Pergamun,* from *Pergamon*"; Lempriere's *Classical Dictionary* says further that the town of Pergamus was founded by Philaeterus, a eunuch, and that parchment has been called the *charta pergamena.*

Derrida: The *Littré Dictionary* which gives the etymology for French makes war responsible for the appearance of "pergamena" or "Pergamina." It is thereby a product of war: one began to write on bodies and animal skins because papyrus was becoming very rare. They say too that parchment was occasionally prepared from the skin of still-born lambs. And according to Pliny, it was out of jealousy that Eumenes, king of Pergamus, turned to parchment. His rival, Ptolemies, the king of Egypt, was so proud of his library that he had only books written on paper. It was necessary to find new bodies of or for writing.

McDonald: I would like to come back to the writing of the dance, the choreography that you mentioned a while back. If we do not yet have a "new" "concept" of woman, because the radicalization of the problem goes beyond the "thought" or the concept, what are our chances of "thinking 'difference' not so much before sexual difference, as you say, as taking off 'from'" it? What would you say is our chance and "who" are we sexually?

Derrida: At the approach of this shadowy area it has always seemed to me that the voice itself had to be divided in order to say that which is given is given to thought or speech. No monological discourse—and by that I mean here monosexual discourse—can dominate with a single voice, a single tone, the space of this half-light, even if the "proffered discourse" is then signed by a sexually marked patronymic. Thus, to limit myself to one account, and not to propose an example, I have felt the necessity for a chorus, for a choreographic text with polysexual signatures.[7] I felt this every time that a legitimacy of the neuter, the apparently least suspect sexual neutrality of "phallocentric or gynocentric" mastery, threatened to immobilize (in silence), colonize, stop, or unilateralize in a subtle or sublime manner what remains no doubt irreducibly dissymmetrical. More directly: a certain dissymmetry is no doubt the law both of sexual difference and the relationship to the other in general (I say this in opposition to a certain kind of violence within the language of "democratic" platitudes, in any case in opposition to a certain democratic ideology), yet the dissymmetry to which I refer is still let us not say symmetrical in turn (which might seem absurd), but doubly, unilaterally inordinate, like a kind of reciprocal, respective, and respectful excessiveness. This double dissymmetry perhaps goes beyond known or coded marks, beyond the grammar and spelling, shall we say (metaphorically), of sexuality. This indeed revives the following question: what if we were to reach, what if we were to approach here (for one does not arrive at this as one would at a determined location) the area of a relationship to the other where the code of sexual marks would no longer be discriminating? The relationship would not be asexual, far from it, but would be sexual otherwise: beyond the binary difference that governs the decorum of all codes, beyond the opposition feminine/masculine, beyond bisexuality as well, beyond homosexuality and heterosexuality which come to the same thing. As I dream of saving the chance that this question offers I would like to believe in the multiplicity of sexually marked voices. I would like to believe in the masses, this indeterminable number of blended voices, this mobile of nonidentified sexual marks whose choreography can carry, divide, multiply the body of each "individual," whether he be classified as "man" or as "woman" according to the criteria of usage. Of course, it is not impossible that desire for a sexuality without number can still protect us, like a dream, from an implacable destiny which immures everything for life in the figure 2. And should this merciless closure arrest desire at the wall of opposition, we would struggle in vain: there will never be but two sexes, neither one more nor one less. Tragedy would leave this strange sense, a contingent one finally, that we must affirm and learn to love instead of dreaming of the innumerable. Yes, perhaps; why not? But where would the "dream" of the innumerable come from, if it is indeed a dream? Does the dream itself not prove that what is dreamt of must be there in order for it to provide the dream? Then too, I ask you, what kind of a dance would there be, or would there be one at all, if the sexes were not exchanged according to rhythms that vary considerably? In a quite rigorous sense, the *exchange* alone could not suffice either, however, because the desire to escape the combinatory itself, to invent incalculable choreographies, would remain.

NOTES

This exchange previously appeared in *Diacritics* 12 (1992). reprinted with permission of The Johns Hopkins University Press.

This text is the result of a written exchange carried on during the fall of 1981. Jacques Derrida wrote his responses in French, and I then translated them into English for publication. It should be noted that I do not ask the following questions in the name of any specific feminist group or ideology. I do nevertheless owe a debt to longstanding conversations on the subject of "Woman" and "Women" with, among others, A. Jardine, C. Lévesque, N. Miller, N. Schor and especially J. McDonald.

1. Jacques Derrida, *Spurs/Eperons* (Chicago: University of Chicago Press, 1978).

2. On August 26, 1970, a group of women calling themselves the Emma Goldman Brigade marched down Fifth Avenue in New York City with many other feminists, chanting: "Emma said it in 1910/Now we're going to say it again."

3. See Roldolphe Gasché, "La bordure interne," and the response by Jacques Derrida, in L'oreille de l'autre: Textes et débats avec Jacques Derrida, ed. C. Lévesque and C. McDonald (Montreal, 1982).

4. The gift is a topic that occurs in a number of recent texts, among others: Glas, Eperons, *La carte postale*. TN.

5. Jacques Derrida refers here to the text *En ce moment même dans cet ouvrage me voici,* in *Textes pour Emmanuel Levinas* (Paris: J. M. Place, 1980). Derrida interprets two texts in particular by Levinas *(Le judaïsme et le féminin,* in *Difficile liberté,* and *Et Dieu créa la femme,* in *Du sacré au saint).* In order to clarify this part of the discussion, I am translating the following passage from Derrida's text in which he quotes from the ten comments upon Levinas's commentary: "The meaning of the 'feminine' will be clarified in this manner by beginning with the human essence; the female Isha [la Isha] begins with Ish: not that the feminine originates in the masculine, but rather the division into masculine and feminine—the dichotomy—starts with what is human. . . . Beyond the personal relationship established between two beings, each born of a discrete creative act, the specificity of the feminine is a secondary matter. It is not woman who is secondary; it is the relationship with woman as woman, and that does not belong to the primordial level of the human element. The first level consists of those tasks that man and woman each accomplishes as a human being. . . . In each of the passages that we are commenting upon right now, the problem lies in the reconciliation of men's and women's humanity with the hypothesis of masculine spirituality; the feminine is not the correlative of the masculine but its corollary; feminine specificity, as the difference between the sexes that it indicates, is not situated straightaway at the level of those opposites which constitute the Spirit.

An audacious question, this one: how can equality of the sexes come from masculine 'ownership' [la propriété du masculin]? . . . A difference was necessary that would not compromise equity: a difference of sex; and from then on, a certain preeminence of man, a woman whose arrival comes later and who is, as woman, the appendix of the human element. Now we understand the lesson. The idea of humanity is not thinkable from two entirely different principles. There must be a sameness [le même] common to others: woman was taken from man, but came after him: the very femininity of woman is in this inaugural afterthought" *(Et Dieu créa la femme, in Du sacré au saint)*. And Derrida follows up, commenting: "It is a strange logic, this 'audacious question.'" One would have to comment each step of the way and verify that the secondariness of sexual difference signifies the secondariness of the feminine in every case (but why indeed?). One would have to verify that the initialness of what is predifferential is always marked by the masculine; the masculine should come, like all sexual marks, only afterward. Such a commentary would be necessary, but I prefer first to underscore the following, in the name of protocol: he himself is commenting and says that he is commenting; one must bear in mind that this is not literally the discourse of E. L. He says, as he is discoursing, that he is commenting on doctors, at this very moment ("the passages upon which we are commenting at this moment," and further along: "I am not taking sides; today I am commenting"). However, the distance of the commentary is not neuter. What he comments upon is consonant with a whole network of his own assertions, or those by him, "him" (53–54). TN.

6. This is an allusion to, among other things, all the passages on the so-called argument of the gaine ("sheath," "girdle"; cognate with "vagina"), in particular pp. 232ff. 250ff. Furthermore, the word "invagination" is always taken within the syntax of the expression "double invagination chiasmatique des bords," in *Living On (Deconstruction and Criticism* [New York: Seabury Press, 1979]) and *The Law of Genre* (in Glyph 7). TN.

7. This is an allusion to Pas, in Gramma 3/4 (1976), *La vérité en peinture* (1978), *En ce moment même dans cet ouvrage me voici,* in *Textes pour Emmanuel Levinas* (1980), *Feu la cendre* (to appear). TN.

Incalculable Choreographies: The Dance Practice of Marie Chouinard

Ann Cooper Albright

Then too, I ask you, what kind of dance would there be, or would there be one at all, if the sexes were not exchanged according to rhythms that vary considerably? In a quite rigorous sense, the exchange alone could not suffice either, however, because the desire to escape the combinatory itself, to invent incalculable choreographies, would remain.

—Jacques Derrida, "Choreographies"

And then if I spoke about a person whom I met and who shook me up, herself being moved and I moved to see her moved, and she, feeling me moved, being moved in turn, and whether this person is a she and a he and a he and a she and a shehe and a heshe, I want to be able not to lie, I don't want to stop her if she trances, I want him, I want her, I will follow her.

—Hélène Cixous, *The Newly Born Woman*

As a dancer and feminist scholar, I am intrigued by these two visions of writing in which sexual identity takes on a certain fluidity of movement. By weaving the language of movement and references to dance throughout their discussions of sexual difference and identity, Jacques Derrida and Hélène Cixous point to the theoretical possibilities of a form of communication predicated on the instability of the body and the resultant displacement of meaning. In this chapter I extend the implications of Derrida's and Cixous's interest in movement and writing by including another kind of text—that written by and on the live dancing body of contemporary Canadian performer Marie Chouinard.[1] For live performance, because it comes *through* the body but is not only *of* the body, can problematize theories of meaning and sexual difference in powerful ways. Learning how to read that body in an attempt to understand all the conflicting layers of meaning in physical motion is a complex task that requires an awareness of the kinesthetic as well as the visual and intellectual implications of dance. I place Chouinard's physical choreography (specifically *Marie Chien Noir*, *S.T.A.B.*, and *La faune*) in the midst of Cixous's and Derrida's theoretical "dances" in order to address what is frequently absent from contemporary theory—an awareness of the material consequences of the live performing body.

This desire to consider the physical body does not stem from a naive belief in a "natural" or even a "biological" body—quite the contrary. Clearly cultural values resonate throughout the bodies that constitute them, and often these structures are physically internalized and thus rendered as "essential" elements of human nature. Dancers, however, can consciously engage in a physical training that seeks to resist oppressive ideologies concerning women and their bodies in performance, effectively challenging the terms of their own representation. Because dance is at once social and personal, internal and external, a dancer can both embody and explode gendered images of the body—simultaneously registering, creating, and subverting cultural conventions. When Marie Chouinard literally and figuratively appropriates Vaslav Nijinsky's body in her interpretation of his dancing, for instance, she opens the question of what it means to be a man by refusing to stay in the role of a woman. By making us aware of her own physical experience while she refuses the categories of social experience, Chouinard destabilizes the usual relationships between the body and gender, language and meaning, extending the direction of Derrida's and Cixous's textual choreographies into physical movement.

In "Choreographies" Christie McDonald prefaces a series of questions to Derrida about his interest in dissolving sexual difference and the place of "the feminine" in this scheme by quoting Emma Goldman's famous line, "If I can't dance I don't want to be part of your revolution."[2] Throughout this interchange the words *choreography* and *dance*—both feminine nouns in French—continually weave their way into a discussion of feminism and sexual difference. Despite the improvisatory and slightly flippant tone of Derrida's remarks, he repeatedly imbues "the dance" (*la danse*) with an almost sacred vitality. Later in this same passage Derrida is more specific: "dance changes place and above all changes *places*" (69). The revolutionary quality of dancing, then, becomes more than the quick footedness to move out of the way; it takes on the refined ability to change places without feeling displaced, to move in a way that shifts the meaning of location.

Throughout much of his interchange with MacDonald, Derrida identifies dancing as a "feminine" subversion par excellence. Theoretically, at least, "the feminine" realm is not connected exclusively to the female body (in fact, it often ends up including the male avant-garde—a move that creates its own set of problems) and serves to signify instead anything that is outside, although certainly not unaffected by, dominant structures of power, and that could potentially be subversive or disturbing to that power.[3] This distinction, however, is elusive and, as we see in Derrida's comment, can slip back into a binary paradigm which implicitly connects "the feminine" with women and dance: "The joyous disturbance of certain women's movements, and of some women in particular, has actually brought with it the chance for a certain risky turbulence in the assigning of places within our small European space" (69). While she is resisting, while she is dancing outside of history, woman is also, of course, constructed by that history. Nowhere is this marked more clearly than on her physical body. Dancing in and around cultural constructions of the female body, she choreographs against the grain of those texts, those histories.

Unwilling to confront the embodied presence of the one who is dancing, Derrida abandons the connection of dancing and women at the end of this improvisatory dialogue. Instead, he traces the word *choreography* back to its etymological root, *khoros,* and refigures dance as a mass chorus of movement: "As I dream . . . I would like to believe in the multiplicity of sexually marked voices. I would like to believe in the masses, this indeterminable number of blended voices, the mobile of non-identified sexual marks whose choreography can carry, divide, multiply the body of each 'individual' whether he be classified as 'man' or as 'woman' according to the criteria of usage" (76). Deftly darting through McDonald's questions about what constitutes "the feminine," Derrida avoids the quagmire implicit of his own theory, which seeks to equate the feminine realm with a subversive stance (or rather, a subversive dance) and the masculine realm with the power of the dominant discourses. By appropriating choreography and dance as deconstructionist tropes—precisely because they are about constant displacement—Derrida attempts to create another category, one constructed in movement, that slips right through sexual difference. While it is tempting to rest a moment in Derrida's dream of a dance that goes beyond gender, envisioning "incalculable choreographies" as a poststructuralist sequel to *Dirty Dancing,* popular culture—tempered with a dose of feminism—has infused me with too literal an imagination. The question keeps darting through my head: What do the "incalculable choreographies" actually look like? Whose body is dancing, and what is it dancing about?

Here, of course, is the crux of the issue. Despite all this fantastic dancing of words across the page, it would be hard to translate Derrida's vision onto the stage. Real dancing bodies carry the signs of sexual difference in much less ambiguous ways; even movement choruses are often divided by sex. Traditionally, a corps de ballet is all women; when there is a group of men onstage, the sexes are divided spatially. There are, nonetheless, ways in which the gender of the dancer can be worked over, played with, and exceeded in an effort to disrupt these traditional dancing roles and disconcert the audience's reception of that bodily image. While we may know whether it is a he or a she on that stage, the action or theatricality of the performance can place that knowledge in jeopardy. By moving *through* instead of locating her(him)self *in* narrative positions, the dancer is able to step out of meaning before it becomes stabilized.

In this sense, then, dance is a wonderful example of Derridian difference. Based on the motion of live bodies, the dancing "text" is singularly elusive. Any isolated movement or gesture is practically meaningless until it is placed in the context of what went before or after it. But that context is continually shifting in time and space, appearing only to disappear an instant later. In order to make sense of the dancing, the viewer must try to remember the flickering traces of earlier movements at the same time as s/he is watching the next series of motions. This ongoing process rarely stops long enough for the connections to catch up, and for this reason dance can be difficult to watch and even more problematic to write about.

In the midst of all this poststructuralist profusion, however, is the dancer's physical body, whose movement constructs a presence as well as a continual absence. Derrida leaves no room to discuss the way this presence can be palpable, indeed, powerful, in the midst of its own erasure. As the dancing body evolves from, say, crawling on the floor to standing upright, the cultural meanings usually attached to those actions shift, but at the same time that these meanings are displaced, another current of meaning is constituted by the very act of moving. What becomes visible then is the movement between two moments marked by recognizable images. By dwelling in these moments, dancers can draw the audience's attention to the dancers' own physical reality, pulling our bodies closer to theirs. This process of making (presence) in the midst of unmaking (absence) allows for an intricate layering of visual, kinesthetic, and cultural meanings in which bodies, sexualities, and identities can begin to restage the terms of their alliance. For if sexual difference can be conceived as physical motion rather than a set of stable ideological positions, the resultant narratives of desire might then be choreographed more imaginatively.

Near the beginning of "Mimas, lune de Saturne," the first segment of the evening-length *Marie Chien Noir*, Chouinard travels across a long diagonal from the back to the front of the stage. Crawling low, she moves first like a lizard and then rolls and tumbles and rises with the silent agility of a fox, finally arriving on her feet as she moves closer to the audience. Chouinard looks out toward the spectators, as she takes her place next to a skeleton positioned downstage in a permanent and ironic plié. Shaping her hand like a swan's neck, she extends her arm in a full arc, slowly raising her face to greet the hand-bird which glides down to her mouth and deeper into her throat. A collective shudder darts through the audience as Chouinard's abdomen contracts convulsively. As she turns to stand with her profile to the audience, her swan hand dips down into her interior again, but this time the audience can see the contraction spawn a series of ripples that spread out like water through her body.[4]

While many of her movements are graceful and sensuous, Chouinard never lets the audience settle back too comfortably into their seats. As soon as we become lulled by the curves and stretches, spirals and suspensions of her dancing, she jerks us out of that contented place by putting a raw and often disturbing edge to her movement. In the sequence I have just described, for example, she creates an edge in her performance (and a certain edginess in the audience) by going too far down into her throat. What may have been an eroticized moment

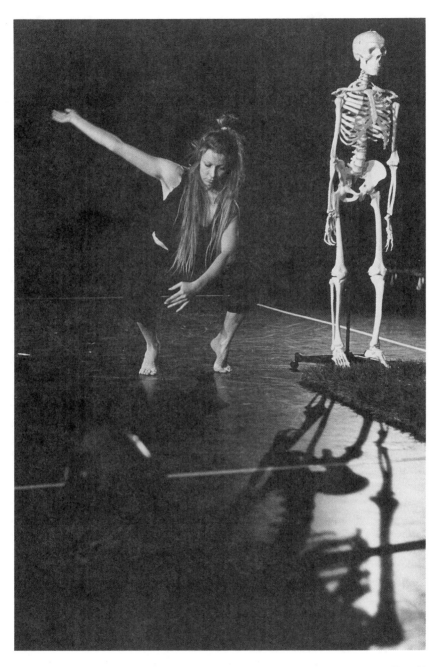

FIG. 18. Marie Chouinard in *Marie Chien Noir*. Photo copyright © Tom Brazil

shifts dynamics as she pulls out a very real gag response over which she has no control but is apparently willing to engage. At this moment in the performance, Chouinard shatters a classically "beautiful" visual image (and the audience's expected pleasure in watching that image) by insisting that we recognize her own physical experience. Metaphorically, she is also pulling out the space of her insides, that invisible realm of female sexuality—a space audience members are rarely able to confront. I suspect it is this enforced intimacy with her somatic experience which brought on the audience's collective shudder.

One of the more radical elements of Chouinard's work, particularly in *Marie Chien Noir*, is her challenge to the representation of feminine desire as a passive (and silent) desire-to-be-desired, a desire to be someone's "other." Traditional Western forms of dance, such as the Romantic ballet, parallel the structures of desire imposed by classic cinema. The voyeuristic gaze of the audience, set up by the three-pronged looks of the director, the camera, and the male protagonist in film, is represented in dance by the looks of the choreographer and the male dancing partner, who literally "presents" the female dancer to the audience's gaze. The solo format that is the basis of Chouinard's performance works against this structure of desire. Since the audience has no danseur's gaze to introduce the terms of this visual economy, and since there is no implied "other" in the dance to whom she is addressing her performing—and in whose shoes we could place ourselves—we must take a leap of faith and believe she is performing for us. But since the usual signs that a dancer is performing for an audience—the projected, eccentric (moving outward) movements, the entertaining smiles and easy nods— are missing, the audience is left in the lurch, often wondering if we should be present at all. Over the course of this ninety-minute solo, the stage becomes her space, a self-contained world of reality and fantasy. Even though she places herself on the stage to be viewed, to be consumed (in the high capitalist sense that one pays to see her), her actions elude a facile interpretation, making it difficult for the audience to construct a narrative of desire in which we can participate in the customary manner.

It is dark when Chouinard enters the performance space. She glides slowly across the black floor. A string of twinkling red lights follows her like a luminous tail. Guiding the lights first into a circle, she slips into the middle. Her body—its whiteness a stark contrast to the black briefs and swimcap she is wearing— glistens in the shadows as she pours oil onto herself and the floor. Then, with the sleepy inertia of a black seal, she launches her body. One small twist is all it takes to send her gliding peacefully across the dark pool. Again and again we see a small movement expand as her body skates across the shiny black surface.

In Chouinard's performances, there is no safe, aestheticized distance from her sticky physicality. Given the size of most experimental performance spaces, Chouinard's dancing inevitably invades the audience's space. When she touches herself, spreads her body on the floor, or drools, her physical experience fills the atmosphere like a dense, mysterious fog. The audience is no longer positioned on the other, anonymous side of the keyhole. We are right there, smack in the room, and that exposure forces us to redefine how we are watching this performance. Her presence forces audience members to recognize their ability to respond in multiple ways, to take responsibility for meeting her energy and participating in the event, even if that response is to squirm uncomfortably in their seats.

Chouinard eschews references to her work as either dance or theater, preferring instead to call herself a body artist. In an interview, Chouinard discusses how in another culture she might be regarded as a priestess or a celebrant, but in this society, in order to make "homages" to the moments and parts of life which she values, she has had to become a performing artist and be content with presenting her work in the theater. Still attuned to that image of the *religieuse,* Chouinard consciously works to "hypnotize," fascinate, the audience in hope of activating our imaginations. She intends to draw the audience into her world and to communicate in a way that is experiential and communal—as in a religious rite. But the fact that Chouinard works so intensively with investigations of her own (female) body complicates her intention to make the audience a responsive witness to her performances.

On another occasion in this same first section of *Marie Chien Noir,* Chouinard dunks her long hair in and out of a tub of water. At first crouching by the washtub, she dunks her head again and again. Rising progressively higher with each repetition, she layers the visual rhythm of her movements with the aural rhythm of the sounds of sloshing water. These rhythms subside into the more erratic sounds of dripping water as she stands and lets the water drain off her hair. Gently folding up her hair in a sensuous manner evocative of Renoir's paintings of women bathing, she walks over to the center of the stage and starts to fling her hair in an arc that sweeps back and loops forward, tracing its trajectory with sprays of water. Her hair sweeps the floor expansively, and it seems at first as if she is simply intent on drying it, until the slapping sounds become more and more insistent. Eventually this slapping on the floor is picked up by Chouinard's hands and transferred to her body. Keeping a steady rhythm going, she alternately slaps her chest, arms, and face.

This moment, like the one where she repeatedly falls and gets up, and like several others in the piece, straddles a peculiar line. Chouinard is not exactly beating herself; the energy here is not particularly masochistic. Her body takes in the slap as it exhales, reducing the pain and producing another rhythmic sound with her breath. At the same time that there is something brutal to what she is doing, there is also a feeling of the body being awakened and refreshed, like diving into a cold Maine pond on a hot day. Breathing throughout, her body does not build up any tension during this episode of rhythmic slapping, and this release allows Chouinard to emerge from this moment right into some very luscious, lyrical, and flowing dancing.

In a panel discussion by the recipients of Calgary's Olympic Arts Festival Modern Dance Commissions, Chouinard talks about what makes her passionate about dance: "It is always a discovery. Maybe the audience thinks it knows the idea we are proposing but, for me, when I am dancing on stage I am doing something that is unknown. . . . When I dance, my body becomes a laboratory for experience . . . physical, mystical and other kinds. By working with the body you can make openings for the flowing of life."[5] Physical and visible—visible in her own physicality—Chouinard dances at once for herself and for an audience. Her performance is thus both encoded in the structure of its own representation and continually—kinesthetically—exceeding that structure. At times her body on stage is so clear, so classically beautiful, so much a part of our cultural repertoire of "woman," that the image of her body takes over the audience's consciousness.[6] At other times, when the movements of her dancing body exceed the boundaries of her skin and extend out to affect the audience *kinesthetically,* we can actually participate in her embodied experience. No longer confined to an image of "woman" or even contained within the limits of her own skin, her body spills out into the audience. This close amorphousness of Chouinard's performing body is often described as creaturelike or otherworldly.[7] Considering that Chouinard reveals so much of and about her body on stage, one might think she would be seen as the female dancer par excellence—a "real" woman, with both the sexist and feminist connotations of that word. But the combination of eccentric, nonnarrative sequences in Chouinard's dances with the terrifying and sometimes messy closeness of her bodily functions situates Chouinard outside of the safe, traditional depictions of the female body. Given our interests in movement and language, we might then ask: How can this dancing body enter the writing—in motion?

In *The Newly Born Woman* and "Coming to Writing," Hélène Cixous brings the metaphorics of physicality into writing.[8] Movement, for Cixous, starts with the breath—that moving upward and outward of a writing voice.

> Writing was in the air around me. Always close, intoxicating, invisible, inaccessible. . . . 'Writing' seized me, gripped me, around the diaphram, between the stomach and the chest, a blast dilated my lungs and I stopped breathing. Suddenly I was filled with a turbulence that knocked the wind out of me and inspired me to wild acts. 'Write.' When I say 'writing' seized me, it wasn't a sentence that had managed to seduce me, there was absolutely nothing written, not a letter, not a line. But in the depths of the flesh, the attack. Pushed. Not penetrated. Invested. Set in motion. ("Coming to Writing" 9)

Cixous's insistence on the physicality of the writing body, especially her focus on metaphors of birth and maternity (blood and milk), seems to imply a direct relationship between the female body and "feminine writing." Because Cixous imbues her notion of the "feminine" within this source of somatic textuality, many feminist scholars, particularly in the Anglo-American tradition, react strongly to what they perceive to be the essentialist overtones of her project.[9] It is true that Cixous takes what Diana Fuss, in her concise survey of the "essentialist/

constructivist" debate in feminist theory, calls "the risk of essence."[10] At times, for instance, Cixous portrays the "feminine" in writing as a "truthful" voice which reflects the presence of the body. And if, as she repeatedly declares, *"In body/Still more:* woman is body more than man is" (*Newly Born Woman* 95), then the figure on the other side of the equals mark is usually a woman. It is important to note that for Cixous, a bodily presence in writing is not necessarily limited to women. It is just that the evangelistic force of her writing in these works is aimed at encouraging women to reverse the dynamics of an oppressive discourse that claims women are *only* their bodies. Although she frequently writes in mystical language that slips away from a historical grounding, Cixous is mindful of the ways that social ideologies influence the somatic and erotic textuality of writing bodies. Often, however, Cixous is writing *from* a historical positioning of women and men in Western political and intellectual history *toward* the possibility of a utopian moment in which the cultural ideologies which structure sexual difference are radically transformed. "And let us imagine a real liberation of sexuality, that is to say, a transformation of each one's relationship to his or her body (and to the other body), an approximation to the vast, material, organic, senuous universe that we are. This cannot be accomplished, of course, without political transformations that are equally radical (Imagine!)" (83).

In *The Newly Born Woman*—which is set up, interestingly, as an authorial pas de deux, Catherine Clément and Hélène Cixous evoke two distinct visions of a dancing woman. Clément's solo essay ("The Guilty One") speaks of the feminine role as that of the sorceress or the hysteric—the dancing image of a madwoman whirling ferociously in a tarantella. Circling, circling, and never going anywhere, Clément's vision of this mad dancer exemplifies a classic psychoanalytic model of the hysterical woman who displays her transgression—her desire for more from the world, the desire to move in it—in a fit of dancing that releases her emotions but also insures her eventual reincorporation into the web of society. In this scene the madwoman's dancing, while certainly a frightening representation of woman's sexuality, also serves to exorcise her madness (she literally dances it out), and she returns to the group exhausted and subdued. Cixous's written solo ("Sorties") is inspired, in part, by this mad dancing woman who dares to get up and dance her passion. But Cixous's dancer is not fated to sit down again. "Unleashed and raging . . . she arises, she approaches, she lifts up, she reaches, covers over, washes ashore, flows embracing the cliff's least undulation, already she is another, arising again" (90). Filled with an explosive, expansive energy (the word *sortie* suggests a pushing out, an outburst, an escape), this newly born woman jumps over historical and social restraints to explore the dancing pleasures of her changing sexuality. "She doesn't hold still, she overflows" (91).

To read Cixous only in terms of her political pragmatism is to severely limit the radical potential of her intervention in the very process of women's inscription in the world—the way their bodies are written onto a cultural slate. In one sense, Cixous joins Derrida in positioning women (by invoking "the feminine") as outside of and therefore subversive to Western metaphysics. But rather than simply relegating women to "other" status (as Derrida seems to do), Cixous explores the sources of that otherness in the female body. This body, however, is neither completely "natural" nor "textual." In fact, it refuses the very logic of those categories. "A body 'read,' finished? A book—a decaying carcass? Stench and falsity. The flesh is writing, and writing is never read: it always remains to be read, studied, sought, invented" ("Coming to Writing" 24). Written over and writing (on and for) itself, this body is engaged in a constant process of splintering and deferring. Here, the body meets the page as a mirror meets another mirror, always already reflecting back the inscription of the other. "Life becomes text starting out from my body. I am already text. History, love, violence, time, work, desire inscribe it in my body" (52). Keeping the body present within texts, Cixous stages the "whole of reality worked upon my flesh" in a written performance that moves through words and into dance (52).

Following Cixous's writing is like being on a roller coaster of images, speeding through dense active descriptions with verbs flying every which way, trying to catch up with that newly born woman who is always just slipping out of sight around the next bend. The cyclical timing of transitional phrases which continuously loop back over the previous ones—traveling over, through, across, and around—creates a breathy abundance of language that spills over its own meaning. The repetitious rhythm of her words and their incessant movement back and forth shape a writing presence that is analagous in many ways to Chouinard's performing presence in *Marie Chien Noir*.

> She doesn't "speak," she throws her trembling body into the air, she lets herself go, she flies, she goes completely into her voice, she vitally defends the "logic" of her discourse with her body; her flesh speaks true . . . she conveys meaning with her body. She *inscribes* what she is saying because she does not deny unconscious drives the unmanageable part they play in speech. ("Sorties," in *Newly Born Woman* 92)

> Her dance is solid, concrete actions; her movement suggests design, even writing; the *voice* surges. Out of her movements, often drawn from bodily functions, emerges a new body language which shatters the traditional notion of dance.[11]

While these two passages come from different historical moments and geographic places—"Sorties" was originally published in France in 1975 and Chouinard's press packet was published ten years later in Montreal—and express different artistic impulses, they both speak of the relationship between body and voice in terms of an embodied language that explodes tidy separations of the physical from the intellectual. These movement images reflect back on a body that spills over, continually exceeding the culture that seeks to contain it. One physical manifestation of that transgression is the voice. For both Cixous and Chouinard, the voice is a meeting of body and discourse. Yet that voice is not an exclusively private or internal calling. Swelling far beyond the body which produces it, the voice emanates into the public domain. Indeed, Cixous seems to be speaking for Chouinard when she writes: "Voice! That, too, is launching forth and effusion without return. Exclamation, cry, breathlessness, yet, vomit, music. . . . And that is how she writes, as one throws a voice—forward, into the void. . . . Woman must write her body, must make up the unimpeded tongue that bursts partitions, classes and rhetorics, orders and codes, must inundate, run through, go beyond the discourse" ("Sorties," in *Newly Born Woman* 94–95).

The edge in Chouinard's dancing which I discussed earlier takes on another form in "Mimas, lune de Saturne." This time the edge is the sound of her voice: her calling, her chanting, her screeching. In the middle of this dance Chouinard again comes forward to face the audience. Looking out with a blank expression, she drops to her hands and knees and waits with her mouth open until enough saliva collects to start dribbling out. She sucks it back up into her mouth and darts back a few feet to repeat the whole procedure. Finally backed into a corner, she begins a walking journey which starts as a lullaby and ends as a fierce war dance. Bent over and swinging her upper body like a pendulum, her arms making a circle which frames her head, she hums a song as she sways from side to side. The soothing sound becomes more urgent as her stepping becomes more insistent and percussive. The stamping pattern takes over her body and crescendos into a driving rhythm. Chouinard lifts her upper body, clenches her hands into fists, and stares vehemently off into the distance. Her voice starts calling fiercely like a pack of angry crows, and her body explodes in fits and starts of motion.

Abruptly, she drops that driven energy and walks over to the washtub. A moment's respite of silence and the sound of her hands in the water gives way to her voice. Chouinard seats herself comfortably on one leg, slips one and then the other sleeve of her shirt off her shoulder and slides her hand down her pants. Her head cradled in one arm, she closes her eyes as if to listen to a song inside herself. A deep, light tremor begins in her breathing. Swelling along with her pleasure, these undertones break out into a vibrato of chants and cries which steer my attention away from the visual spectacle of a woman masturbating toward another, imagined, one, of an archaic mourning ritual. Contrary to popular opinion, dance is not a "silent" art form. Most people find it difficult to dance without an audible breath, and vocal sounds can help the dancer achieve various qualities of movement. In this moment, Chouinard's voice is like another limb, stretching out into the space of the performance.

Over the course of a discussion concerning her use of vocal sounds in performance, Chouinard described her feelings about the human voice. Frustrated by the narrow limits of our usual monotone speech and feeling as if the traditional notes on a musical scale did not allow for a full expression of her individual voice, Chouinard chooses to explore instead the vocalization of her own body's movements and pleasures. In this way, as in the song of orgasm in "Mimas, lune de Saturne," she feels she finds a voice that expresses the uniqueness of her somatic experience, the sound of her body in motion. Vibrating through the air,

Chouinard's voice gives the audience a palpable kinesthetic experience of her body. Yet while her breath clearly generates the chanting, these sounds seem to turn around and repossess her. This cyclical looping out of her voice into the performance space and then back into her interior body creates a fascinating and important disjunction. Rather than affirming the voyeuristic potential of the scene, her eerie voice slices through that objectifying gaze, once again pulling the audience away from a comfortable state of passive watching.

For Derrida, voice suggests a metaphorics of "presence," which he sees as an outdated remnant of Western metaphysics. In this philosophical tradition, vocal expression is seen as the transcendent signifier of an authentic self—as if somehow one's voice always does what one wants it to—as if the voice is, in fact, consonant with the self. Eschewing voice in favor of writing, Derrida points to the deferral or suspension of direct reference in written texts. Ironically, he describes this textual free play as the "performativity" of writing. I doubt Derrida has ever seen Marie Chouinard; nor, I suspect, has he spent much time actually listening to the human voice. The fleshy presence of the voice in performance often exceeds or counters the body which sponsors it. And certainly in the above example, the voice pulls away from, instead of reinforcing or unifying, a "coherent" image of "a woman dancer." What we see in Chouinard's performance is the same kind of "performativity" with which Derrida imbues writing, but we see it through a live body and voice. Herein lies a crucial difference for feminist theory.

In her book *Thinking Fragments*, Jane Flax critiques Derrida for not including any discussion of the material condition of discourse in his discussion of sexual difference and writing. "What is still 'absent' (forbidden) is the in-corporation of 'woman' *qua* embodied, desiring, and concrete and differentiated being(s) *within* culture, language, ruling, or thinking *on our own terms* and not as man's 'other,' 'Object of desire,' or linguistic construct" (215). The reluctance on the part of many poststructuralists to deal critically and phenomenologically with the live female body is fear, I suspect, of being too weighed down with a kind of essentialist mass. This fear (which many feminists also share) is based on an oppressive image of the body as unconscious matter which tends to burp, fart, or menstruate at inconvenient and embarrassing moments. But simplistic biologism obviously doesn't begin to account for the many ways in which our bodies structure our consciousness. Looking at live dance performances and analyzing how those performers use their articulate bodies (and voices) help us reexamine the discussions of physicality and sexual identity so critical to contemporary feminist thought. In performance, women can consciously, creatively, confront what Mary Ann Doane calls the "double bind" of representation: "On the one hand, there is a danger in grounding a politics on a conceptualization of the body because the body has always been the site of women's oppression, posited as the final and undeniable guarantee of a difference and a lack; but, on the other hand, there is a potential gain as well—it is precisely because the body has been a major site of oppression that perhaps it must be the site of the battle to be waged."[12] Chouinard continues to wage that battle in her 1986 dance *S.T.A.B. (Space, Time and Beyond)*.

Naked, her body painted red and her face painted white, Chouinard emerges from the wings onto a vast, darkened, unadorned stage. Each step she makes resounds with the clank of her tin shoes. Enclosed within an aviator's helmet which sprouts a long white tube curving down to the floor, her head seems heavy

FIG. 19. Marie Chouinard in *S.T.A.B. (Space, Time, and Beyond)*. Photo: Louise Oligny

and slightly detached. Her movements are much less fluid than in *Marie Chien Noir*. Close, almost bound to the body, her movements are cautious and jerky, as if she is feeling out a new environment, testing the quality of the space around her. Soon the microphone attached to the helmet is amplifying her breathing as her body twists and turns. The microphone modulates her voice, and the sound projected out into the theater seems to come from deep inside her throat. Almost all of her motion is concentrated in her central torso, which twitches and convulses like that of an amphibian about to regurgitate a meal. Often Chouinard stands in one spot as the contractions of her body send up a harrowing series of screeching, gulping, growling. These sounds explode out to boomerang back into her body, sponsoring a new cycle of convulsions.

The cumulative effect of this twenty-minute solo is, well, weird. The no-man's land of the stage space and its otherwordly lighting effects give Chouinard's presence on stage a mystical, almost possessed, materiality. Gradually increasing in intensity and frequency throughout the course of her dance, Chouinard's vocalizations begin to echo themselves in an ongoing, layered conversation. Then, after a loud emission of these peculiar bodily sounds has faded out, Chouinard calmly takes off her headpiece and stands holding the white tube next to her as the lights dim in a very long fade.

What intrigues me in *S.T.A.B.* is the way the embodied languages of movement and voice work in tandem to create an opportunity for what Derrida identified as "a certain risky turbulence" in the representation of the female dancing body. Specifically, I am interested in how Chouinard's voice and movement create an ambiguous image in which it is unclear whether the vocal sounds are motivating the movement or the movement is forcing the body to speak. The technological frame of *S.T.A.B.* further enhances those peculiar moments by giving this image a slight shift in synchrony produced by the voice's amplification. As Doane documents in "The Voice in the Cinema: The Articulation of Body and Space," advances in filmic sound technology have allowed cinema to present an image (what she calls the "fantasmic" body) whose visual and vocal movements create a convincing embodied presence on the screen. Through the use of synchronous dialogue and the addition of various "natural" room sounds, the filmic soundtrack is "married" to the image to reinforce the blissful unity of illusion that is the backbone of traditional film. The sound enacts—makes real—the space framed by the story. Even the voice from off the screen (voice-off) belongs to a character situated in a space that is presumed just beyond the camera's focus. In this way, Doane argues, the voice is always tied to a visible (or imagined) body: "The voice-off is always 'submitted to the destiny of the body'" (35).

Breaking this blissful unity, however, is another use of vocal sound in film, the interior monologue, which employs the voice to display "what is inaccessible to the image, what exceeds the visible; the 'inner life' of the character" (41). Doane calls this a "disembodied" voice and discusses the subversive potential in its position outside a representation of the body. "It is its radical otherness with respect to the diegesis which endows this voice with a certain authority. . . . It is precisely because the voice is not localizable, because it cannot be yoked to a body, that it is capable of interpreting the image, producing its truth" (42). Presumably, then, this authority of the voice-over in the interior monologue could be used to present a fuller picture of a female character. Escaping the image of her body which is caught and held as an object-to-be-viewed in the apparatus of filmmaking, her voice could conceivably move with a great deal more freedom, commenting on the "truth" of the image.

Unfortunately, as Kaja Silverman demonstrates in the *The Acoustic Mirror: The Female Voice in Psychoanalysis and Cinema*, the female voice may be even less a woman's own than her body.[13] In traditional film, these voice-overs are what Silverman calls "thick with body"—desperate, breathing heavily, screaming, or about to die. The mechanisms of unity that Doane discusses in her article work, for Silverman, to resubmerge the female voice within the female body. In Silverman's analysis, for a voice to be "thick with body" is not (as it is for Cixous and Chouinard) liberating. Quite the contrary: Hollywood film in this light most often presents the female-embodied voice as a nonlinguistic, nondiscursive black hole.

In a chapter on feminist cinema, Silverman discusses the representation of the female body and the place of that body's voice in experimental film. Silverman contrasts the work of such women as Bette Gordon, Yvonne Rainer, Patricia Gruben, and Sally Potter, who try in their films to disengage the female's voice from the image of her body, with the "embodied" writing of *écriture féminine,* specifically the work of Luce Irigaray. In doing so, she sets up an unnecessarily narrow field of choice: a fatally embodied voice—"only at the price of its own impoverishment and entrapment" (141)—or a tragically disembodied one. Over the course of a careful intertexual analysis of Irigaray's work and that of experimental feminist filmmakers, Silverman argues convincingly for the potential of representing a female subject through the skillful use of the embodied voice. While she criticizes Irigaray's conflation of a discursive "writing the body" with real female bodies, Silverman seems to be recommending a deflation of the female subject down to her disembodied voice. What I object to most strongly, and why I see Chouinard's *S.T.A.B.* as a way out of this feminist maze of voice and body, is the sense that there is no freedom of movement in between the poles of a "silent" body and a bodiless voice—an implication which suggests that when it comes to the female body, every choreography is somehow already calculated.

"Thick with body," Chouinard's voice in *S.T.A.B.* serves as an extension of her body. Although it "exceeds the visible" and turns the body inside out (her voice comes from inside and is projected out), it is not exactly an interior monologue; the audience can plainly see the body which engenders the voice. The struggles of the body to produce the peculiar modulations of Chouinard's voice and the slight lapse of time between her speaking and its projection through the sound system create a rupture or an edge that makes the stage image strange. Her voice

FIG. 20. Marie Chouinard in *S.T.A.B. (Space, Time, and Beyond)*. Photo: Louise Oligny

hangs in the space between being fully embodied and completely disembodied, because the sounds don't seem to come "naturally" from her body. They don't even sound like what we might expect her voice to sound like. Distorted by her inhaling and exhaling while she talks, her voice roars in a throaty vibration not easily described as either feminine or masculine. In the midst of a performance completely predicated on the dialogue between the body and the voice, the effect of this slight echo is powerful indeed.

Suspended between her breath and its vocal amplification, Chouinard occupies a curious space in *S.T.A.B.* Aurally close yet visually distanced, her body drifts somewhere in between presence and absence. This double movement of coming forward and receding is the focus of Derrida's literary essay "Pas" (in a volume of collected writings on Maurice Blanchot titled *Parages*).[14] The word *pas* is a soft, short exhalation in French, a one-syllable word with a hundred different meanings. In its affirmative sense, *pas* can mean anything from "step," "pace," "footprint," "trace," "stride," "walk," "gait," "pass," "strait" to "dance," as in "pas de deux"—a dance for two. As an adverb, *pas* joins with *ne* to negate the statement at hand. Ringing like a mantra whose repetition gradually loosens meaning from its semantic moorings—"Passivité, passion, passé, pas" (54)—*pas* travels over all these possible references, forcing us to recognize the slipperiness of definitions. Submerged in Blanchot's liquid language, Derrida acts like a sponge, allowing Blanchot's words to expand and influence his own writing. In this piece, Derrida's language soaks up the sensuality of the moving body, presenting its texture within his text. Here the abstract theoretical take on dancing, as well as the clipped tone of his responses to MacDonald's questions in "Choreographies," gives way to a more sensual meditation.

In the midst of this ocean of Blanchot's work, Derrida drifts back and forth within the wavelike motions of *Parages* (literally "waters" in French). Caught in this double movement of coming and going within "Pas," Derrida moves beyond the usual parameters of literary criticism as he bathes in the moisture of Blanchot's work. Foregrounding the sensuality of the writing body, his words surround and are surrounded by another's tongue as citations of Blanchot's work mingle with Derrida's textual responsiveness. In this sense, "Pas" becomes a pas de deux, a love duet whose homoeroticism is both stunning and scriptural. Viens. Come. Those voices call to one another throughout the essay, and yet they can never actually meet, for the *pas* are always in transit. Their tango glides smoothly back and forth, back and forth, because for each step toward, there is always a complementary step away—theirs is a tango that refuses entanglement.

The palpable physicality in "Pas" is not unlike that in Cixous's writings. Although their rhythms are radically different (Cixous's work almost always pulsates with a constant, driving beat), their willingness to become immersed in the humidity of another's language and the erotic closeness to their subjects bring these different writers in "step" (*pas*) with one another. In "Coming to Writing," for instance, Cixous extends a meaning of the French word *pas* in a discussion that curiously echoes some of the literary implications of Derrida's own essay: "carving out a pass: the door, the route, wanting to go ahead, to keep exceeding the language of a text; to break with it and to make it a point of departure" (23). Cixous describes in this last phrase the double (and doubling) movements of "Pas," in which Derrida repeatedly interrupts the text in order to engage with it from a different perspective. Stepping away only to step back, he meets the text by crossing over boundaries of time and space to suspend it in his own writing. This movement is repeatedly marked by the list of prepositions and prepositional phrases with which Derrida describes his own approach to literary texts: "the literary texts I write *about, with, toward, for, . . . in the name of, in honor of, against,* perhaps too, *on the way toward.*"[15] This movement across—this trans/*pas*/ition—animates the various duets in "Pas." "I wrote a text, which in the face of the event of another's text, as it comes to me at a particular, quite singular, moment, tries to 'respond' or to 'countersign,' in an idiom which turns out to be mine" (62).

Cixous also speaks of writing about other texts as a crossing-over. But this circulation, the transition or translation of the other's text into one's own writing, includes for Cixous a different kind of transformation. "It is me, I, with the other, the other within me, it's one gender going into the other, one language going through the other."[16] Joined by the mesmerizing rhythm of their partnering, this couple exchanges roles, alternatively absorbing or being absorbed by one another's gender and language. This pas de deux implies a movement from the self into an other and vice versa. For Cixous, this interchange is predicated on a willingness to give and receive on both a physical as well as a textual level. Although this transformation of "self" into "other" does not collapse difference, it does radically redefine their "boundaries." The separation of language in terms of gender is thus treated less as an immutable fact of social discourse and more as a space to move through—an invitation to dance across sexual difference.

> One of the most important, most remarkable turnings or transitions or transits in writing is the one from one sex to the other—either imaginary or real, either for instance, the experience of going over from heterosexuality to homosexuality, or the one that Clarice Lispector tried to inscribe in *The Hour of the Star*, that extraordinary fact of her suddenly having to become a male writer, in order to be able to write on a particular character who is 'a woman.' Everything that has to do with 'trans,' including translation, has to do with sexuality, and as difference. (14)

In 1987 Chouinard created a dance based on photographs of Nijinski's *L'après-midi d'un faune*, called *La faune*.[17] In the same ways that *S.T.A.B.* deconstructs the image of a unified body, *La faune* works against traditional representations of sexual difference in dance. The story line of the original ballet is a classic narrative of male sexuality—what dance historian Lynn Garafola calls "a work of adolescent sexual awakening."[18] In her extensively researched book on art and enterprise in the Ballets Russes, Garafola distinguishes the poetic inspiration of Stéphane Mallarmé's poem of the same name from the actual performance. "Where the poem blurs the line between dream and reality, the ballet presents the erotic theme as lived experience: the reality of the Nymphs, like the scarf that sates the Faun's desire, is never in question" (56). Indeed, the narrative plot of the dance is quite simple: a faun sees a group of beautiful nymphs dancing around, gets excited, and chases them. The nymphs flee, but one drops a scarf which the faun retrieves and fetishizes, later "making love" to it in the infamous orgasmic ending of the dance. The ballet was experimental for its time (it premiered in Paris in 1912) in its use of stark two-dimensional profile positions and severely bound stylized movements. These innovations served to heighten the intensity of Nijinski's final phallic pose, which created an explosive scandal throughout the Parisian art world.

Working always in profile, Chouinard uses only a thin downstage slice of the space, traversing the stage laterally, back and forth, back and forth. She is dressed in a skin-colored unitard with extra padding on one thigh and the other calf, and a headpiece consisting of two large ramlike horns. Still, poised with the attentiveness of a hunter, her gaze steadily scans the horizon as a soundtrack of repetitive breathing gradually crescendos. Her steps are bulky and uneven, belying a fiercely bound sexual energy which explodes unexpectedly in thrusts and quivers of her pelvis. Time and again a contraction grips her body, bringing her to her knees. As the breathing becomes louder and louder, it takes on an industrial, almost menacing quality. What was once an internal accompaniment to Chouinard's movements becomes an external, oppressive sound, forcing her to continue. Images of an injured animal, a predator, a bacchant, even of Nijinski himself dart across this tableau. Then Chouinard breaks off a section of her horn and attaches it to her crotch. What previously had been an image, a movement quality, crystallizes into a surreal moment as Chouinard, exhausted after an increasingly forceful series of pelvic thrusts, moves into Nijinski's final pose.

Explaining her interest in experimenting with Nijinski's dance, Chouinard emphasizes this great dancer's performing presence and his ability to transform himself on stage. "He could transform himself, become totally unrecognizable. I am inspired by his complex vocabulary of movements and am drawn physically as much as intellectually to his strength and the strangeness of his movements."[19] A note on the program of the 1987 Festival International de Nouvelle Danse describes Chouinard's presence in this piece as "other than human." Although Nijinski was famous for being able to completely transform himself into the character he was dancing, his role in *L'après-midi d'un faune* is rarely seen by the reviewers of his time as "other than human": even though his movements and demeanor are strange or animal-like, he still takes on the traditional male sexual role in this narrative movement of desire. In translating this role onto her own body, Chouinard takes on the physical intensity of that desire, but she breaks up its erotic narrative by replacing the central object of Nijinski's desire (first the nymph and then the scarf) with an evanescent sign—rays of light. She connects her interpretation of *L'après-midi d'un faune* to Mallarmé's pastoral poem in which he asks, "Did I dream that love?" Chouinard explains: "The Nymphs don't really interest me. It's the ambivalence of the object of desire that I find marvelous."[20]

Chouinard has reshaped Nijinski's dance in two central and seemingly contradictory ways. By concentrating her focus on the intensity of the faun's desire, Chouinard at once affirms that desire and makes it strange. No matter how impressive Chouinard is in her intense, almost hungry physicality, the audience is always aware that she is a woman in the position of a man. Yet she does not seem awkward or out of place. The female body in the place of male desire does not negate the position or the movement. Rather, like Chouinard's voice in *S.T.A.B.*, her body at once completes and fractures that desire. Somehow, there seems to be

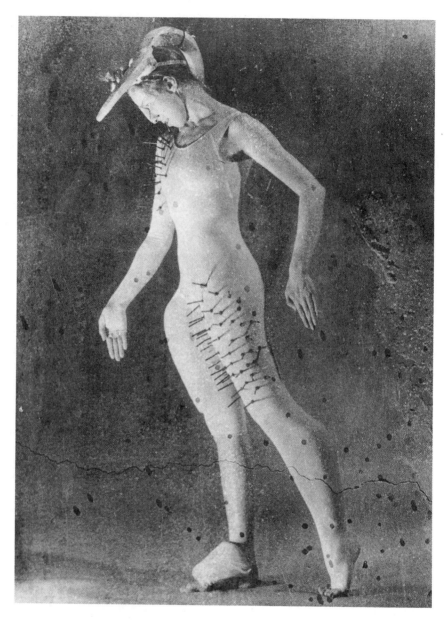

F<small>IG</small>. 21. Marie Chouinard in *La faune*. Photo: Benny Chou

a physical reality in her representation of the faun's desire that also feeds the integrity of her own body. Becoming a heshe on stage does not erase the material sheness of Chouinard's body, but it does begin to question a number of assumptions about the polarity of male and female desire.

Chouinard's use of lighting effects as a diaphanous stand-in for the nymph and her scarf further complicates this scenario. At the same time that she seriously enacts this scene of male yearning (there is no sense of campiness during this solo), Chouinard frames it somewhat ironically. In order to take on the phallus, she has to first break it off her head—an action which, taken out of context, suggests some humorous images. On a less comic level, her costume has dartlike projections attached to it, and it is ambiguous whether they symbolize horns of the faun, the literal expression of the faun's sexuality, or the arrows of a hunter. In *La faune*, male desire, which is generally predicated on an object—an "other"—is given a vivid representation in the midst of an absence of the other. By becoming invisible in the scenario of *La faune*, the other—the nymph, the woman—becomes visible in another (an "other") light, one projected by the narrative of her own desire.

Intellectually, Chouinard's reconstruction/deconstruction of Nijinski's dance is both witty and provocative. But it is also deeply compelling in a way we haven't yet developed a language to describe. The shifting triad of desire— Chouinard's desire to capture Nijinski's physical presence, the faun's desire for the nymph who eludes him, and Chouinard's translation of that desire into her body—flows in and around the choreography like a series of small waves, gently tugging the audience back and forth. Swept up in this co-motion, Chouinard embodies both the textual and the physical referents of Nijinski's *L'après-midi d'un faune.*

Seeing Chouinard physicalize her own yearning in the midst of embodying the historic choreography of a mythic dancer and the classic narrative of a mythic faun, one begins to recognize how completely layered with representation and innovation our bodies can be. In addition to physicalizing the faun's desire, she also occupies the spotlight of that which is desired: the nymph, the scarf, the woman, the "other." Shifting in and out of this intangible light, Chouinard "steps" back and forth between writer and dancer, faun and nymph, Nijinski and herself, body and text. As in the writing of Derrida and Cixous discussed earlier in this essay, Chouinard's performance of *La faune* crosses over these boundaries of "self" and "other" so frequently that the very categories begin to lose their meaning. What is left, then, is the dance created by the movement between those places. Chouinard's transformations back and forth from female to male and vice versa are rarely definite and are never complete. The minute shaking movements which are a result of the determined tension in her body vibrate with the traces of both sexes, confounding the audience at the very same moment that the shaking excites us. In this sense, Chouinard's *La faune* embodies both Derrida's dream for a "choreography [which] can carry, divide, multiply the body of each

FIG. 22. Marie Chouinard in *La faune*. Photo: Benny Chou

'individual' whether he be classified as 'man' or as 'woman' according to the criteria of usage," and Cixous's vision of "texts that are made of flesh. When you read these texts, you receive them as such. You feel the rhythm of the body, you feel the breathing" ("Difficult Joys" 27). That Chouinard accomplishes this without sacrificing the material presence of her own physicality shows us how much feminist theory can learn from dance performances.

By actually—physically—dancing across sexual difference, Chouinard's *La faune* severs any essentialist bonds between a biological body and its appropriate sexuality. On the other hand, by being physically present in this performance, Chouinard also refuses the slippery poststructuralist notion of difference which, in its most absolute manifestation, seems never to reside in *any body*. Chouinard's choreography stretches the theoretical terms of our discourse and forces us to recognize that it is not the *fact* of her body (or its absence) on which we must focus our attention, but rather it is *how* that body is dancing which is critical here. Realizing the physical presence of the writer and the reader, the dancer and the audience—the body and the text—doesn't mean we have to reconstitute an authentic interpretation or a definitive exchange of meanings (either sexual, textual, or in movement) within those interactions. As consciously trained and creatively choreographed, Chouinard's dancing body enacts a thoughtful engagement with her own representation which urges us to consider a more complex and experiential understanding of physical bodies and social discourse. By bringing Derrida, Cixous, and Chouinard into dialogue with one another, I have shown that discursive bodies and real ones can lean on one another in a mutual dependence that provides a point of contact through which ideas, inspirations, and ultimately movements can travel. The dances born of this interdependence can play with new motions—both theoretical and physical—and sift through a variety of choreographies. Rather than defining a single position (either theoretical or physical) for the female body, I am interested in exploring the intertextuality between writing and dancing bodies, knowing that, however incalculable, these are never inconsequential choreographies.

NOTES ⎯ ⎯ ⎯ ⎯ ⎯ ⎯ ⎯

1. After studying a multitude of diverse movement techniques, including ballet, t'ai chi, modern dance, and contact improvisation, Chouinard began to shape her own style of performance in 1978. For a long time her publicity information insistently underscored her solo status: "Marie Chouinard's work is resolutely

personal. . . . An independent choreographer, she dances solo and interprets only her own pieces." Recently, however, she has begun to work with her own dance company. During the eighties, Chouinard's work coincided with an explosion of experimental dance in Quebec, and she is well known as part of the dance renaissance in Montreal.

2. Jacques Derrida and Christie MacDonald, "Choreographies," *Diacritics* 12.2 (1982): 66–76, reprinted in this volume.

3. For a more in-depth discussion of this problematic move in Derrida, see Jane Flax, *Thinking Fragments* (Berkeley: University of California Press, 1990); and Diana Fuss, *Essentially Speaking: Feminism, Nature, and Difference* (New York: Routledge, 1989).

4. *Marie Chien Noir* premiered in 1982; I saw the first section, "Mimas, lune de Saturne," at Dance Theater Workshop in New York City in October 1985.

5. "Panel: Canadian Choreography—The Development and Practise of the Craft" (transcript), *Dance Connection*, March/April 1988, pp. 19–23.

6. In an interview with the author (Montreal, October 15, 1988), Chouinard registered her exasperation with the critical reception of her work which focuses only on the afterimage of her body, not the actual presence of its performance: "It's incredible! . . . they [the critics] never speak of my dance, how I move, only the impression I made upon them."

7. "She is part woman, part animal, switching back and forth until one loses any sense of her as human. She becomes a mythic vision from another world, a creature who moves and screeches, warbles and screams with unparalleled intensity" (Linda Howe-Beck, *Montreal Gazette*, April 1986). "Chouinard dances like an extraterrestrial creature" (Ine Rietsap, N.R.C. Amsterdam, 1986). Out of ten reviews of Chouinard's work (describing three different dances), eight described her persona as either a "creature," "sorceress," or "witch."

8. Hélène Cixous and Catherine Clément, *The Newly Born Woman* (Minneapolis: University of Minnesota Press, 1986); Hélène Cixous, "Coming to Writing," in *"Coming to Writing" and Other Essays*, ed. Deborah Jenson (Cambridge: Harvard University Press, 1991).

9. The relationship of the body to writing has been extremely problematic in feminist theory. During the 1980s, this discussion often ended up staged as a debate between Anglo-American and French feminist theorists. The scope of this chapter does not allow me to take up the terms of this debate, but many anthologies and essays have focused on this issue. For general discussions of French feminist thought see Elaine Marks and Isabelle de Courtivron, eds., *New French Feminisms* (New York: Schocken Books, 1981); Toril Moi, *Sexual/Textual Politics* (New York: Methuen, 1985); and Nancy Fraser and Sandra Lee Bartky, eds., *Revaluing French Feminism* (Bloomington: Indiana University Press, 1992). For discussions of the role of "feminine writing" in Cixous's work, see Helen Wilcox, Keith McWatters, Ann Thompson, and Linda Williams, eds.,

The Body and the Text: Hélèn Cixous, Reading and Teaching (New York: St. Martin's Press, 1990); and Verena Conley, *Hélène Cixous: Writing the Feminine* (Lincoln: University of Nebraska Press, 1984).

10. See Fuss, esp. chap. 1.

11. Marie Chouinard, publicity materials, 1985.

12. Mary Ann Doane, "The Voice in the Cinema: The Articulation of Body and Space," *Yale French Studies*, no. 60 (1980): 33–50.

13. Kaja Silverman, *The Acoustic Mirror: The Female Voice in Psychoanalysis and Cinema* (Bloomington: Indiana University Press, 1988).

14. Jacques Derrida, "Pas," in *Parages* (Paris: Éditions Galilée, 1986), 9–116.

15. "This Strange Institution Called Literature," an interview with Jacques Derrida by Derek Attridge, in Jacques Derrida, *Acts of Literature*, ed. Derek Attridge (New York: Routledge, 1992), 41.

16. Hélène Cixous, "Difficult Joys," in *The Body and the Text*, 14.

17. This work premiered on July 9, 1987, at the Ottawa National Arts Center. I saw its U.S. premiere two days later, on July 11, 1987, at the Pepsico Summer-fare Festival, N.Y. The photographs of Nijinski in *L'après-midi d'un faune*, by Adolphe de Meyer, on which Chouinard's dance is based, were published in 1983 in a book of the same title by Dance Horizons Press, New York. Although the 1987 programs give the title as *La faune*, later publicity packets—in an interesting slippage of the original and the copy—refer to the dance as either *Le faune*, or *L'après-midi d'un faune*.

18. Lynn Garafola, *Diaghilev's Ballets Russes* (New York: Oxford University Press, 1989), 56.

19. Chouinard, publicity materials, 1987.

20. Interview with the author, Montreal, October 15, 1988.

Force and Form in Faulkner's Light in August

Ellen W. Goellner

Halfway through chapter 15 of *Light in August*, William Faulkner describes the movement of gossip through his fictional community:

> Through the long afternoon they clotted about the square and before the jail—the clerks, the idle, the countrymen in overalls; the talk. It went here and there about the town, dying and borning again like a wind or a fire until in the lengthening shadows the country people began to depart in wagons and dusty cars and the townspeople began to move supperward. The talk flared again, momentarily revived, to wives and families about supper tables in electrically lighted rooms and in remote hill cabins with kerosene lamps. And the next day, the slow, pleasant country Sunday while they squatted in their clean shirts and decorated suspenders, with peaceful pipes about country churches or about the shady dooryards of houses where the visiting teams and cars were tethered and parked along the fence and the womenfolks were in the kitchen, getting dinner, they told it again.[1]

Joe Christmas has been captured; the Hineses have arrived. This description of "the talk" circulating through Mottstown and the surrounding countryside, "dying and borning again like a wind or a fire," and of how "the talk flared again, momentarily revived" characterizes not only most of the town's action and presence in Faulkner's novel, and not only that of certain prominent characters, but—in some crucial ways—the very dynamics of Faulkner's textual practice. Like gossip's dance through his fictional community, Faulkner's assays and experiments in *Light in August* work not toward a single, climactic, and revelatory moment, but instead as a continual redirection and transformation of textual energy through his characters' recountings and retellings, both of their lives and the lives of others. In their gossip—their reinvention of what happened and why—and in the ceaseless repetitions—of names and family configurations, images and fears, solitude and remembering—that mark their stories, Faulkner creates the centripetal and centrifugal patterns that are *Light in August*. In his novel, Faulkner continues to take structural and stylistic risks that he had taken in the earlier novels, then complicates and polishes those moves. What he was after in

Light in August was what he sought earlier in *The Sound and the Fury, As I Lay Dying*, and *Sanctuary*, and would achieve brilliantly in *Absalom, Absalom!*: to have his stories formally enact "the furious motion of being alive."[2]

In looking at the narrative dynamics of *Light in August*, I propose a shift away from the conceptual framework found in largely male-coded narrative theories, limited by analogies between narrative principles and psychoanalytic (usually Freudian) principles.[3] The prominence of Freud's theory of homeostatic desire in current narrative theory makes it difficult to separate the conception of how a narrative works from the psychoanalytic workings of a narrative's characters. I find it crucial to make this separation when reading Faulkner, however, for while characters such as Joe Christmas from *Light in August* seem indeed to strive toward a passive state, to be in pursuit of those inner freedoms from tension which signal a return to quiescence, the novel does not unfold toward that state, nor is my experience of reading Faulkner's novel analogous to his characters' psychosexual strivings.

The idea that narrative desire ultimately seeks and achieves discharge in a moment of epiphanic or heuristic climax, and that that desire must be bound in place lest it discharge prematurely, is antithetical to the working of energy in *Light in August*. Most desire theorists (e.g., Peter Brooks, Leo Bersani, the Barthes of *The Pleasure of the Text*) see a text's energy accruing in order to discharge, so that controlling the relatively short supply of the novel's textual energy becomes a matter of careful accumulation and expenditure by the author. According to this framework, *Light in August* would fail either because it lacks adequate discharge (of the force of its plotting and characterization) or because its structures do not sufficiently rein in the narrative energy.

I believe Faulkner is after a very different kind of energetics.[4] Faulkner's seventh novel is a system that requires motion nearly for its own sake, much as dance does; it sets up relations of tension, exhibiting textual forces and their effects in order to represent the dynamic forces and regulations of the southern town. In contrast to models of gathered energy and controlled discharge, *Light in August*'s energy is *excessive*. This results in a dynamic system that is very nearly—but never quite—out of control. Faulkner is not attempting a narrative that comes to a satisfying rest but is exploring dynamic patterns that ceaselessly redirect energy as do the particular structures of modern dance; his problems in *Light in August* lie in counterbalancing the novel's centrifugal forces with its centripetal forces.

If, as reader-response theorist Wolfgang Iser explains, reading "causes the literary work to unfold its inherently dynamic character" and sets the literary work in motion,[5] a descriptive study of *Light in August* must reveal the dynamism that is part of the work's read totality. This immediately re-creates for the critic of *Light in August* the problem that Faulkner continually confronted in writing and one that continually confronts dance critics. The literary critic, like the dance critic, must of necessity freeze that motion temporarily in order to study it.[6] It would thus seem a given irony that only by slowing down and separating a literary or dance text into static and discrete parts can we talk about the dynamics of that text. But as literary critics, our analytic discourse is particularly ill-equipped for the study of things in flux or for considering the motions of bodies and nervous systems. By contrast, the language of dance and its attendant ideas of motion, inertia, movment dynamics, even gravity, may allow the literary critic ways to conceive anew both motion and energy—in this case, textual energy, but also the "social energy" recently described by Stephen Greenblatt[7]—and to see relationships between this motion and that.

The suggestion that "read" bodily movement and read narrative are seriously analogous is not as far-fetched as it may at first sound. In his essay "The Tensor," comparing textual practices, Jean-François Lyotard addresses semioticians on reading signs or signifiers, and offers a provocative, if incidental, analogy between dance and reading:

> we read it differently. You say it speaks to you? It sets us in motion. . . . We don't start off by saying to ourselves: someone or something is speaking to us here, so I must try to understand. To understand, to be intelligent, is not our overriding passion. We strive instead to be set in motion. This is why our passion would be more like the dance that Nietzsche wanted, and that Cage and Cunningham continue to look for.[8]

Drawing on investigations in anthropology, psychology, philosophy, and semiotics, literary theory since the 1950s has turned to languages of the body, most often sexual and erotic experience, for saying things about narrative and textual practices. Theorists such as Roland Barthes and Julia Kristeva, however, tend to re-estrange the body through abstract psychocultural reconstructions of desire and sexuality. I want to insist on the importance of the material body for understanding the way a text—in this case, Faulkner's *Light in August*—does its work. The analogy of narrative dynamics to dance allows this in ways that psychoanalytically based conceptions do not.

A dance understanding of *Light in August* both foregrounds the gendered and raced bodies in Faulkner's novel and directs our attention to formal elements, such as the narrative device of gossip, which act as infusions of or drains on the energy that animates (and is) our reading of that text. Indeed, my misgivings about current desire theories arise in part from how much they hypostatize readings, fix points of steady reference and sequence. This fixity and progressivism cannot address *Light in August*'s thematic concern with "lawlessness" and unintelligibility. Moreover, if looked at through this alternative energy model, *Light in August* neither fails to reach climax nor climaxes and ends prematurely. Events do not necessarily develop over time, lead inexorably toward climaxes, and die away; nor is there a final moment of completion, in which the total pattern of the work becomes instantaneously clear. In some respects, *Light in August* even works to sabotage our expectation of development and resolution as it instructs us in how to perceive its much freer play of energy.

In a literary text as in a movement sequence, it is possible, once the work's underlying kinetic logic has been intuited, to identify and describe specific formal elements that govern that logic. For instance, where centripetal forces dominate in nineteenth-century fiction and classical ballet, stability is achieved partially through a principle of hierarchic order among the parts: subordinate centers of interest play "minor" roles formally and thematically. Highly dissipative and unstable dynamics tend to dominate modernist and postmodernist fiction, and especially postmodernist choreography. In such works, a multiplicity of centers (i.e., of principal characters or events) and antiprotagonist, antihierarchical structures require the writer's or choreographer's balancing of many individual coequal or nearly coequal parts. In this regard, dances by Merce Cunningham, Trisha Brown, Lucinda Childs, Steve Paxton, and Meredith Monk have taught dance audiences not to need a principal dancer and not to have to see everything that happens on the dance stage, that is, all the bodies, their connections, progressions, and movements. Like these choreographers, Faulkner risks frustrating his audience's expectations—in this case, by making it impossible to follow all the myriad connections, repetitions, and progressions in his novel. Faulkner once explained that writing style is "like anything else, to be alive it must be in motion too. If it becomes fixed, then it's dead, it's just rhetoric" (*Faulkner in the University* 279).

So in *Light in August*, I see particular elements directing textual energies in integrative patterns to pull the story toward stability: genealogical structures, logico-temporal chains, repetition-as-connection, symmetry, represented bonds of love or blood. Likewise, I identify highly dissipative patterns that work to destabilize the novel: the nonclosure of individual stories within the novel, the novel's open frame, polyphonic storytelling, multiple centers of judgment, repetition-as-difference or -deferral, destructive or transgressive versions of kinship, violence, and eroticism. Gossip is one site where the above tensions play out.

Broadly put, gossip is the main mode of communication and storytelling in *Light in August*: Byron gossips to Hightower and Hightower to Byron, Joanna to Joe, Joe to Bobbie and to Joanna, Lena to Byron and Mrs. Armstid, Mrs. Hines to Hightower, the deputy sheriff to the townspeople, Gavin Stevens to his visiting friend, Doc Hines to anyone who can bear to listen to him, and sundry town and country people in and around Jefferson and Mottstown to each other. Not surprisingly, *Light in August* is convoluted. Most of the action takes place in and around Jefferson and Mottstown during a week in August, beginning with the arrival on foot of very pregnant and unwed Lena Grove on the day Joanna Burden's nearly decapitated body is found outside her burning house. The stories unfold as Lena tracks the fleeing father of her unborn baby and the townspeople hunt Joanna's murderer.

Faulkner's use of the social act of gossip—and the literal and figurative acts of reading which gossip entails—allows him to explore the possibility of locating the self within (or outside or behind) the community, the family, and the social status quo.[9] The communities in the novel act through their refashioning of events, their attempts to get the story fixed and unfixed. In this refashioning of the narrative world, Faulkner's community is threatened—disequilibriated—at all its edges by both events and talk, and his "major" characters (marginal members of the little society when the novel opens) are in like fashion threatened and disequilibriated by the community. The assumptions and fears of the culture that Faulkner writes about in *Light in August* allow only a narrowly circumscribed area for the self-representations and self-inventions of blacks, women, the poor, and for those not part of the monogamous heterosexual mainstream. In giving voices to Lena, Joanna, Byron, Joe, and Hightower—if only through the indirect discourse of the overarching narrative voice—Faulkner allows these traditionally marginalized figures to occupy an area usually ascribed to upper-class, white, heterosexual men, townsmen like Gavin Stevens and the sheriff.[10] Faulkner's reliance on more marginalized voices to tell a large part of his story results in an authorial skepticism unmasking what Wesley Morris and Barbara Alverson Morris call "discursive repression."[11] As such, *Light in August*'s principal narrative voice in effect swings both ways: it becomes the public voice of the community, and it presents the private voices of individuals marginal to that community. Both ways, it seems, lie gossip: first, as a dispersed public voice representing a community judgment; second, as nonmainstream, alternative, subversive sets of histories.

Gossip, of course, has some straight-ahead commonalities with narration: it discloses plot, for instance, and Faulkner presents much of what happens in the novel through gossip. Chapter 2 begins, "Byron Bunch knows this: It was one Friday morning three years ago" (31), and goes on to reveal information about Joe's arrival in Jefferson, his early move to the Burden plantation, and his alliance with Lucas Burch and their whiskey business. Gossip chronicles Lena's tracking of Lucas Burch and the town's pursuit of Joanna Burden's murderer. There is more to it, though: the texture of the reading—and the open inquiries and ambiguous emotions it prompts—are especially linked to gossip. While social storytelling can lay down a sequential path of "plot" through the text, revelation by revelation, it can also restlessly wipe away previously "established" events and leave readers uncomfortable with the status or context of the information they get.

The voices of the gossiping characters join Faulkner's writing and our reading. Using gossip as narration, Faulkner attempts a story whose very telling is fundamentally open to change and restatement, negations, reinterpretation. Exemplifying what the Morrises call Faulkner's "aesthetics of revision" (61), the gossip in *Light in August* tends to be busy about the piecing together of information, filling in the gaps around what is known in order to make a meaningful, if not truly seamless, whole. This tendency to integration is in large part what I mean by *centripetal*: seeing gossip as a thematic pattern or a structure of communication helps make *Light in August* intelligible as a performance, and intelligible for the characters and readers who take part.

The sense that the reader makes of a character or story is always provisional exactly because the characters and stories are held together in a continual play of shifting connections, as in dance. Sometimes a character's story bears an uncanny resemblance to a story told by another distant and unrelated character—stories about Joanna's and Hightower's fathers and grandfathers, for instance. One character's story may even seem to the reader to continue a story told earlier by or about an unrelated character, as happens between the Milly Hines and Lena Grove accounts. Because the lives of such characters never intersect, because only the reader is positioned to hear all the stories, and because there is no sustained hierarchical order setting one story or character as foil to another, the meaning of the momentary mirrorings of lives and stories is not easily discerned. From the meta-analyst reader's interpretive vantage point, then, the multivocal and restlessly provisional qualities of *Light in August*'s gossip keep judgment from forming—keep a moral or circumstance or single voice from asserting itself and dominating interpretation. And this is largely what I mean by *centrifugal* textual energies.

Although I am interested in constructions of the integrative as well as explosive movement of bodies, I am most interested in how gossip in *Light in August* countervails the steadier centripetal pulls of Faulkner's novel. In some specific ways, gossip redirects the textual energy of Faulkner's story outward into increasingly complex fractal-like patterns; this formal design involves the reader intimately—as a voyeur of the town's or characters' proper knowledge, and as a visitor subject in part to the bewildering instability, caprice, and violence of their world. What follows is a look at a few of the ways that gossip, as an element of narrative design, sets up and counters the integrative pulls of Faulkner's novel.

Faulkner's shift in this novel toward "community" knowing includes returning some power and privilege to the community and underlining the physicality of the (re)making of knowledge and law. Talk is staged, contextualized, respected; it is understood as the property of the participants. One measure of that proprietary nature of the talk and knowing is the uncomfortable voyeuristic experience of witnessing as well as overhearing. As the characters share news and stories, Faulkner brings their bodies into momentary proximity or union, moving narrative energy through connected bodies rather than abstracted words and disembodied space. Before either Byron or Hightower utters a word in their evening gossip together (chap. 4), Faulkner describes their physical positions: "They sit facing one another across the desk. The study is lighted now, by a greenshaded reading lamp sitting upon the desk. Hightower sits behind it, in an ancient swivel chair, Byron in a straight chair opposite. Both their faces are just without the direct downward pool of light from the shaded lamp" (77). In this and other accounts of gossiping characters, Faulkner uses physical space and the placement of actual bodies to figure the closeness or possibilities of closeness between characters: they face one another, study one another, sit across from or beside one another. Faulkner has his characters encounter the other and the self in the other through the physical relationships that the dance of gossip entails—both in the intimacies of its telling and in the intimate concerns it addresses. *Light in August* teases readers in and out of the gossiped world—in much the same way that we are included in or excluded from the gossip marking our own lives. The edginess this may bring to readers is marked, too, by the discomforts of the characters: very often, the light familiarity we tend to think of as a setting for gossip is replaced by darkness, by watchfulness, by the characters' faces "just without the . . . pool of light" (77).

In her discussion of old age and "the struggle to stay alive . . . to maintain one's extension out into the world," theorist of the body Elaine Scarry explains that "the voice becomes a final source of self-extension; so long as one is speaking, the self extends out beyond the boundaries of the body, occupies a space much larger than the body."[12] Through their voices, Faulkner's characters are able to expand and interconnect. Patricia Meyer Spacks explains that the "value of gossip at its highest level involves its capacity to create and intensify human connection" (19). In *Light in August*, to engage in gossip as listener or teller signals the social movement of a character and the terms of that individual's engagement with or disengagement from others. As social performance, the absence of telling or hearing by a character serves to underscore that character's (or, as above, the reader's) position outside the community. The novel's characters form a network, organized to move with tensions and resolutions, balance and imbalance, in a precarious unity. This network of relations weaves itself into a centripetal momentum, to rein in the novel's burgeoning group of seemingly disparate characters—and its flood of words.

But the creation of these social boundaries and intrapersonal identities requires a huge aggregation of talk and cross-talk and no-talk, which in its very unwieldiness threatens to fall apart. The fragility of this world, the real sense of danger and of invention that it invokes, provides us in Faulkner's design with a very complex experience (or threat) of self-disintegration—importantly like that which Joe, Hightower, and Joanna undergo within a racist and misogynist culture.

Perhaps a stronger counter that gossip in *Light in August* presents to the gathering centripetal movement of Faulkner's novel is its subject matter. In discussing the power and attraction of gossip, Spacks explains that its "fascination bears some relation to that of pornography. . . . Gossip, even when it avoids the sexual, bears about it a faint flavor of the erotic. . . . The atmosphere of erotic titillation suggests gossip's implicit voyeurism. . . . A relatively innocent form of the erotics of power . . . this excitement includes the heady experience of imaginative control: gossip claims other people's experience by interpreting it into story" (11). Topics of gossip in *Light in August* include illegitimacy, rape, homosexuality, "nymphomania," sodomy, miscegenation, violence on the part of the Ku

Klux Klan, lynching, castration, decapitation. There's gossip about Lena's illegitimate pregnancy and Byron's fascination with her. There has been in the novel's past a great deal of talk about Hightower's "unnatural" sexuality. Joe's presence electrifies the town with talk of interracial sex—either because he is himself believed to be the product of miscegenation, or because, as he is perceived to be a black man (hence sexually rapacious) able to pass as white, he is thought to be an insidious sexual threat to white women. Jacquelyn Dowd Hall explains that rape and rumors of rape in the South during 1900–1940 (and thus at the time Faulkner was writing *Light in August*) had become a kind of "folk pornography."[13] Any one of these topics of gossip can be volatile material for a story, but Faulkner packs them all into *Light in August*. Oddly, critics of *Light in August* tend to play down and diffuse the violent and erotic subjects of the novel. And though no single violent or erotic event or subject is what Faulkner's novel is about—that is, we would not say that *Light in August* is *about* rape or miscegenation, the KKK, or alleged homosexuality—collectively, the energy-effects of its content play a crucial role in the dynamics of the narrative.

Faulkner, of course, knew that literary pornography and violence, overdone or done poorly, could be dull. But he was also well aware of the shock value that violent and erotic literature can have—as his own story of Temple Drake and Popeye had had a year earlier—and of the saleability of detective-story potboilers. As he had done in *Sanctuary*, Faulkner taps into the volatility of violent and pornographic subject matter in *Light in August* and transforms that subject matter into something more than the stuff of "pulp novels or trashy magazine photos that serve up their fantasies straight."[14] In *Light in August,* violent and erotic episodes and images work against the closure of representation. These elements threaten to disintegrate Faulkner's representational project with expressions and confessions of perverse or transgressive desire, that is, desire that twists away, often violently, from the conventional and familiar. In "Pornography, Transgression, and the Avant-Garde," Susan Rubin Suleiman discusses pornography, modern writing, and the "metaphoric equivalences between textual violation and the violation of bodies" (123); the essay traces the "transfer . . . of the notion of transgression from the realm of experience . . . to the realm of words" (120) in the French tradition of "transgressive writing" founded by Marquis de Sade and running through Georges Bataille. She sees the elaboration of a "metaphoric equivalence between the violation of *sexual* taboos and the violation of *discursive* norms" (119). Leo Bersani also looks at Bataille's fiction, although not nearly as thoughtfully as Suleiman, and analyzes the relation between literary pornography, especially violent pornography, and writing. He offers the useful insight that violent and erotic images or scenes in literature can be charged and used to attack and break down both cultural structures and the psychic continuity of characters.[15]

In keeping with Suleiman's version of the avant-garde—and against the backdrop of the pulps—Faulkner's representations of violent and erotic moments are not conventionally explicit. Their power comes from the salient detail—"the buckle raking across the negro's back" during the sheriff's interrogation (293); Joe's (possibly "nigger") "hand . . . slow and quiet on [Bobbie's] invisible flank" as the two lie naked together in the dark (196)—and from what he withholds from the prurient gaze. As violence and erotics are subjects of gossip and triggers to repulsion, outrage, or arousal, they create an energetics of overload in Faulkner's text. Restrained and stylized depictions as they may be, the explosive events accumulate to rock Faulkner's novel, send it reeling off balance; they even threaten to destroy the novel by virtue of their volatility—their taboo and horrific status. The novel asks to be put down, or turned away from, as it invites the gaze.

And if, as Spacks notes, the erotic/violent content is parceled with "imaginative control," the prevalent and destructive powers of gossip in the hands of the community place a premium on regaining control of one's representation and one's voice. Both the text of *Light in August* and the emblematic figures of Joe and Joanna show the stakes and the precarious, ambiguous nature of that control. For instance, when the stories Faulkner's characters tell one another do not give up their secrets easily—as Joanna's story does not—when their gossip stalls or breaks off, or when a character snatches part of a story away from another character-narrator and refashions it, the novel's gossip interrupts narrative continuity and directs its textual energy outward and around into more intricate patterns. In chapter 16, for example, the narrative that Byron and Mrs. Hines construct for Hightower is threatened by Doc Hines's repeated and raging interruptions: "Bitchery and abomination! . . . he shouts the three words with outrageous and prophetlike suddeness, and that is all" (370–371). Byron tries to explain Doc Hines to Hightower, but before he gets very far, the "old man interrupts again, with that startling suddenness. But he does not shout this time: his voice now is calm and logical as Byron's own" (371). Byron and Mrs. Hines eventually manage to get the telling back from Doc Hines, but only for a short while. "'It's God's abomination of womanflesh!' the old man cries suddenly. Then his voice drops, lowers; it is as though he were merely gaining attention. He talks again rapidly, his tone plausible, vague, fanatic, speaking of himself again in the third person. 'He knowed. Old Doc Hines knowed'" (373–374).

Voice and story are pitted in this scene against voice and story, destroying dialogue, bifurcating the story to be told, and leaving the reader, like Hightower, hard-pressed to see a point in all the argumentative gossip. Eventually, however, Byron and Mrs. Hines win back their telling and are able to give Hightower details of Joe's mother's family. But their shared disclosure only *appears* to advance the novel's story at this point. Their unasked-for telling actually feels to Hightower like a violation of his privacy and isolation, and he becomes increasingly anxious to know *why* they have made him listen to their story: "'What is it they want me to do? What must I do now? Byron! Byron? What is it? What are they asking of me now?' . . . I am not clairvoyant, like you. . . . What is it you want me to do? Shall I go plead guilty to the murder? Is that it?'" (386). The chapter ends, of course, with Byron's explosive proposition to Hightower: "'You could say he was here with you that night'" (390). Byron's proposition carries powerful force precisely because it taps into and is the attempt to exploit the past gossip about Hightower's homosexuality.

His proposition gains even more force as Hightower and readers share the listener's position in this interchange, not knowing how "it" will turn out or what is to be done about "it." In a discomfiting strategy, Hightower and readers are linked as effete and menaced, helpless as events begin to loom and the worst of bad histories is reinvoked. We first hear of Hightower's sexual history almost three hundred pages earlier in what would look and feel in a conventional novel like a disclosure scene—Byron's recollection in chapter 3 of the town gossip he heard when he arrived in Jefferson seven years earlier. Faulkner, however, uses this gossip both to check the forward movement begun in chapters 1 and 2 and to establish an atmosphere and context of violence for the events and relationships that follow in later chapters. The gossip about Hightower also works to undermine the reader's easy identification with and confidence in the principal narrator.

The principal narrator observes, in chapter 3, that gossip can be the willful spread of misinformation and lies. Concerning the rumor that Hightower hired someone to murder his wife so that he could collect insurance money, the narrator concedes: "But everyone knew that this was not so, including the ones who told it and repeated it and the ones who listened when it was told" (71). This sort of gossip that promulgates misinformation, which, in turn, damages the lives of the novel's characters, complicates and challenges the reader's meaning-making. One of the most powerful examples of the thematic and structural destructiveness of gossip is in the town's construction of and belief in Hightower's homosexuality and sexual perversion. It is important to keep in mind that the town not only constructs Hightower's homosexuality (Faulkner supplies no more "proof" of Hightower's actual homosexuality than he does of Joe's father's blackness), but that the town's understanding of homosexuality is itself a culturally and historically relative construction. Hightower's alleged homosexuality is worth attention because it is rarely mentioned by critics even though it plays a crucial role in Faulkner's story. Moreover, Faulkner's oblique presentation of the town's construction of Hightower's homosexuality itself serves as an example of the social and political restraints he critiques in his novel, restraints that defined and regulated sexual and racial as well as gender behavior in the United States in the early part of this century.

We learn in chapter 3 what Byron was told seven years earlier: that the congregation had been outraged not only by Hightower's "profane" sermons, but by his wife, who "had jumped or fallen from a hotel window in Memphis [one] Saturday night, and was dead. [And because] there had been a man in the room with her" (67). We also learn from Byron that after Hightower agreed to resign his pulpit under pressure from the elders of the church, he would not further oblige the town by leaving Jefferson. Soon after, "the whispering began" about Hightower and his cook, a black woman. The town gossiped about "how he had made his wife go bad and commit suicide because he was not a natural husband, a natural man, and that the negro woman was the reason. And that's all it took; all that was lacking" (71). In Byron's recollection of the public record over the novel's next two pages, Faulkner carefully presents parts of the story in a way that traces the cause and effect of each new installment that the town created. Note how what happened, the cook's quitting, generated more gossip to explain *why*—why she quit, why she was terrorized, why blacks were deemed more degenerate than whites, why Hightower's degeneracy was worst of all:

> One day the cook quit. They heard how one night a party of carelessly masked men went to the minister's house and ordered him to fire her. Then they heard how the next day the woman told that she quit herself because her employer asked her to do something which she said was against God and nature. And it was said that some masked men had scared her into quitting because she was what is known as a high brown and it was known that there were two or three men in the town who would object to her doing whatever it was which she considered contrary to God and nature, since, as some of the younger men said, if a nigger woman considered it against God and nature, it must be pretty bad. (71)

In this passage, acts of gossip peel away the event—the cook's quitting—and reveal the underworkings of the town's racist and homophobic ideology.[16]

After the cook quit, the matter seemed settled and the gossiping over, "until they heard one day that he had a negro man to cook for him, and that finished him, sure enough" (72). Having a male cook "finished" Hightower in the eyes of the town not because he had been ordered by the KKK to do his own cooking forever afterward, but because he now kept a *male* cook in his house. The implication here is, of course, that Hightower hired a male cook for purposes of even more degenerate, more "unnatural" sex. The day this news hit the gossip circuit, "some men, not masked either, took the negro man out and whipped him" (72). The KKK next left Hightower a note tied around a brick and thrown through his study window "commanding him to get out of town by sunset." Hightower doesn't leave, and he is found the following morning "in the woods about a mile from town. He had been tied to a tree and beaten unconscious" (72), which ritually completed his secular excommunication. The violence done to the minister and his cooks becomes, in the illogic of the town's gossip, the *proof* that Hightower had transgressed the norms of white heterosexuality. The homophobia expressed in that gossip functions to suppress recognition of the homosociality on which patriarchal domination depends. Further, the KKK's violent conduct can be understood to express its members' own repressed homoerotic desires. Trudier Harris, writing of lynching and burning rituals, argues that those who participated in or even attended violent gatherings (like that of the KKK in *Light in August*) "engaged in a communal orgiastic climax which made the sexual nature of the ritual explicit."[17]

Byron seems not to believe the gossip about Hightower. At the close of his recollection of what he had heard years ago, Byron doubts to himself that anyone in town now even knows "what the inside of [Hightower's] house looks like. And they dont even know that I know, or likely they'd take us both out and whip us" (73). Although the furor of twenty years ago has died down, Byron still visits the minister only in secret because he believes in the force and longevity of the town's gossip and the repressed sexual energies that gossip could direct against him.

Suffering the allegations of sexual perversion and the brutal violence that accompanied them is, as Hightower repeatedly tells himself and Byron, the payment he has made for his "immunity"—his right to forego any further involvement in the town or in the affairs of others. In urging Hightower to become involved, to say that Joe was with him the night of Joanna's murder, Byron explains that Hightower could shore up the lie by telling the town that all the nights Lucas Burch claims to have seen Joe "go up to the big house and go in it," Joe was actually going to Hightower's house. Byron recognizes that in the white heterosexual hierarchy of sexual acts,[18] interracial homosexuality between Hightower and Joe (who the town now believes is black) is more perverse—and therefore more fascinating—than the rape of a white woman by a black man, but less threatening than consensual sex between a white woman and a black man.[19] Byron assures Hightower on this point, "They would believe that, anyway. They would rather believe that about you than to believe that he lived with her like a husband and then killed her" (390).

Joe does, of course, run to Hightower's house rather than away from Jefferson. The gossip in chapter 19 on this event reactivates the old gossip—long accepted as fact—about Hightower's homosexuality. "There were many reasons, opinions, as to why he had fled to Hightower's house at the last. 'Like to like,' the easy, the immediate, ones said, remembering the old tales about the minister" (443). When Grimm and his lynch mob chase Joe into Hightower's house, Hightower at last tries to stop them with Byron's lie. "'Men!' he cried. 'Listen to me. He was here that night. He was with me the night of the murder. I swear to God—'" (464). Grimm does not claim disbelief at Hightower's assertion as he pushes the ex-minister out of the way, but confirms his self-righteous disgust with the lot of the town's "perverts": "'Jesus Christ!' Grimm cried, his young voice clear and outraged like that of a young priest. 'Has every preacher and old maid in Jefferson taken their pants down to the yellowbellied son of a bitch?'" (464).

Against the corrosive menace of the town's lurid suppositions—a taste for talk about taboos and for violence against them—safety is in silence: physical safety in not being the subject of gossip, ethical safety in not participating in it. Joe's life story, more than any other character's in the novel, is the history of the shutting down of his voice and of the menace of speech. In the institutionalized and impersonal world of the orphanage, not only is Joe never encouraged to talk, he is actively discouraged from doing so by the dietician and by the nurses and children who call him "nigger." In ever more violent ways, the world outside the orphanage silences Joe.

From his adopted father's hard, cold Presbyterianism, Joe learns that the essence of being male is being silent and stoic. A man of few words and no tenderness, McEachern demands silent obedience from his wife and adopted son. Joe also learns how to resist McEachern's tyranny with silence. Early in chapter 7, the principal narrator tells the chilling story of Joe's refusal to learn the catechism as McEachern requires him to do each Sunday. For refusing to recite the lesson, McEachern whips Joe. He orders the eight-year-old boy to the barn: "'Take down your pants,' he said. 'We'll not soil them.'. . . When the strap fell [Joe] did not flinch, no quiver passed over his face. He was looking straight ahead, with a rapt, calm expression like a monk in a picture. McEachern began to strike methodically, with slow and deliberate force, still without heat or anger. It would have been hard to say which face was the more rapt, more calm, more convinced" (149–150). After this, Joe is forced to stand with his "trousers [still] collapsed about his feet" for another hour to learn the catechism. At the end of the hour, Joe still refuses to speak the words McEachern wants him to say and so is whipped again. This exchange is repeated until Joe collapses and is carried to his bed in the late afternoon.

Joe's silence throughout the day has been a small but decisive and hard-edged victory over McEachern. Joe can, of course, speak, but chooses not to. As a child, Joe learns "to keep silence" as a way of resistance, of hiding himself, and of keeping himself intact even at the expense of the violation of his body. As a man, Joe will endure more beatings, many he deliberately provokes, because he refuses to speak, to explain, to risk telling himself in words.

Women too threaten Joe because they do talk and, worse, because they want him to talk. Joe sees the women in his life as seeking to open his mouth: they give him food, they tell him their secrets, and they try to get him to tell them his. But Joe, believing "he was doomed to conceal always something from the women who surrounded him" (262), seeks to conceal the self that women seem to recognize in him—a phatic self, trusting and vulnerable. On Joe's first night in the McEachern house, Mrs. McEachern hovers around him performing welcoming kindnesses that the child cannot understand or believe in. "He didn't know what she was trying to do, not even when he was sitting with his cold feet in the warm water. He didn't know that that was all, because it felt too good. He was waiting for the rest of it to begin; the part that would not be pleasant, whatever it would be" (166). Mrs. McEachern stays with Joe in his room that night to comfort him with her presence and talk until he falls asleep. But Joe cannot understand such gestures or "that soft kindness which he believed himself doomed to be forever victim of and which he hated worse than he did the hard and ruthless justice of men. 'She is trying to make me cry,' he thought, lying cold and rigid in his bed . . . 'She was trying to make me cry. Then she thinks that they would have had me'" (169). For Joe, even as a young boy, talking and listening to another person come to equal surrender to the other.

Eventually for Joe, intimate bodily relations with others precede intimate verbal interactions. For a while, physical intimacy provides Joe with the only context he finds safe enough in which to risk words. In describing a patient's loss and recovery of her voice, Merleau-Ponty explains that "the memory or the voice is recovered when the body once more opens itself to others and once more (in the active sense) acquires significance beyond itself."[20] So for Joe. In that context alone, he will talk with Bobbie, and later with other women including Joanna, about his racial identity. Consider the following scene, which occurs after Joe and Bobbie have been lovers for a month:

> That night they talked. They lay in the bed, in the dark, talking. Or he talked, that is. All the time he was thinking, 'Jesus. Jesus. So this is it.' He lay naked too, beside her, touching her with his hand and talking about her. Not about where she had come from and what she had even done, but about her body as if no one had ever done this before, with her or with anyone else. It was as if with speech he were learning about women's bodies, with the curiosity of a child. She told him about the sickness of the first night. It did not shock him now. Like the nakedness and the physical shape, it was like something which had never happened or existed before. So he told her in turn what he knew to tell. He told her quietly and peacefully, lying beside her, touching her. Perhaps he could not even have said if she listened or not. Then he said, 'You noticed my skin, my hair,' waiting for her to answer, his hand slow on her body. (195–196)

In this context of physical intimacy, Joe is about to reveal to Bobbie what for him is his strongest secret—that one of his parents may have been black.

Verbal intimacy, even that accompanied by bodily intimacy, becomes increasingly difficult for Joe to achieve after what he perceives as his betrayal by Bobbie. By the time he is involved with Joanna, Joe can share a sexual relationship with a woman without letting that physical intimacy penetrate his verbal isolation; in Joanna, however, his own silence is matched. Even after they are lovers for four or five months, Joanna and Joe do not let shared talk draw them together. Instead, when they would meet by day, they "would stand for a while and talk almost like strangers" (233), while at night they share nothing of themselves beyond their bodies:

> She told him very little, anyway. They talked very little, and that casually, even after he was the lover of her spinster's bed. Sometimes he could almost believe that they did not talk at all, that he didn't know her at all. It was as though there were two people: the one whom he saw now and then by day and looked at while they spoke to one another with speech that told nothing at all since it didn't try to and didn't intend to; the other with whom he lay at night and didn't even see, speak to at all. (232)

That Joanna so little engages in meaningful talk about herself, perhaps even that she seems so little interested in hearing from him, begins to bother Joe. Although she had let him subdue her physically, Joanna's surrender to Joe does not feel complete to him until she gives herself up to him "in words":

> Thinking, knowing *She has come to talk to me* Two hours she was still talking, they sitting side by side on the cot in the now dark cabin. . . . Sitting beside her on the dark cot while the light failed and at last her voice was without source, steady, interminable, pitched almost like the voice of a man, Christmas thought, 'She is like all the rest of them. Whether they are seventeen or fortyseven, when they finally come to surrender, completely, it's going to be in words.' (240–241)

When Joanna finally does speak of herself to Joe after nearly a year of sexual relations with him, Joe sees this as her capitulation and her fully relinquishing to him control of their relationship. Joe will discover shortly after Joanna's visit to his cabin, of course, that he is mistaken in his assessment of her surrender. And Joanna, having opened herself physically and verbally to Joe, discovers the erotic power of language: "She had an avidity for the forbidden wordsymbols; an insatiable appetite for the sound of them on his tongue and on her own. She revealed the terrible and impersonal curiosity of a child about forbidden subjects and objects; that rapt and tireless and detached interest of a surgeon in the physical body and its possibilities" (258). Joe and Joanna's newfound verbal intimacy signals an intensification in their relationship and sends them—and Faulkner's story—reeling into what feels to Joe like a "sewer" or "swamp" of emotional corruption and sexual fury. Unlike Joanna, whose self-gossip he has listened to for hours, Joe is rarely compelled to break into speech. He has no voice of presence to himself; for him, there is very little "being" in language. Thus, in Joe, Faulkner dramatizes the struggle not only of the black man silenced, but, behind this, of the white southern writer trying vainly to unsilence the black presence in literature.

Joanna's impulse to tell her family history is, in part, the impulse to take possession of what is on the point of becoming lost and forgotten and, by her, never understood. And in part Joanna's impulse is simply to keep talking, to keep others listening, to assert causal chains and relations, to stave off failure—the end of her story, the end of her family line, the end of her relationship with Joe—in essence, to keep language from vitiating itself and leaving her alone in silence. Scarry explains that "ceaseless talk articulates [one's] unspoken understanding that only in silence do the edges of the self become coterminous with the edges of the body it will die with" (33). For Joanna, talk comes to feel like survival. Later in chapter 12, after she discovers she is too old to become pregnant and after her months-long silence to Joe, Joanna's impulse to talk changes. In what Joe sees as the "third phase" of their relationship, Joanna's talking at Joe becomes truly incessant and expresses the desperation and hopelessness she feels:

She stayed him with a single word; for the first time he looked at her face: he looked upon a face cold, remote, and fanatic. 'Do you realise,' she said, 'that you are wasting your life?' And he sat looking at her like a stone, as if he could not believe his own ears. . . . She sat looking into the fire her face cold, still, brooding, talking to him as if he were a stranger. . . . She had the plan all elaborated. She recited it to him in detail. . . . He would go on into the house and mount the stairs. Already he would be hearing her voice. It would increase as he mounted and until he reached the door to the bedroom. The door would be shut, locked; from beyond it the monotonous steady voice came. He could not distinguish the words, only the ceaseless monotone. (268, 278–279)

Here Joanna uses her voice as a weapon—seemingly against Joe, but actually against herself. At one point in this "third phase," as she lay on her bed, her mouth bleeding from slaps and punches Joe has given her to force her to "Shut up. Shut up that drivel" (277), Joanna says back to Joe, " 'Maybe it would be better if we were both dead' " (278).

Even in her very first long talk to Joe, Joanna finds it nearly impossible, once she begins, to be silent about what obsesses her. She does her telling to Joe, making him listen to the story of Nathaniel, Calvin, Nathaniel, and Calvin in some effort to explain to him and to herself not only why she lives in Jefferson, but why she is its most famous spinster, why she refuses to leave the town, why she persists in her "Negro work," why she is his lover, and to reveal her buried rages. In her mind, her telling answers all of this—and so binds Joe closer to her—and none of it: she ends her hours-long accounting with the crushing and simple, "I think that was it." Despite all her revelations, Joanna has no definitive or soundly convincing explanations, only answers that don't really answer or resolve, answers that instead raise further questions that are, in turn, an opportunity for her further invention. Of Joanna's and other characters' efforts, David Dowling observes that "none of *Light in August*'s many narrators finds peace in explanation."[21] Indeed, in no very satisfying way does Joanna's telling enable her or the reader to understand the woman who waits for Joe each night, who tries to murder her lover and herself with an ancient pistol, and who ends both de-flowered and decapitated, beheaded but not beloved.

Whatever formal risks Faulkner took in his 1930 novel, he did so to match the stories he dared to tell and the portraits he created: intimate, appalling, over-complicated, tender. In the process, he devised a language to impart the fleetness, and paradoxical stillness, of lives in motion. *Light in August*'s classic "reader-in-the-text" moment is a scene in chapter 5 in which Faulkner shows Joe reading a pulp detective-story magazine—the "type whose covers bear either pictures of young women in underclothes or pictures of men in the act of shooting one another with pistols" (110)—"straight through as though it were a novel" (111). In the quiet clearing by the spring on Joanna's property, moments before he rises to make his way to her house where he will brutally slash her throat, Joe turns the pages in steady progression, though now and then he would seem to linger upon one page, one line, perhaps one word. He would not look up then. He would not move, apparently arrested and held immobile by a single word which had perhaps not impacted, his whole being suspended by the single trivial combination of letters in quiet and sunny space, so that hanging motionless and without physical weight he seemed to watch the slow flowing of time beneath him. (112)

Faulkner's picture of Joe reading works reflexively to make us, as readers of Faulkner's novel, self-conscious of our efforts to find meaning in the "trivial combination of letters," the shifting and disputed signs that are *Light in August*; it may make us even more uncomfortable with its broad suggestions about what we really like to look at or listen to.[22] As readers, we may feel that we understand Faulkner's novel by participating in its gossipy world, but, to a large degree, we find in it what Joe finds all around him: the dis-integration and dis-quiet of the social world of speaking, the laying bare and appropriation of secrets we need to keep close. Joe tries to resist that world and the dangers it holds for him by being silent, and, as a result, more than any of the other characters in *Light in August*, Joe resists being read.

So too does Faulkner's text: with its intricate and complex internal design, the reader finds that the "cold, implacable . . . printed words" (149) of *Light in August*—like Faulkner's hunted, indecipherable character—resist easy reading. And the culture of which Faulkner writes, whose half-hidden scenes lure and repulse us, is a culture of pulp-readers and pulp-inventors living in a world of their own fearful creation. This brutal, anti-folk picture of the creative life of the community—its dance, its literature—might suggest to us why *Light in August* is singularly ambivalent about its own "artistry." And perhaps, for readers in the United States today, this novel's conclusions are still too disturbing to voice.

NOTES

This chapter is based on research first published in *Narrative* 1.2 (May 1993): 105–123. Copyright © 1993 Ohio State University Press. All rights reserved.

I thank William Veeder, Arthur Evenchik, and Gwen Bergner for their valuable editorial suggestions. I am especially grateful to Douglas Kincade for his generous and insightful comments on this piece and the longer study from which it is drawn.

1. William Faulkner, *Light in August: The Corrected Text* (New York: Vintage Books, 1990), 348–349. All further references to this novel are from this edition.

2. "The furious motion of being alive, that's all my story is. You catch this fluidity which is human life and you focus a light on it and you stop it long enough for people to be able to see it." William Faulkner, *Faulkner in the University: Class Conferences at the University of Virginia, 1957–1958*, ed. Frederick L. Gwynn and Joseph L. Blotner (New York: Random House, 1965), 239.

3. Other critics have begun to look indirectly at the narrative dynamics of *Light in August*: Martin Kreiswirth, "Plots and Counterplots: The Structure of *Light in August*," in *New Essays on Light in August*, ed. Michael Millgate (New York: Cambridge University Press, 1987); Eric J. Sundquist, *The House Divided* (Baltimore: Johns Hopkins University Press, 1983), 71–76; Donald M. Kartiganer, *The Fragile Thread: The Meaning of Form in Faulkner's Novels* (Amherst: University of Massachusetts Press, 1979), 41. But each, for different reasons, falls back on models of stability, homeostasis, or what Sundquist calls "a kind of psychological exhaustion" (73) to explain the novel's energetics; Kartiganer finds that *Light in August* fails to achieve unity or coherence. Kreiswirth's identification of particular narrative forms is excellent, but even he is not so much concerned with the textual energy or with the play of that energy as he is with the progression of Faulkner's plotting.

4. Desire theory paradigms similarly fall short of describing the energetics of other novels, for instance, Gabriel García Márquez's *One Hundred Years of Solitude* and Toni Morrison's *Beloved*.

5. Wolgang Iser, *The Implied Reader: Patterns of Communication in Prose Fiction from Bunyan to Beckett* (Baltimore: Johns Hopkins University Press, 1974), 275.

6. This is not unlike the "bracketing" of the phenomenologists, most obviously, the narrative theory of Paul Ricoeur; Maurice Merleau-Ponty and Iris Marion Young are also important to my thinking. The phenomenological theory of perception provides a way to recognize the contributions of the reader to the creation of *Light in August* without ignoring that novel's objective authorial or artistic forms. It allows us to maintain the artistic integrity of Faulkner's novel and account for our capacity to read the same work (the same organization of narrative forms) variably.

Iris Marion Young, "Throwing Like a Girl: A Phenomenology of Feminine Body Comportment, Motility, and Spatiality," in *Throwing Like a Girl and Other Essays in Feminist Philosophy and Social Theory* (Bloomington: Indiana University Press, 1990), 141–159. See also Young's critique of existential phenomenology's tradition of "inattention to embodied experience as specifically sexed and gendered" in "Introduction," in *Throwing Like a Girl*, 1–18; and, Judith Butler, "Sexual Ideology and Phenomenological Description: A Feminist Critique of

Merleau-Ponty's *Phenomenology of Perception*," in *The Thinking Muse: Feminism and Modern French Philosphy*, ed. Jeffner Allen and Iris Marion Young (Bloomington: Indiana University Press, 1985), 85–100.

7. Stephen Greenblatt, *Shakespearean Negotiations: The Circulation of Social Energy in Renaissance England* (Berkeley: University of California Press, 1988).

8. Jean-François Lyotard, *The Lyotard Reader*, ed. Andrew Benjamin (Cambridge, Mass.: Basil Blackwell, 1989), 8–9.

9. The thematics of gossip has been treated most importantly, of course, in Patricia Meyer Spacks, *Gossip* (Chicago: University of Chicago Press, 1986). General notions of community talk are discussed in connection with Faulkner's fiction in Peter Brooks, *Reading for the Plot: Design and Intention in Narrative* (New York: Vintage Books, 1985); John Duvall, "Murder and the Communities: Ideology in and around *Light in August*," in *William Faulkner's "Light in August": Modern Critical Interpretations*, ed. Harold Bloom (New York: Chelsea House, 1988) 135–157; and John T. Irwin, *Doubling and Incest, Repetition and Revenge: A Speculative Reading of Faulkner* (Baltimore: Johns Hopkins University Press, 1975).

10. Richard Pearce also examines what he calls the "authority" of the narrative voice in *Light in August* and its powers of disrupting the novel's narrative structures. See Pearce, *The Politics of Narration: James Joyce, William Faulkner, and Virginia Woolf* (New Brunswick, N.J.: Rutgers University Press, 1991), 97–110.

11. Wesley Morris and Barbara Alverson Morris, *Reading Faulkner* (Madison: University of Wisconsin Press, 1989), 132.

12. Elaine Scarry, *The Body in Pain: The Making and Unmaking of the World* (New York: Oxford University Press, 1985), 33; see also 280–290.

13. Jacquelyn Dowd Hall, "'The Mind That Burns in Each Body': Women, Rape, and Racial Violence," in *Powers of Desire: The Politics of Sexuality*, ed. Ann Snitow, Christine Stansell, and Sharon Thompson (New York: New Feminist Library, 1983), 328–349; quotation, 335.

14. Susan Rubin Suleiman, distinguishing Georges Bataille's pornographic fiction from other pornography, in "Pornography, Transgression, and the Avant-Garde: Bataille's *Story of the Eye*," in *The Poetics of Gender*, ed. Nancy K. Miller (New York: Columbia University Press, 1985), 115–136.

15. Especially see "Murderous Lovers," in Leo Bersani, *A Future for Astyanax: Character and Desire in Literature* (New York: Columbia University Press, 1984), 3–17.

16. Accordingly, the acts the terrorized woman reportedly alleges Hightower "asked her to do"—acts that went "against God and nature"—would likely not refer simply to interracial vaginal intercourse, which, although harshly stigmatized, was not unheard of in southern culture of the 1930s. What Hightower allegedly asked the woman to do was something so "wicked" as to be unmentionable and very nearly unimaginable. This kind of evasive language is also found in laws prohibiting heterosexual as well as homosexual sodomy (laws still on the books in Mississippi and nineteen other states), and seems designed to pique and play to the culture's prurient sensibilities and racist and homophobic fears: sodomy may refer to anal sex between members of the same or opposite sex, but it may also refer to sexual acts defined only as "too heinous to mention."

17. Trudier Harris, *Exorcising Blackness: Historical and Literary Lynching and Burning Rituals* (Bloomington: Indiana University Press, 1984), 22.

18. For the notion of a sex hierarchy, I am indebted to Gayle Rubin, "Thinking Sex: Notes for a Radical Theory of the Politics of Sexuality," in *Pleasure and Danger: Exploring Female Sexuality*, ed. Carole Vance (Boston: Routledge and Kegan Paul, 1984), 267–319, esp. 275–284. Rubin's hierarchy, however, does not include interracial sex.

19. On the unthinkableness in white racist ideology of consensual sexual relations between white women and black men, see Hall, especially her discussion of the 1931 Scottsboro trial.

20. Maurice Merleau-Ponty, *Phenomenology of Perception* trans. Colin Smith (New York: Routledge and Kegan Paul, 1986), 165.

21. David Dowling, *William Faulkner* (London: Macmillan, 1989), 80.

22. Robert Dale Parker reads this scene as a "stereotype of how fiction and novels are supposed to be read" (87), and his concern is with how Faulkner defies "the notion that plot should move in a straight line" (87). In Parker, *Faulkner and the Novelistic Imagination* (Champaign-Urbana: University of Illinois Press, 1985).

READING WRITING
ABOUT DANCE

Mimique

Mark Franko

> We would have to choose then, between writing and dance.
> —Jacques Derrida, "Force and Signification"

Must we choose between writing and dance? Has deconstruction set us at liberty to believe dance and writing are identical forms of inscription? And is the mirror-opposite belief—that dance is writing's absolute other—not just a comparable assertion of their "sameness-in-difference"? Under the sign of play, dance has become a new identity of writing within Jacques Derrida's deconstruction of the transcendental ego as "presence." Yet, when Derrida treats the play of dance or the subject of performance, distinctions between presence and difference become uncharacteristically slippery. In an essay on Antonin Artaud, for example, Derrida concludes that Artaud is after "pure presence as pure difference."[1] This statement hints that Artaud's project locates dance neither in writing nor in writing's other.[2] Instead, dance becomes located *outside* a "closure" that bounds the play of differences itself, outside a "closure of representation" from which Derrida declares Artaud, in fact, unable to escape. Whereas in other of Derrida's writings from the sixties, play is boundless precisely because it exceeds the closure of (structuralism's) structure against which he wrote, in his second essay on Artaud play becomes uncharacteristically bound within an enclosure. Meanwhile, the play of dance (of cruel theater) occupies an impossible outside. Its impossibility, however, is significantly situated in a possible space, "outside" the possible. As Mark Wigley has written: "whatever philosophy places outside is still inside precisely because it is 'placed.'"[3] Such ambivalence is the price of Derrida's opening gambit in "La parole soufflée" where he refuses to allow Artaud's madness to become an exemplary case for literature.[4] Let us follow suit by refusing to consider dance a "case" (even an exemplary one) for literature. It is to Stéphane Mallarmé, however, that I turn as a literary locus of the danced as writing, the written as dancing, and too, as a rendezvous of deconstructive thought.

Mallarmé's dancer at the inception of modernism—an unwritten body writing—represents a strong moment of conjuncture between dance and literature. The poet as danseuse has pointed literary critics from literature to performance theory and back, introducing a mimetic relation between dance and writing.

Recent studies of Mallarmé's performance theories by Evlyn Gould and Mary Lewis Shaw position dance relative to literature in suggestive ways.[5] Since both critics have contended with Derrida's influential reading of Mallarmé's "Mimique" in "The Double Session," I move from Gould and Shaw toward a consideration of Derrida's concept of trace and its import for performance theory.[6] I argue that the disappearing presence of the trace—unrepeatable but not for that reason culturally irrecuperable—is the "being" of performance, its "once" as memorable, its inscription as "enduringly" worldly. This is to write with but also against Derrida because my argument rehabilitates "primary mimesis," a concept purely of operative value for Derrida's reading of Mallarmé.

It is apparently ironic that a poet associated with the autonomous work of words should have reemerged in poststructuralist theory of the late 1960s as a champion of the body's claims vis-à-vis literature. Mallarmé's proposal that the work of art does not *exist,* that its presence denotes an absence, has decided resonance for performance studies.[7] In rethinking Mallarmé's poetics, the old trope of dance's ephemerality becomes rejuvenated and essentially transformed into that of the "disappearing body." Whereas "ephemerality" had glorified but also trivialized and marginalized dance as that profoundly apolitical activity (its deepest nature unplanned, its most essential sense irrecuperable), the "disappearance" trope recasts the body's provisional interventions in space or theory as a textuality of its own making. Dance's change of cast has deconstruction to thank. Furthermore, ephemerality-as-disappearance is a synonym of the Derridian trace: "The very thing that has no meaning, is ceaselessly re-marking itself— that is, disappearing" ("Double Session" 250). Yet parity with the trace can prove problematic, for it removes another sort of presence from dancing: the presence of dancing subjects themselves in their gendered, cultural, and political distinctiveness. Having thankfully graduated from the "elegant gratuitousness of the dance" as a critic once phrased it apropos of Paul Valéry, we still abide—at least as long as we read Mallarmé—with the essential conditions of meaning in modernism/postmodernism: mobility, indeterminacy, multiplicity, reflexivity.[8] The palpability and concreteness of differences get lost in Derrida's trace. Hence the question that dance raises: How can difference itself display difference?

Evlyn Gould focuses on the relation between virtuality and actuality in Mallarmé's thought on performance. She argues he was the first to develop a performative writing enabled by his notion of virtuality: "Mallarmé's reconciliation of a virtual with an actual theatricality creates an important link between the metaphor of the theater to describe the functioning of a psychical apparatus and the relationship of this apparatus to actual performing arts" (142). Dance, in other terms, is virtual writing, and writing virtual dance. For Gould, theatrical virtuality resides in a mobility of subject positions engaged in an experience of staging. But Gould focuses on Mallarmé's performance theory through the lens of his "virtual plays." Here literature can appropriate dance as a way of rendering performance imaginary.

In a more recent article, Gould addresses Mallarmé's writings on ballet.[9] This essay clarifies how the reading of a literary text *about* performance leads to a theory *of* performance. The "difficulty" of Mallarmé's prose (his ballet reviews), made up of "potential associations among words" and "a constant confusion of subjects of discussion and their interlocutors," is said by Gould to "approximate the imaginary representations or, what I also call 'virtual theater,' that accompany any attendance at a theatrical performance" (98). Here, dance becomes truly virtual, and thus paradigmatic for literature. The link between dance and poetry, Gould claims, is that both offer an experience of reading/spectatorship in which there is a confusion of subject and object, where no meaning is fixed, but all are projected onto a psychic stage in a play of memory and forgetfulness. "The stage is transformed into an ephemeral two-way mirror making it unclear if the reviewer [Mallarmé] translates the ballet performance in his writing or if the ballerina translates the reviewer's mental (virtual) performance in hers" (104). The virtuality of performance can be turned inside out to reveal poetry's performativity. Dance and writing become mirrored in one another, but their ensuing mimetic rapport only renders further exploration of performance illusory: the two-way mirror is "ephemeral." In this second version of virtual theater, a notion of performative writing as the only possible response to dance—and of dance as a "writing" whose imaginary suspends interpretation—gains focus but still appears quite limited as an explanation of anyone's save Mallarmé's spectatorship. It does not account for what may be lost in Mallarmé's translation. Gould's remarks speak above all to the lack of a unified "point of view" which makes performance a difficult object of study, actually not an object at all. But, there she stops. To organize that multiplicity, to confront its intersubjective complexity in historically grounded instances of cultural practice, remains the task of performance studies and not literary studies. "The corps-graphy or body writing on stage" is for Gould "that part of the spectacle one cannot quite remember" (101). I return later to why it is important and also revealing that memory be omitted from poststructuralist theories of bodily writing.

Mary Lewis Shaw's treatment of dance's place in Mallarmé's poetic is more exhaustive than Gould's, but also surprisingly restrictive. Shaw insists on a Cartesian rhetoric wherein dance expresses "the inherently corporeal and contingent" (9).[10] In the chiasmas she sets up between dance and literature, "literature and the performing arts reflect each other as identical contraries" (27). This chiasmas is designed to show dance as "a negative poetic sign." Performance indicates the poetry it is not (thus, its status as "unwritten poem"). Poetry, for its part, although also tangible because "writing or print on paper," actually "directly (i.e. verbally) transcribes thought" (59, 58).[11] Shaw's analysis of the place of dance in Mallarmé's poetic neglects the preponderance of signifier over signified, the productive web of connotations. Moreover, the sheerly negative apprehension of performance as missing literature (with all its damning weight of the accusation of illiteracy) undermines the very ramifications of dance as a model for this productivity: "Whereas he [Mallarmé] considers literature . . . as a means of access to the *intangible* presence of the idea through acts of language that abolish nature, he sees the performing arts as a means of access to the *tangible* presence of the idea through nonverbal, corporeal acts that conversely nullify *la parole*" (16). To abolish nature is obviously to foster the Idea; to "nullify *la parole*" is to be "a negative form of writing" (17). This analysis is unsatisfying for the way it undervalues the productivity uniting performance and literature in modernism. Without that union, there would be little attraction to Mallarmé as performance theorist.

Although both Gould and Shaw are influenced by and also reacting against Derrida, his formulations seem to engage performance more directly. Perhaps this is because French poststructuralist thought of the 1960s employed the terms "stage" (*scène*) and "gesturality" as models of deconstructed philosophy, as if performance were that "outside" always denied an ontological dimension in thought. Poststructuralist critical theory self-consciously constituted itself as a performative enterprise, indeed, as the project of a theater through its emphasis on the gestural.[12] Even if this critical language designated no existing performance, it suggested the possibility of one: the performance of "inexpressive" gesture. Deconstruction indirectly undermined the foundations of expressive performance by destabilizing the ontological dimension of the term "expression" itself.[13] More particularly, it constructed gesture as a polemical weapon against phenomenology (although Merleau-Ponty was significantly left out of this polemic). Opposing the privilege of the voice, gesture was equated with writing (the trace). In "The Double Session" the gesture of Mallarmé's mime becomes Derrida's model for the trace. And in Derrida's analysis, Mallarmé's texts on dance are never far in the background.

Like the cogito, Mallarmé's mime engages in a mute soliloquy, and thus raises issues of mimesis (both as self-presence and as imitation) and of mimicry (as simulation) to which Derrida devotes considerable attention. He establishes a primary sense of mimesis as *eidos,* the presentation of the thing itself which occurs in the cogito in the form of an image: "*Logos,*" remarks Derrida, "must indeed be shaped according to the model of the *eidos*" ("Double Session" 188).[14] "Even before it can be translated as imitation, *mimesis* signifies the presentation of the thing itself, of nature, of the phusis that produces itself. . . . In this sense, *mneme* and *mimesis* are on a par since *mneme* too is an unveiling (an un-forgetting), *aletheia*" (193).[15] Appearing form is material provided by sense perception for the "idea." The return of appearing form as an image in the wake of sense perception is a function of memory. Thus "*mneme* and *mimesis* are on a par." This "movement of the *phusis*" is actually "the ideality—*for* a subject—of what is" (193, 194). Thus the ambivalent relationship of Cartesian metaphysics to imagination and memory. On the one hand, Descartes conceptualizes ideas as images: "ideas exist in me as pictures or images."[16] On the other: "this power of imagination which I possess, in as far as it differs from the power of conceiving, is in no way necessary to my [nature or] essence, that is, to the essence of my mind" (112). In traditional metaphysics from Descartes to Husserl, memory as repeatable experience yields only probable or inferential knowledge. Production/ reproduction cannot compete with the cogito as presence of the self-same, empirical certainty, truth. The image and memory are evicted from the cogito, along with the body, as figures of space. Conversely, primary mimesis does not imply reproduction of the self-same; it is the taking of bodily form by bodies, the material occasion for the presentation and transmission of behavior. Mihai Spariosu has identified primary mimesis as a pre-rational form of play, which he calls "mimesis-play" as distinguished from "mimesis-imitation."[17] Prior to Plato, as Spariosu explains,

> the *mimesis* semantic group was employed in a ritualistic-dramatic context, designating a performative function that we moderns associate with play. Consequently, this semantic group, at least before Plato, should not be understood as conveying the idea of imitation in the sense of 'representation or reproduction of an original or a model,' but rather the idea of 'miming,' 'simulating,' or even 'presencing' (invoking, calling something forth). (*Dionysus Reborn* 17)

Given the frequency with which Derrida has linked the trace to play, primary mimesis would seem to describe how or what performance traces, how dance is a particular form of "spacing."[18]

Nevertheless, primary mimesis quickly disappears from Derrida's reading of "Mimique." He understands Mallarmé's mime at first to be nonimitative: "there is no imitation. The mime imitates nothing. . . . There is nothing prior to the writing of his gestures" ("Double Session" 194).[19] But Derrida does not focus on performance theory in deference to "Mimique" as written text: "Before we investigate this proposition, let us consider what Mallarmé is *doing* in *Mimique*. We read *Mimique*" (198). Reading writing about the unwritten body's trace, Derrida nets the performing body thematically but only mimics its theory. In this sense, performance itself appears in "The Double Session" in the very guise of primary mimesis: it both appears without naming its source and withdraws back into the work of performance, leaving its status as theory ambiguous.

Mallarmé's own proposition regarding performance is nevertheless entertained. Derrida writes: "Since the mime imitates nothing, reproduces nothing, opens up in its origin the very thing he is tracing out, presenting, or producing, *he must be the very movement of truth*" (205; my emphasis). The movement of truth, stresses Derrida, would not be any form of superior mimesis involving an imitator and an imitated, but rather "truth as the present unveiling of the present: monstration, manifestation, production, *aletheia*" (206). Derrida discounts this approach, however, as "one of the most typical and tempting metaphysical reappropriations of writing" (206). "One could indeed push Mallarmé back into the most 'originary' metaphysics of truth if all mimicry [*mimique*] had indeed disappeared, if it had effaced itself in the scriptural production of truth" (206). But this is not the case because "*There is* mimicry. . . . We are faced then with mimicry imitating nothing . . . a reference without a referent" (206).

The contradiction Derrida locates in "Mimique" is between the copresence of "mimesis-play" and "mimesis-imitation." No-thing is being imitated. Yet, as Spariosu shows, the pre-rational tradition of primary mimesis goes beyond a visual unveiling. It *does* have to do with an imitator and an imitated. Historically associated with dance and music, primary mimesis is a doing, a physical participation. A certain performance logic seems required to explain that no-thing (substantively) be imitated. As Merleau-Ponty has pointed out: "The cultivation of habit as a rearrangement and renewal of the body image presents great difficulties to traditional philosophies, which are always inclined to conceive synthesis as intellectual synthesis."[20] It is possible that memory itself and its physical manifestations in habit imitate no-thing. The issue becomes how to understand the projection of the habitual past into a future governed neither by conscious representation nor irrational (empty) reflex. Only "praxis" avoids these two extremes, and I wish to theorize dance as "praxis."[21] Although Mallarmé's text on mime may unfailingly posit mimicry, as Derrida claims it does, such mimicry does not inevitably undo the movement wherein the *eidos* is formed, the movement of the *phusis* as *mneme*.

Primary mimesis does not entail an originary metaphysics so much as a project of becoming. If one conceives the danced trace as primary mimesis, dance need not be identified with an originary metaphysics on one hand, nor with referenceless reference on the other. As Carol Barko has remarked, the dancer Loie Fuller "illustrates his [Mallarmé's] principle of the expansion of the book from the letter."[22] Barko's example is of the dancer inside her enveloping fabrics, whose undulating and metamorphosing shapes danced, thereby suggesting different natural forms to Mallarmé and finally, in their entirety, a poem. According to Barko, this occurred through a "tension between its [the body's] center (self) and its expanding periphery (its production as emanation)" (179). Derrida leaves out of his discussion a productive aspect of appearances in which "utterance means production" ("énoncer signifie produire").[23]

Derrida only considers primary mimesis in a rational perspective as being rather than as becoming. "The Double Session" appropriates mime, and dance as well, to the logic of the trace as "hymen"—that which disappears in the course of its own inscription.[24] When deconstruction brings about the convergence of dance and writing, one surmises an unwitting replay of metaphysics's reservations with respect to memory.

Frances A. Yates has shown that classical arts of memory operate by situating bodies mentally in architectural spaces. Yates refers to these spaces as "inner writing": "A *locus* is a place easily grasped by the memory, such as a house, an intercolumnar space, a corner, an arch, or the like. Images are forms, marks or simulacra (*formae, notae, simulacra*) of what we wish to remember. . . . The art of memory is like an inner writing."[25] By the same token, Mallarmé's dancer as unwritten body writing suggests through its very engagement with space the recuperability of its own passage. What the movements (spacings) of dance establish is a *space* charged with absent presence, a space that intends to become. Mallarmé identifies the movement of Loie Fuller's voluminous costumes with a becoming of place ("the withdrawal of skirt or wing instituting a place"—"les retraits de jupe ou d'aile instituant un lieu" [308–309]). Movement through space leaves the trace of place that would have made movement possible, architecturally inevitable. In other terms, dance is reverse architecture, taking down what was not there. This is its monumentality. The architectural fantasm of dance is impermanent but not unstable, under erasure but not as "non-sense."[26] Movement both evokes and shapes a surviving social response as a physical environment. Dance, in other terms, calls social space into being. In "Choreographies," Derrida asserts, "The dance changes place and above all changes *places*. In its wake they can no longer be recognized" (69). I differ. Its places are noted and retained. Dance is about the enactment of future place through the memory of "spacing." The places of dance always *will be* recognized. They are habitually absent.

Derrida's framing of mime as "reference without a referent" denies or significantly underplays the inscriptive *force* of gesture necessary to the claims I make for dancing bodies.[27] For Derrida, corporeal inscription is nothing more than an "*index sui*," "the same as not being a sign . . . present to itself without indicative detour" (*Speech and Phenomena* 61). By becoming "reflective," the performed trace becomes "unproductive." The trace, as presented in "The Double Session," is too formalist an entity to encompass what performance re-presents, what its persistence re-marks. It is entirely reliant on the negative residue of deconstructed metaphysics. Derrida's trace is what movement leaves behind, sense as fade, vector becoming shapeless. "For difference," writes Derrida, "is the necessary interval, the suspense between two outcomes, the 'lapse of time' between two shots, two roles, two chances" ("Double Session" 277). Yet between self-referential mimicry and trace lies performance as what can materialize, and therefore "retain" what is not, re-call it. I invoke memory not as reproduction (copy) but as the capacity to perform anew, although always differently, to reproduce by repetitive otherness. In other words, time in performance is not only given as a "spacing out" passing toward itself as nothing, but also as a "spacing in," an introjection of uncertainty about something to be readdressed (redressed). Through the memory implied by such repetition, the unrepeatable avoids being irrecuperable.

"What takes place," in "The Double Session," "is only the *entre,* the place, the spacing, which is nothing, the ideality (as nothingness) of the idea" (214). Having exposed the metaphorical ideality of "full presence," Derrida develops a conceivable notion of time as non-self-presence (gesture rather than voice) with only a virtual body to inhabit that time. His prodigious gesture reaches out from nobody. It is an abstraction of difference as the nonessential. For performance studies, the ideality of movement as trace begs reformulation. Instead of emptied space "between" two virtualities, I propose the following rewriting: the indicative function of the trace is forceful action taken on behalf of what is not. Let us imagine "spacing" itself as subject to a black or red spot, like the eyes of Paul Margueritte's mime in the libretto Mallarmé read prior to writing "Mimique." To be faithful to that libretto, the mime is not, as Derrida claims, white on white (the blank), a symbol of mimicry as referenceless reference. "His [the mime's] head is marked, eyes and lips, as black and red" ("la tête, yeux et lèvres, s'y marquent, qui de noir, qui de rouge").²⁸ Theatrical presence emerges as memory hastening melancholy deferral toward fully artificial presence, "fictive or momentaneous" ("fictif ou momentané" [Mallarmé 296]). Having given up "the most 'originary' of metaphysics of truth," we can welcome nevertheless the uniqueness of each re-marked moment, dancing as the "flesh of *différance.*"²⁹ The uniqueness of difference (the plurality of differences) needs to be understood as performances. Dance performs still nonexistent social spaces constructed from the memory of what is not, and never was, "under a false appearance of a present."³⁰ Taken in this sense, dance presents itself as a project, which is also to say, "a direction of action that is not free from dangers and uncontrollable ambiguities."³¹ The very fact that its performance occupies no present enables the memory its presence incurs to be a memory for some politics. A setting, perhaps, rather than a *scène:* what remains is the place, repeatable through the impossibility of its inhabitation.³²

NOTES ‒ ‒ ‒ ‒ ‒ ‒ ‒

I thank Sam Gillespie, Christian Herold, Randy Martin, and Theresa Senft for their helpful comments during the preparation of this chapter.

1. Jacques Derrida, "The Theater of Cruelty and the Closure of Representation," in *Writing and Difference*, trans. Alan Bass (Chicago: University of Chicago Press, 1978), 247.

2. Artaud's radical vision of theater, as is well known, relied on rendering conventions of theater more like those of dance.

3. Mark Wigley, *The Architecture of Deconstruction: Derrida's Haunt* (Cambridge, Mass.: MIT Press, 1993), 158. The convolutedness of dance/play as a figure of deconstruction parallels Wigley's analysis of the architectural figure and "a thinking of architecture" in Derrida's writing.

4. See Jacques Derrida, "La parole soufflée," in *Writing and Difference*, 169–174.

5. Evlyn Gould, *Virtual Theater from Diderot to Mallarmé* (Baltimore: Johns Hopkins University Press, 1989); and Mary Lewis Shaw, *Performance in the Texts of Mallarmé: The Passage from Art to Ritual* (University Park, Pa.: Pennsylvania State University Press, 1993).

6. Jacques Derrida, "The Double Session," in *Dissemination*, trans. Barbara Johnson (Chicago: University of Chicago Press, 1981), 174–285.

7. Maurice Blanchot describes Mallarmé's project with reference to precursor Joseph Joubert. Both are concerned with "The power to represent through absence and to manifest through remoteness, a power that lies at the center of art, that seems to move things away in order to say them, to keep them at a remove so that they may become clear, a power of transformation, of translation, in which it is this very removal (space) that transforms and translates, that makes invisible things visible, that makes visible things transparent, that thus makes itself visible in them and then discovers itself to be the luminous depth of invisibility and irreality from which everything comes and in which everything is concluded." Maurice Blanchot, "Joubert and Space," in *The Notebooks of Joseph Joubert: A Selection*, ed. and trans. Paul Auster (San Francisco: North Point Press, 1983), 170.

8. "Valéry's prose often attains the elegant gratuitousness of the dance," writes Victor Brombert. "This is why," the same critic concludes, "he rarely went to the far end of his own thought." Brombert, "Valéry: The Dance of Words," *Hudson Review* 21.4 (Winter 1968–1969): 675, 686, respectively. In an interview with Christie V. McDonald, Derrida defines dance as "surprise." "It should happen only once, neither grow heavy nor ever plunge too deep." See Derrida and McDonald, "Choreographies," *Diacritics* 12 (1982): 66; reprinted in this volume. Derrida and Brombert seem almost to be in agreement, which is disturbing. For a useful comparison of Mallarmé and Valéry on dance, see Magalie D. Hanquier, "Je pense donc je danse?—Danse/Poésie, Mallarmé/Valéry," in *Bulletin des Etudes Valeryennes* 64 (November 1993):111–127.

9. Evlyn Gould, "Penciling and Erasing Mallarmé's Ballets," *Performing Arts Journal* 15.1 (January 1993): 97–105.

10. Mallarmé is said to have "a deep-rooted awareness of the mind/body duality" (27) thanks to which "what dance signifies most keenly is the physical dimension of the human self" (62).

11. "Literature," Shaw notes, "is more closely associated [than is performance] with the signified, the immaterial concept" (57).

12. For a perceptive analysis of the transition between theater semiology and poststructuralist theatricality, see Maria Minich Brewer, "Performing Theory," *Theatre Journal* 37.1 (March 1985), esp., 16–19. See also Michel Foucault, "Theatrum Philosophicum," in *Language, Counter-Memory, Practice*, trans. Donald F. Bouchard and Sherry Simon (Ithaca, N.Y.: Cornell University Press, 1977), 165–196; Jean-François Lyotard, "The Tooth, the Palm," *Substance* 15 (1976): 105–110. The process through which Derrida arrived at indexical (inexpressive) gesture was the deconstruction of Husserlian phenomenology, particularly in Derrida, *Speech and Phenomena and Other Essays on Husserl's Theory of Signs*, trans. David B. Allison (Evanston, Ill.: Northwestern University Press, 1973). To outline his itinerary is beyond the scope of this essay, but let us note that gesture displaces voice, which historically had subsumed it. On the historical background of this contest between gesture and voice, see Mark Franko, "Ut Vox Corpus," in *Dance as Text: Ideologies of the Baroque Body* (Cambridge: Cambridge University Press, 1993), 32–51.

13. If truly displaced into the domain of performance, deconstruction says that within every expressive gesture is an inexpressive gesture that renders expression possible.

14. *Eidos* could be thought of as the form something takes: "*Logos* . . . arises as a sort of primary painting, profound and invisible" (189). This "psychic painting" "gives us the image of the thing itself, what communicates to us the direct intuition, the immediate vision of the thing, freed from the discourse that accompanied it, or even encumbered it" (189–190).

15. This primary form of mimesis which is actually an operation of memory as appearance is important for my ensuing argument.

16. René Descartes, *Discourse on Method and Meditations*, trans. John Veitch (Buffalo, N.Y.: Prometheus Books, 1989), 91.

17. See Mihai I. Spariosu, "Introduction," in *Mimesis in Contemporary Theory: An Interdisciplinary Approach*, vol. 1, *The Literary and Philosophical Debate* (Philadelphia: John Benjamins Publishing, 1984), i–xxix. For a full discussion of the "*atopian* quality of play as the Other of Western Metaphysics" (3), see Spariosu, *Dionysus Reborn: Play and the Aesthetic Dimension in Modern Philosophical and Scientific Discourse* (Ithaca, N.Y.: Cornell University Press, 1989). Philippe Lacoue-Labarthe also deals interestingly with a parallel distinction between "restricted" and "general" mimesis in modernity, showing that theater itself is the model of "general" or primary mimesis. See Lacoue-Labarthe, *L'imitation des modernes: Typographies II* (Paris: Galilée, 1986).

18. "Spacing" (*espacement*) is a term Derrida adopted from Mallarmé. As Mark Wigley points out, "*Spacing*, as distinct from space, is first and foremost not a thing but a movement" (73).

19. This is Derrida's response to the following lines of Mallarmé: "The scene illustrates but the idea, not any actual action, in a hymen (out of which flows Dream), tainted with vice yet sacred, between desire and fulfillment, perpetration and remembrance: here anticipating, there recalling, in the future, in the past, *under the false appearance of a present.* That is how the Mime operates, whose act is confined to a perpetual allusion without breaking the ice or the mirror: he thus sets up a medium, a pure medium, of fiction." I am following here the translation reproduced in "The Double Session" (175).

20. Maurice Merleau-Ponty, *The Phenomenology of Perception*, trans. Colin Smith (London: Routledge and Kegan Paul, 1962), 142.

21. In a parallel manner, Michael Taussig's retheorization of "contact" in the "copy" concept of mimesis is relevant to my argument. See Taussig, *Mimesis and Alterity: A Particular History of the Senses* (New York: Routledge, 1993).

22. Carol Barko, "The Dancer and the Becoming of Language," *Yale French Studies* 54 (1977):179.

23. Stéphane Mallarmé, "Crayonné au théâtre," in *Oeuvres complètes* (Paris: Gallimard, 1945), 295. This is a fundamental difference between Derrida and Heidegger. See Timothy Clark, "Being in Mime: Heidegger and Derrida on the Ontology of Literary Language," *Modern Language Notes* 101.5 (December 1986):1003–1021. Julia Kristeva gets at this practice of productivity by plumbing beneath the surface of language toward the semiotic material (best exemplified in her terms by chance and music) that underlies and disrupts it. This amounts to another form of mirroring that ingeniously dodges metaphysical fixity because its "originary metaphysics" is motility itself without spatial coordinates. See Julia Kristeva, *Revolution in Poetic Language*, trans. Margaret Waller (New York: Columbia University Press, 1984). Derrida discusses the relationship of "production as mimesis" to Western aesthetic theory in his "Economimesis," *Diacritics* 11 (1981):3–25.

24. The reading of "hymen" as both union and barrier should be understood as the inability of the signifier to wed its signified and unite with it. It is the very productivity of language that the notion of barrier introduces, rather than, as in Robert Greer Cohen's critique, a grotesque misreading. See Robert Greer Cohen, "Mallarmé on Derrida," *French Review* 61.6 (May 1988):884–889.

25. Frances A. Yates, *The Art of Memory* (Chicago: University of Chicago Press, 1966), 6.

26. Derrida remarks that the trace "re-marks itself forever as disappearance, erasure, non-sense" ("Double Session" 253).

27. Derrida's early writings that incriminate structuralism, particularly "Force and Signification" (1963) and "Structure, Sign and Play in the Discourse of the Human Sciences" (1966), both reprinted in *Writing and Difference*, thematize play and theorize the trace as force. Later, notably in "The Double Session," he theorizes the trace as death (the introduction of alterity into presence as the self-same). Yet this apprehension of spacing as death is only convincing inasmuch as it "performs" a critique of presence. The more Derrida broaches the subject of performance per se in which movement acquires its own consistency the more there appears a nostalgia for presence in his texts.

28. See "Double Session" 195; and Paul Margueritte, *Pierrot assassin de sa femme* (Paris: Paul Schmidt, 1882), 1.

29. See Mark Yount, "Two Reversibilities: Merleau-Ponty and Derrida," *Philosophy Today* 34.2 (Summer 1990):139.

30. Derrida's interpretation of mime hinges on the moment in "Mimique" when Mallarmé envisions performance as a union (hymen) of the past and the future "under the false appearance of a present" ("sous une apparence fausse de présent").

31. Remo Guidieri and Francesco Pellizzi, "Shadows: Nineteen Tableaux on the Cult of the Dead in Malekula, Eastern Melanesia," *Res* 2 (Autumn 1981):67.

32. Here I concur with Spariosu's perspective according to which "art and play are not a subversion of or an alternative to power, but an older, more immediate form of it" (*Dionysus Reborn* 96). For a more specific delineation of this view in dance modernism, see Mark Franko, "The Invention of Modern Dance," in *Objects of Movement: The Politics of Expression in Modern Dance* (Bloomington: Indiana University Press, 1995).

Stéphane Mallarmé, Loie Fuller, and the Theater of Femininity

Felicia McCarren

A déduire le point philosophique auquel est située l'impersonnalité de la danseuse, entre sa féminine apparence et un objet mimé, pour quel hymen: elle le pique d'une sûre pointe, le pose.

—Stéphane Mallarmé, "Crayonné au théâtre"

"NOT A WOMAN DANCING"

Stéphane Mallarmé's famous remarks on dancers, collected in the essays "Crayonné au théâtre" (Sketched at the theater),[1] describe the dance as a form of his idealized Literature, removed from writing by the dancer, who functions in it as a Sign. Of all the arts, only dance is able to capture the Mallarméan literary "idea": "Dance alone capable, in its summary writing, of translating the fleeting and the sudden all the way to the Idea" (541). But for the dancer to operate as poetry par excellence, she herself must remain outside of language, unable to manipulate it, and unconscious of the revelations she brings to the poet watching her.

Mallarmé's simultaneous idealization of the dance and dehumanization of the dancer is a familiar chapter in the nineteenth-century tradition of French dance writing. But his theory of literature and the dancer's relevance to it move beyond this double-edged appreciation and appropriation of the dance familiar from Théophile Gautier and others. Mallarmé is interested not in using dance to do what writing alone cannot do (this is Gautier's implicit motivation for writing ballets), or in writing like dance (a commonplace in Romantic poetics), but rather to do in writing what the dancer does with her body. Mallarmé's dance writing and the theory included in it reveal a reconception of the writer's subjectivity along the lines of that of the dance: a de-individuated, disappearing, or dead poet performing a number of roles and yet never entirely present in any one of them.

Despite Mallarmé's general distaste for the theater of his time, his notion of theater and the role of female dancers in that conception of theater are foundational to his literary thinking. Theoretical approaches which have sounded that thinking have largely left the dancer in the position of semiotic operator,[2] and while the poet's subjectivity has been explored in a broader context, Mallarmé's dehumanization of the dancer has remained unchallenged by consideration of the dancers informing his writing, most notably the American dancer Loie Fuller, whose work is analyzed in "Crayonné au théâtre." A closer look at Fuller's dances with huge panels of silk swirled on long sticks under electric lights reveals to what extent her work, and the nature of the dancing body in that work, shaped Mallarmé's theory.

Mallarmé's formulation of the dancer's impersonality is located in this problematic passage from "Crayonné au théâtre":

> To understand that the dancer *is not a woman dancing,* for the juxtaposed causes that she *is not a woman,* but a metaphor summarizing one of the elementary aspects of our form, sword, cup, flower, etc., and *that she does not dance,* suggesting, by the prodigy of shortcuts or energies, with a corporeal writing that would necessitate paragraphs of prose in dialogue as well as description to express, in editing: poem disengaged from all writing apparatus. (304)

This passage, denying both the dancer's sex and her work, is rarely read in the context of its inspiration. A closer examination of both Fuller's dances and Mallarmé's writing about them reveals that it is this real dancer, and her dances, which suggests to Mallarmé the dehumanized, semiotic subjectivity which he also applies to the poet. More than the simple referent or object of study, the subject about which Mallarmé is writing, Fuller's work, examined through Mallarmé's texts, visual images, and her own writings, suggests to what extent the female body dancing is at the center, rather than the margins, of his formulation.

Mallarmé locates the dancer's impersonality between her "feminine appearance"—the body onstage—and "a mimed object," the referential content of her dance; that is, between subject and object, or what is presented onstage and what is represented there. The dance form created by the female form raises for Mallarmé the most important philosophical questions of artistic signification and the artist's subjectivity: "To deduce the philosophical point at which is situated the [female] dancer's impersonality, between her feminine appearance and a mimed object, for what hymen: she stings it with a sure point, puts it down" (296).[3]

In Loie Fuller's dance, however, subject and object become confused, and the line between presentation and representation, or reference and reflexivity, is blurred. This is precisely the philosophical conundrum that Fuller's dance creates: how the dancer manages such anonymity when she is not hiding behind the character, costume, or speeches of conventional drama; how she manages to make herself an object though she is also, ultimately, the only subject of her dance. Fuller is both signifier and signified. In her work, it is impossible to distinguish a signified content from a signifying body, and the dance is itself also both a content and the act of producing that content.

Fuller's work allows Mallarmé the occasion for a critique of the narrow visuality of the contemporary theater—the possibility of a new way of seeing and the importance of that more profound seeing both for art and the artist. Mallarmé is critical of all forms of theater which clutter the stage with the trappings of plot, set, and costumes. He is critical as well of the frenzied viewing of dandy voyeurs who attended the ballet, like the vaudeville, armed with opera glasses for privatized possession of the performer's visual images.[4] In "Crayonné au théâtre," Mallarmé describes Théophile Gautier at the vaudeville as a displeased spectator who is blinded by his opera glasses but unwilling to put them down:

> Sitting before the immediate and mad triumph of the monster, or Mediocrity, parading in the holy site, I love Gautier applying to his jaded eye the black opera glass as if in a voluntary blindness and exclaiming before the curtain "It is such a gross art . . . so abject"; but as it did not occur to him, because of disgust, to annul on his part the prerogatives of the seer, it was all the more ironic, the sentence: "There should only be one vaudeville—with a few changes made from time to time." (313)

For Mallarmé, the problem with the contemporary theater is not only one of monstrous mediocrity invading the "holy site," but a larger problem of spectating, a problem created by the theater, but also potentially addressed by it. Mallarmé goes to the theater not simply to see what is happening there, but to study the problem of seeing. Yet the current state of the theater threatens to make such investigation impossible:

> —I went only rarely to the theater: from whence, perhaps, the chimerical exactitude of such observations, and when I indicated there some alienation for the pamphlets or reviews after which, professional and marvelous, of a Gautier, of Janin, of Saint-Victor, of Banville, no, I did not seriously think, not at all, that the genre, honored by these great men of letters, would resuscitate today and produce an outburst that allied itself with theirs, for all, clear, supreme, imposing, with Catulle Mendes capable of producing magnificent daily articles about middling events: I try, before such curtains of reason, prestige, loyalty, and charm, on that which continues for me, a lack of interest or the current theater practice, with fury and magic draped, not to perceive the contemporary emptiness behind. (1562)

If Gautier and others went to the theater to see something, and write about it, Mallarmé here describes trying *not* to see, going to the theater—reluctantly—to see if there is anything to see. Despite a lot of looking, there seems to be very little of what he would define as seeing, and very little that satisfies his desire to do something more than the incomplete looking which bad theater demands. Offering a lot to look at—overly decorated sets, overly emphatic gesture, costumes, characters, plots—bad theater makes impossible what Mallarmé would consider "seeing." His response is to try not to perceive this theater's lack, to imagine a more complete theater beyond it—the theater of what he calls "Idée."

"Crayonné au théâtre" begins with the author at the theater, with "lost looks" and "features already tired of [the] nothing" (293). He has come to the theater hoping to find in the performance the elusive "idée," which he defines as a collective coming together, the production or presence of divinity in the "holy site" of the theater: "if we must see in this a soul or even our idea (that is, divinity present to the mind of man)" (293). He wants to see something that is not visible: a divine presence manifested in the audience but not represented onstage.[5] While the horizon glows each evening, he notes, other people do the same; society goes to the theater, as if hungry, to be fed by "the social arrangement" (294) of stage and spectators. This "idea" Mallarmé is looking for is theater itself; the two are equated in his notes for the project of Le livre: "d'où Théâtre = idée" (429). Theater brings the "idée" to light, not by presenting it onstage but by causing it to be present in this social ordering; the stage creates "pleasures enjoyed in common" and is "the majestic opening onto the mystery which we are in the world to envision" (314). The theater is not a place for watching a representation but for envisioning a mystery; ordinary theater "shows only a representation, for those having not at all to see the things themselves" (294). Representation is a shadow or screen obscuring "the things themselves," preventing the viewer from "seeing" them. If Mallarmé goes to the theater, it is because it offers "The charm, perhaps unknown in literature, to strictly extinguish one by one every view that would shine with purity" (298).

In the prose poem "Un spectacle interrompu," Mallarmé describes his way of seeing—what he calls "my poet's gaze" (276)—and how it differs from that of the average spectator. If, for Gautier, the dance makes the writer's words visible, and thus seems to allow everything to be said,[6] it requires a scrutiny of the female body onstage which Mallarmé is the first to describe as blindness. For Mallarmé, looking with a poet's eyes means seeing more than what is visible. Rather than being nothing but eyes, like the dandy armed with opera glasses, reducing all perception to the metaphor of sight, it means broadening the metaphor of sight to describe all forms of perception, that is, using one's mind as if it were eyes, making the organs of sense perception and the mind into eyes.

In "Un spectacle interrompu," Mallarmé deems his "way of seeing" not only superior but true, because it depends on insight rather than sight. He generally goes to the theater to see what is not there, that is, to "see" both what is missing ("the contemporary emptiness behind") and what cannot be seen in the first place, an emptiness which is not a lack but rather the full potential of ideal theater. For Mallarmé, it is a question not of seeing some thing, but rather of seeing what he defines as "nothing." The visual metaphor remains important even though the objects, subjects, or matter being seen are differently defined.

For Gautier and other grands lettrés, theater's capacity for visualization prompted the poet to write texts both for performance and about performance.

For Mallarmé, the ideal theater provides what he calls "l'occasion de rien dire" (297) (the opportunity to say nothing), which could be rephrased as "l'occasion de dire le Rien" (the opportunity to say the Nothing); it provides the opportunity not only to see this "nothing," but to write it. This "rien" that the poet aims to express is something created out of emptiness, silence, blankness; nothingness is itself the subject and material of Mallarmé's poetry, from the opening "Rien" of the collected poems opening "Salut," through the notes for the never-written "Livre."

The Mallarméan poetics set out in "Crise de vers" defines the relationship between words and things as one in which poetry makes present, through evocation, what is absent.[7] The subject of poetry, then, will not be things themselves (365–366). In Mallarméan poetics, language does not so much represent what is absent by naming it, but rather evokes the presence of what Mallarmé calls "mystère" or "énigme," the mysterious functioning of language, the enigma of poetry. A certain Platonism can be read into this poetics: the word *flower*—the famous example—evokes not a real flower, but an ideal form of flower which will never be found in any bouquet. Such a poetics works, Maurice Blanchot has pointed out, not only by making an ideal object present to the eye of the imagination, but by banishing the real object.[8]

Mallarmé defines his interest in this mystery of language, or in the book as a "spiritual instrument," against the proliferation of empty words in newspapers, bad poetry, and pamphlets. "Billet à Whistler," written to welcome Whistler's journal *The Whirlwind*, describes the new publication as a dancer bringing a mysterious excitement to a city full of bad writing, a gust of fresh air to streets cluttered with scandal sheets.

The dance is like good writing, or poetry, in its swift succession of images and in its concentrated form. The dance is the only art capable of presenting the Idea—but only to the extent that it is a "summary writing" and not a representation: "Only the charm of the libretto's pages does not work in the performance" ("Crayonné au théâtre" 303). The dance signifies like language, and its signification can be read; the spectator is drawn to ask: "'What can this mean,' or better, to read it with inspiration" (307). Like poetry, dance is a concentrated or coded form "that would take paragraphs in dialogic and descriptive prose to express, in the editing" (304).

The dance comes closer to the Mallarméan poetics of an ideal theater by making-present, rather than visually representing, "l'idée." It provides the spectator with the opportunity to imagine, rather than simply to see: "the ballet gives only a little: it is the genre of the imagination." The description of the ballet as the "genre imaginatif" in the opening pages of "Crayonné au théâtre" becomes a description of the relationship between dancer and sign:

When a sign of the scattered general beauty isolates itself for the gaze, flower, wave, cloud and jewel, etc., if, for us, the exclusive means of knowing it consists in juxtaposing its appearance to our spiritual nudity in order for it to feel analogous and adapt itself in some exquisite confusion between it and this form in flight—nothing but through the rite, there, enunciation of the Idea, does not the dancer seem half the element in question, half humanity apt at being confused there, in the floating revery? The operation, or poetry, par excellence, and the theater. Immediately the ballet turns out allegorical. (295–296)

Seeing the dance becomes for Mallarmé an act of the imagination, an act of imagining—or rather, imaging—the dancer. The dance is a succession of signs which the viewer projects or juxtaposes against his own "spiritual nudity," like Hamlet's "traditional, Goya-esque, somber near-nudity" (300); the sign then becomes a "form in flight." The dancer here is half-human, half responsible for these signs and for their merging with the viewer's own "idea" or imagination. She is the agent or catalyst, sending these images out in her "operation." The ballet's allegory depends on her "half-humanity," the fact that she is, after all, the body incorporating and generating these signs.

Her "operation"—the enunciation of the Idea—is also a rite; "a ritual takes place there" (296). And the dancer's nature as both female body and pure idea is resolved by Mallarmé into the philosophical puzzle of the point between subject and object where the dancer is situated.

In the worst ballet, Mallarmé finds a "manque hautain de signification" (a haughty lack of signification). Poetry comes off the page only to become stuck in the trappings of the ballet onstage: "Poetry, or animated nature, comes out of the text to be fixed in cardboard maneuvers and the dazzling stagnation of muslin" (303). But a good dancer, in this case, La Cornalba, ravishes Mallarmé because she dances as if "undressed" (303)—devoid of trappings or tricks. The best dancer is one whose personality, sex, and humanity disappear during the performance; the dancer who becomes "the nonindividual . . . never anything but an emblem not at all someone" (304).[9]

Thus Mallarmé moves beyond the gendered relationship of writer and dancer, affirming that onstage the dancer is not a woman at all, and does not work—or rather, dance. Like the objects meditated upon in the poems, the idealized dancer is both something and nothing; as a woman she is "unlettered" (307), but as an artist, or work of art, she is "Sign" or "hieroglyph." At the ballet, Mallarmé claims to be concerned exclusively with the dance as a form of writing:

The unique training of the imagination consists, in the regular hours of frequenting the sites of Dance without seeking anything preconceived: patiently and passively to wonder, at each step, each strange attitude, these pointes and *taquetés, allongés* or *ballons*, "What can this mean?" or better, to read it with inspiration. Surely one will operate in full revery but adequate: vaporous, clean and ample, or restrained, only such that it encloses her in its circuits or transports by a fugue the unlettered ballerina delivering herself to the games of her profession. Yes, that one (would you be lost in the audience, very foreign spectator, Friend) for little that you deposit with submission at the feet of this unconscious revealer, just as the roses that the play of her pale satin vertiginous slippers raises and flings into the visibility of higher realms, first the Flower of your poetic instinct, expecting from nothing else the making evident and in the real daylight of a thousand latent imaginations: then, through a commerce which her smile seems to spill the secret of, without hesitation she delivers to you across the final veil which always remains, the nudity of your concepts and will silently write your vision in the manner of a Sign, which she is. (307)[10]

At the ballet, the poet leaves at the dancer's remarkable feet the flower of his poetic instinct. She is his unlettered, unconscious "révélatrice," unaware of her poetic power to make visible to the poet what might not be there. In the state of "full revery" she is nonetheless capable of "adequation," the function of language. But more importantly, signifying across the veil which always remains, the female dancer's enigma, and that of her body, is inextricably linked to the enigma of language.

Thus the dance is not simply like writing, but an alternate form of writing. The dancer, unaware that she is a poem, is not here a model for the dandy-poet whose person is his own best creation as she is in Baudelaire's *La Fanfarlo*, but rather the image of the artist who has managed successfully to lose all identity in the work. She can write the poet's vision because onstage she becomes a pure sign. The dancer's way of signifying as a sign ultimately goes beyond the written word. Simple questions like What can this mean? cannot be answered; the dance can only be "read" with inspiration, taken on faith. In this way, it re-creates the enigma Mallarmé believes literature must have—the mystery present in language itself.

How does the dancer do this? Behind her knowing smile, Mallarmé says, she is unaware of her ability. Yet from behind the veil that never falls, through this veil, the dancer speaks to the poet of the "nudity" of his concepts. It is only across the veil—enigma—that this laying-bare takes place. The last veil is not the veil of obscurity but the veil that guarantees truth. Mallarmé calls this veiling "evocation," "allusion," "suggestion," but denies that its effect is one of hiding: "Monuments, the sea, the human face, in their plenitude, native, conserving an otherwise attractive virtue that a description will not veil, called evocation, allusion I know, suggestion" "La musique et les lettres" (645). Language can make present the object which is not there—which may not even have a real existence—and can thus create the flower absent from all bouquets.

Across her veils, the dancer is herself Sign, hieroglyph, but behind them she knows no eloquence other than her own vocabulary of movements: "The librettist does not usually know that the dancer, who expresses herself in steps, understands no other eloquence, even gesture" ("Crayonné au théâtre" 306). An artist whose body is a sign, who signifies the fact of signification and knows no other form of expression, cannot be a woman and cannot be simply dancing.

HYMEN AND *HYSTEROS*

Yet beyond this familiar idealization of dance, with its dehumanizing underside, "Crayonné au théâtre" provides a different, richer view of the dancer. On another level, Mallarmé is far from ignoring the dancer's sex and is fascinated by the subjectivity of the dancer. Her ability to signify from behind the veil, to write on the outside world, depends on the relationship between her sex and the material of her dance. The dancer's femaleness, "sa féminine apparence" (296)—that is, her body—and the material that makes up her dance ("un objet mimé") appear to be at opposite poles; the body in its literality presents itself onstage, and the "objet mimé" is represented by it. Yet sex and matter come together, or become indistinguishable, in the work of Loie Fuller.

Mallarmé is referring to the ballet and not to Fuller in the passage which describes both the dancer's sex and her art through use of the word "hymen." This "hymen" is the means by which she signifies: "elle le pique d'une sûre pointe, le pose." In the ballet, the dancer's feet seem both to poke through the veil of the stage space and to hold it in place. The image recalls the Romantic ballet as shaped by Gautier, the simultaneous covering and revealing of the female body; the dandy bored with what he sees but unwilling to put down his opera glasses; the voyeur or fetishist frustrated by what he cannot see, yet determined to look.

What is this veil through which, or by which, the dancer's signification is projected? The "idée" can be seen in the dance because of a veil which allows it to be seen, not unlike the way in which the dancer's transparent costume covers her body without hiding its form.[11] Under the electric light, the veil-like panels of silk increase the apparent speed of the dancer's movement and allow its imagery to be writ large on the performance space:

> In the terrible bath of fabrics fans out, radiant, cold, the performer who illustrates many spinning themes from which extends a distant fading warp, giant petal and butterfly, unfurling, all in a clear and elemental way. Her fusion with the nuances of speed shedding their lime-light phantasmagoria of dusk and grotto, such rapidity of passions, delight, mourning, anger: to move them, prismatic, with violence or diluted, it takes the vertigo of a soul as if airborne on artifice. (308)

With the excitement of fireworks, the fantasy of dusk and dark, the performance creates in the viewer a rapid series of passionate reactions to the performer's abstract actions. Or is Mallarmé attributing these passions to the dancer herself? For at the center of these seemingly self-generating images there is a woman dancing: "a woman associates the flight of clothing to the powerful or vast dance at the point of supporting them, infinitely, as her own expansion" (308). It is a woman who is controlling these tremendous wings or petals, a woman fusing an abstract representation of images and the real emotions they create.

Mallarmé closely links the theatrical space—ideally full of nothing—to the woman in it, describing how Fuller's manipulation of her costume creates or constitutes that space: "The magic that Loie Fuller creates, with instinct, with exaggeration, the contraction of skirt or wing, instituting a place. The enchantress creates the ambience, draws it out of herself and goes into it, in the palpitating silence of crêpe de chine" (309). This description plays on the aural resemblance between "soi" and "soie," casting the woman herself (*soi*) as silk (*soie*); the space which Fuller draws out from inside herself becomes the space in which she moves. It also plays on a comparison of the empty, idealized theatrical space to a female body; working against the floorboards, this dancer—unlike the ballerina—does not pierce any imagined veil or "hymen," but rather reinforces the space's "virginity": "When, at the rising of the curtain in a gala audience, entirely local, thus appears like a (snow)flake blown from where? furious, the dancer: the floorboards avoided by bounds or hard to the pointes, acquires a virginity of site undreamt of, that isolates, the figure will build, will flower" (308). The space's virginity allows Fuller's images to flower. This "hymen" is both the "nothing" represented by this ideal form of theater and the means by which it is presented: "here, rendered unto Ballet is atmosphere or nothing, visions scattered as soon as they are known, their limpid evocation" (309).

More than a simple alternation of a dilating body and a reified, statuesque frame, the changes of this body, and the poet's changing views of it, suggest the intimate, undissolvable connection within the body between hard and soft, expansion and control, liberating flights and centering structure. Just as the fantastic images created by huge wings of silk are made possible by the artist manipulating them, so the dance itself—the dilation of the body into images—is impossible without the anchoring structure of bone and muscle.

As Mallarmé sits at Loie Fuller's spectacle, he attempts an explanation of the contradictions of an art generated by the body and ultimately detached from the body, an art of rapidly changing images spun out of a body that is itself described as changing despite its stability. In the dancing body, there can be no clear demarcation of inside and outside; the dancer seems to contain the space in which she is contained. She is a box full of images filling the space and also simply another image in that box of space. She is both the generator and the product, or artist and artwork; she is both mother and child of her dance, inexhaustibly recreating herself; her dance is a hatching or birth, an "éclosion contemporaine" (a contemporary birthing) (309).

Fuller's dance of veils inspires more than looking and resembles Mallarmé's ideal theater because, principally, the veils moving across the body work like music: "Is there anything, better, resembling gauze than Music!" (309). Like music, like poetry at its best, Fuller's veils work rhythmically. For Mallarmé, rhythm makes evocation, allusion, or suggestion possible because it functions in language like the veil, seeming to hide, while in fact it reveals. And, like the veil, rhythm works through condensation; it is an overlapping rather than an excision or deletion.[12]

For Mallarmé, rhythm is a way to describe the form that structures both poetry and dance. He cites Rodenbach's remarks on the ballerina's usual tendency to "complicate with all sorts of vaporous finery the sorcery of dances, where their body appears only as the rhythm on which everything depends but which hides it" (311). For Rodenbach, the ballet costume hides the dancer just as programmatic orchestral music covers over its structural underpinnings with melody. To describe how Loie Fuller manifests rather than hides this structuring "rhythm" of the body, Mallarmé uses the word *armature,* playing on the resonance between the body and music: "An armature, which is of no particular woman, and thus instable, across the veil of generality, draws onto such a revealed fragment of the form and there drinks the flash that renders it divine; or exhales, in return, by the undulation of fabrics, floating, palpitating, scattered this ecstasy" (311).[13] What is this "inner form" which structures both the body and the dance, but cannot be seen, the form which allows the *idée* to be generated, fleshed out with visible form, translated from "sonorités" to "tissus"? The form structuring the body but hidden, itself, in the body?

Read in the context of Mallarmé's problematization of spectating at the Opéra, his reaction to Gautier's passionate but blind gaze, the inner rhythm which Mallarmé finds so crucial for the dance can be taken as a metaphor for what the dandy armed with opera glasses hoped to but could not see: the dancer's sex under her skirt. Against the voyeuristic or fetishistic gaze of the dandy ballet-goer, defining feminine sexuality as lack or deviance in the visual realm and substituting other, visible parts of her body for that lack, Mallarmé defines the dancer's femininity in rhythmic rather than purely visual terms.

For Mallarmé, Loie Fuller's dance, like the word *rhythm* itself,[14] describes a form neither exclusively visual nor exclusively metrical, neither exclusively plastic or poetic, but somewhere between the two—a form defined by its movement between realms, and defined as movement. Only glimpses of this form are possible; or rather, the form can only be seen as a fragment. Fragmented glimpses or glimpses of fragment suggest a rhythmic viewing, alternating between seeing too much and too little: "Yes, the suspense of the Dance, the contradictory fear or wish to see too much and not enough, requires a transparent prolongation" (311).

What is this contradictory fear and wish to see both too much and not enough? And what is the transparent prolongation which the dance requires, or suspends? In Mallarmé's formulation, seeing too much and not seeing enough are not contradictory: "to see too much *and* not enough." The contradiction comes only in the alternation of fear and desire for this kind of seeing; it could be read as "fear, or contradictory wish," although here again there is a kind of equivalence being set up between two apparent opposites—fear is equal to a contradictory desire.

This looking-at-what-is-there-or-not, like the gaze of Gautier voluntarily blinding himself with opera glasses, can only construct a female body which, in its anatomical difference from the male, can only be seen as lacking. But here Mallarmé offers an alternative way of looking, focusing on the structure of the body ("armature") that we cannot see, though we know it is there. Hidden by the "veil of generality," unseen because of the obscuring gaze of an overly avid public, the body's inner form eludes the gaze.

Requiring insight rather than sight, allowing the "transparent prolongation" of the look, dance allows to be seen not emptiness or lack, but the "nothing" which Mallarmé locates at the heart of theater. In Loie Fuller's dance, the visible expansion and representation of feminine "matter," we see a complex construction of artistic and sexual identity which depends on the movement between passion and control, nothing and something, abstraction and femaleness. The female form in Loie Fuller's dancing redefines femininity as a series of roles, a series of images, the rapid movement from role to role or image to image; her dance redefines the female form not as lack but as the ability to create multiplicity from nothing and return it to nothing, to create images which succeed one another and then disappear. It is a theatrical subjectivity theorized by Mallarmé as the role of the poet himself, the poet who disappears in his enunciation, but also casts himself in a series of roles of which absence is only one.[15]

The two women Mallarmé finds in Fuller's dance, the artist of inebriation and the technical wizard identified, respectively, as the non-woman and the woman, exist side by side in Fuller's own assessment of herself. Her autobiography describes both her aggrandisement in the public eye and her self-deprecation, a split or multiple personality that finds expression in her dances.[16] The use of electric light which makes Fuller's work so effective, the "industrial accomplishment" whose effect Mallarmé so carefully notes in her spectacle, highlights the multiplied subjectivity which allows her to perform.

Fuller's "éclosion," then, her rhythmic production of images, offers a creative way to deal with potentially hysterical *rythmos,* by making the theater into a feminine space, transforming its womblike emptiness from a space of potential hysteria traditionally located in *hysteros,* the uterus, into a space of theatrical expression. Her dance presents, and represents, a different theatrical possibility for *hysteros,* an interior theater that Mallarmé theorizes in his writings on her in "Crayonné au théâtre." Beyond the mediocre theater of the nineteenth century, and the century's theatrical hysterics, beyond the theater tradition in which it is hymen that traditionally closes comedy or opens tragedy, it is the woman dancing who moves Mallarmé to figure a different theatrical "hymen," from the inside out.

NOTES ⸺⸺⸺⸺⸺⸺

1. "To deduce the philosophical point at which is situated the [female] dancer's impersonality, between her feminine appearance and a mimed object, for what hymen: she stings it with a sure point, puts it down." Stéphane Mallarmé, *Oeuvres complètes*, ed. Henri Mondor and G. Jean-Aubry (Paris: Bibliothèque de la Pléiade, 1945), 296. All essays by Mallarmé cited in this chapter come from this edition of his *Oeuvres complètes*. All translations are my own except where otherwise noted.

2.   In "Les Fleurs du Mal Armé," Barbara Johnson recognizes that Mallarmé's "feminine" writing, or adopting a "feminine" voice in his poetry, is quite different from considering or presenting the real voices of real women. Unfortunately, Johnson's feminist critique of Mallarmé's identification of femininity with textuality does not extend to the dancer; the dancer's real existence as a woman is ignored in Johnson's work, which describes Mallarmé's relation to the dancer as "completely depsychologized" (125). This is of course a recapitulation of Mallarmé's own statements on the topic, which I suggest need to be re-read. Barbara Johnson, "Les Fleurs du Mal Armé," in *A World of Difference* (Baltimore: Johns Hopkins University Press, 1987), 116–133.

3.   In French, several alternative meanings are suggested by both vocabulary and syntax (see epigraph): *pique* has been alternately translated as "pricks" by Barbara Johnson, and "ticks off" (as on a list or chart) by Robert G. Cohn, whose translations and readings of passages from "Crayonné au théâtre" differ greatly from mine. Cf. Johnson 116–133, and Robert G. Cohn, *Mallarmé's "Divagations"; a Guide and Commentary* (New York: Peter Lang, 1990), 119–212. *Pointe* refers also to the blocked shoe of the ballerina, which Loie Fuller did not wear.

4.   On the spectatorship of the *loges infernales* at the Paris Opéra, see Lynn Garafola, "The Travesty Dancer in Nineteenth-Century Ballet," *Dance Research Journal* 17.2 and 18.1 (1985–1986): 35–40; Ivor Guest, *The Romantic Ballet in Paris* (London: Sir Isaac Pitman and Sons, Ltd., 1966); Martine Kahane, ed., *Le foyer de la danse* (Paris: Editions de la Réunion des Musées Nationaux, 1988); Abigail Solomon-Godeau, "The Legs of the Countess," *October* 39 (Winter 1986): 65–108. A comic view of the experience of spectatorship at the ballet of the Opéra is presented by the anonymous authors of *Musée Philipon périodique dit album de tout le monde,* collection of the Bibliothèque de l'Opéra de Paris.

5.   In *Musica Ficta (figures de Wagner)* (Paris: Bourgois, 1991), 95–160, Philippe Lacoue-Labarthe argues that Mallarmé's theater attempts to keep the chorus of the Greek drama without the scenic representation. Here and elsewhere in this chapter I am influenced by Lacoue-Labarthe's readings of Mallarmé's texts on theater and religion.

6.   In *L'art romantique* (Paris: Editions de la NRF, 1923), 103, Charles Baudelaire quotes Gautier as having said: "L'inexprimable n'existe pas" (The inexpressible does not exist). Gautier's recourse to the ballet can be interpreted as an attempt to fulfill his romantic doctrine of finding words for every idea, for being capable of what he called "saying everything." And, more than repeating Romantic doctrine, this formulation suggests the links between Gautier's ballets and the

most explicit of his pornographic writings. Gautier's Romantic ballet repeats, on the surface, themes from his poems, particularly those of *Emaux et camées*; yet their latent misogyny echoes that of his pornography, collected in *Oeuvres erotiques*.

7. "Je dis: une fleur! et, hors de l'oubli où ma voix relègue aucun contour, en tant que quelque chose d'autre que les calices sus, musicalement se lève, idée même et suave, l'absente de tous bouquets" (367). This sentence has produced many readings, and thus many different translations. "I say: one flower! and, outside of the forgetting where my voice relegates any contour, as anything other than the known calyxes, musically arises, the idea itself and suave, the absent (flower) of all bouquets."

8. Maurice Blanchot, "Le mythe de Mallarmé," in *La part du feu* (Paris: Gallimard, 1949), 37.

9. Mallarmé also uses the word "emblème" to describe the subjectivity of the dead Gautier, in "Toast funèbre" ("à Théophile Gautier"). This description of the dancer in the same terms as the dead poet echoes Mallarmé's famous denial of his own existence in letters written during the composition of "Hérodiade" in the 1860s; later theorized as the "disparition élocutoire du poète" (elocutionary disappearance of the poet), in "Crise de vers" (Crisis of verse).

10. For a slightly different translation of this passage and commentary, see Johnson 127.

11. Baudelaire's comment in *La Fanfarlo* on the way in which the Romantic ballerina's veiling exposes rather than hides the body is adapted and extended by Mallarmé.

12. See Julia Kristeva, *La revolution du langage poétique* (Paris: Editions du Seuil, 1974), 237, for a discussion of these lines from Mallarmé's "Hommage": "Le sens trop précis rature/Ta vague littérature" (73).

13. The electrical connotation of the word *armature* should not be ignored either, as Fuller's use of electricity is crucial to her stage illusion. I have discussed this in "The 'Symptomatic Act' circa 1900: Hysteria, Electricity, Dance" (in press).

14. In "La notion de 'rythme' dans son expression linguistique," Emile Benveniste traces the origins of *rhythm* to the Greek *ruthmos*, and considers its shift in meaning from a term used to describe spatial form to a term used to describe aural form. Benveniste attributes the modern meaning of *rhythm* to Plato, who uses the word in its traditional meaning of spatial form, disposition, or proportion, but also gives it a new meaning by applying it to the dance. In Benveniste's reading, the dance is the art in which the form and the content are not simply inseparable, but indistinguishable; and both can be described by the word *form*. Dance is inseparable from the human form dancing it; thus, to some extent, the formal aspect of dance is itself the human form. The dancing body thus provides the meeting ground for the overlap of rhythm in its human and extrahuman, concrete and abstract senses: the form or shape of the body ("attitudes

corporelles") and the formal movement of that body in space and time ("mesure" or "metre" of the movement). See Emile Benveniste, "La notion de 'rythme' dans son expression linguistique," in *Problèmes de linguistique generale* (Paris: Gallimard, 1966), 1:327–335.

15. This disappearance or death of the poet, described by Mallarmé in letters written during the composition of the first version of "Hérodiade," and later theorized in "Crise de vers" (366), is also linked by Johnson (126) to the impersonality of the female dancer.

16. Loie Fuller, *Fifteen Years of a Dancer's Life; with Some Account of Her Distinguished Friends* (London: Herbert Jenkins, 1913). Fuller describes here her experiments with electricity and amateur hypnosis as well as her experience of electroshock therapy. Her self-descriptions include statements about her inability to be "Loie Fuller" to admirers backstage and the multiplication of her images by imitators calling themselves Loie Fuller. I have analyzed these passages at greater length in "The 'Symptomatic Act.'"

Textual Evidances

Susan L. Foster

ORGANIZING DANCE'S HISTORY

Dance's Origins

In 1682 Claude François Menestrier, a Jesuit writing on the history of dance, summarized its origins as follows:

> The dance that today serves as entertainment for all peoples and persons of quality was in its origin a kind of mysterious ritual and ceremony. The Jews, to whom God himself gave his laws and the ceremonies that they observe, introduced dance into their festivities, and the pagan peoples following them worshiped their gods in dance.[1]

Seventy-two years later Louis de Cahusac, author of several entries on dance and gesture for Denis Diderot's *Encyclopédie*, proposed this alternative beginning:

> Man had sensations at the first moment that he breathed; and the tones of his voice, the play of his features, the movements of his body, were simply expressions of what he felt. . . .
> The body was peaceful or agitated; the eyes flamed or smouldered; the arms opened or closed, rose toward heaven or sank to the earth; the feet formed steps slow or rapid; all the body, in short, responded by postures, attitudes, leaps, shudders to the sound with which the soul expressed its emotions. Thus song, which is the primitive expression of feeling, developed from itself a second which is in man, and it is this expression that we have named dance.[2]

For Menestrier, dance's murky origins are embedded in the social practices that constitute ritual and religion. His description evokes a group dance, both ceremonial and celebratory, and weighted with a symbolic significance passed down from one generation of performers to the next. The first records indicate that it was performed by Jews and subsequently by Egyptians and then Greeks, whose civilizations developed dancing over centuries. For Cahusac, dance's origin is both psychological and universal. His portrait of originary dance depicts a solo, a moment of discovery by a sensitive and responsive everyman moved by the power of feeling. Dance thereby existed as an innate human response prior to any social conventions that came to govern it. For Menestrier the connection between dances past and present resides in the fact of their performance at both moments in history. Cahusac attributes such continuity to the enduring structure of the human psyche.

Tables of Contents

Menestrier, whose work is widely acclaimed as the first extant history of dance, continues his description of dance's origins by listing the various instances of dance—by Moses and Miriam at the parting of the Red Sea, by the daughters of Silo, by David before the Ark of the Covenant—known to scholars through references in ancient texts. With the seeming spontaneity of a raconteur, Menestrier discovers each new topic or feature of dance nestled close to its predecessor. David's dance at the Ark reminds Menestrier of sacred Spanish dances, which remind him of something Lucian said about dance, and so forth. Each topic inspires the next by sharing some attribute of the dance with it.

Cahusac, who had studied Menestrier's text, describes these same dances, including much of Menestrier's commentary about them, but not before categorizing them with respect to their nature and function. In his history these dances occupy a particular place within a much larger taxonomic organization: first, they are examples of "Sacred Dances," and, within that broad category, they are instances of "Sacred Dances of the Jews." In much the same way that Cahusac's description of dance's origins segments the body, vividly cataloging its repertoire of movements, so his history itemizes dances in so far as they conform to one of several main types. Thus he describes sacred dances of Jews, Egyptians, Greeks, Romans, Christians and Turks, followed by an examination of the "Profane or Secular Dances" of these same peoples, and then concludes with a treatment of their "Theatrical" dance forms. The arrangement of the chapters on the pages renders the body of Cahusac's book as clearly jointed as the originary dancer he describes. White spaces and centered titles frame each chapter at predictable five-to seven-page intervals.

No such exoskeletal organization supports Menestrier's history. A glance at a section of the table of contents is sufficient to violate all categorizing sensibilities:

> . . . On figures in the ballet.
> On movements.
> Criminals exposed to suffering and death in performance.
> On harmony.
> On paraphernalia.
> On machines.
> On costumes.
> The Crowning of Petrarch.
> Horse ballets. . . .

Yet Menestrier leads the reader with ease from costumes to "The Crowning of Petrarch" to "Horse ballets": Petrarch's coronation made use of exemplary costumes and, as a procession, recalls other similar processions, some using horses, which in turn invites comments on horse ballets in general. And he moves just as convincingly through the entire history of dance from its earliest occurrences to the invention of the ballet, to an analysis of different aspects of the ballet, with descriptions of specific ballets interspersed throughout. The chapter titles, appearing in the margins of an otherwise seamless text, simply add another level of commentary, marking noteworthy people, features of dance, or dances rather than junctures in a developing logic.[3]

STAGING HISTORIES OF DANCE

Menestrier's and Cahusac's histories, so deliciously, excruciatingly different from one another, frame the historical period in which European theatrical dance undergoes the processes of both professionalization and narrativization. During this period theatrical dance loses its cast of amateurs and promotes instead the highly skilled accomplishments of professional dancers trained in a codified and delimited repertoire of steps and gestures. Selected and salaried at the king's behest, these master dancers exert enormous influence over pedagogical, stylistic, and evaluative procedures. Their designation as specialists and the sheer number of hours they can devote to dance training set these performers apart. The skills they demonstrate, while clearly issuing from the aesthetic matrix of the social dance lexicon, increasingly exceed the amateur's grasp. The same period witnesses the first experiments with dance movement as a vehicle through which a coherent narrative can be conveyed. In these danced stories, characters enact soliloquies and dialogues using gesture, dramatic posture, and facial expression. Unlike the opera-ballets, where singing characters move the plot forward and danced interludes establish a corporeal and emotional ambiance for the story, these new story ballets attempt to shift from mimetic movements to the virtuoso vocabulary of ballet steps and back again. These experiments eventually allow theatrical dance to separate from opera and develop as an autonomous genre of spectacle.

The two dance histories likewise document the changing conceptions of the body which ensue from the challenge to absolutism undertaken during the Enlightenment. Menestrier's history, written at a moment of supreme monarchic control by Louis XIV, presumes a world of physicalized sociability which the king has helped shape. All social classes, but especially aristocrats, rely on systems of corporeal signification to convey status and identity. Louis's issuance of the patents that authorize a professional cadre of dancers only extends his authority over bodily discipline, a domain he has begun to regulate as early as the 1640s through his proscriptive behavior for proper comportment at court and his insistence on social dance occasions as performances. Cahusac's history, in contrast, participates in the Enlightenment privileging of the category of the individual human being over political and religious social formations. Enlightenment concern with expressive gesture, with gesture that depicts the intimate feelings of each character in a story, stems from its capacity to portray individual sensibilities rather than social standing. Gestural expression has the status of a kind of universal language to which all humans have equal access. Even the story ballet's use of gesture grows out of the fair theater productions that were specifically designed as an affront and challenge to royal authority.

The shift from Louis XIV's absolutism to an Enlightenment humanism encumbers the body with a new and distinctive expressive function, and it also specifies a new relation between writing and dancing. In Menestrier's time both practices are conceptualized as forms of inscription. Each medium is equally capable of articulateness; each can represent many different things. Both forms of inscription circulate within a rigidly fixed social and political hierarchy. The chain of meaning that descends from god to king to social classes enables but also requires the body to speak. Its corporeality must be cultivated so as to insure control over the contents of its communications. By the time Cahusac writes his history, words and movements, while each forming the vocabulary of a kind of language, are apprehended as unique in their expressive abilities. Words can translate directly into movements, as the scenarios for the story ballets demonstrate, yet movement's message appeals to heart and soul in a way that words cannot. The body's expressive movements thereby secure a private place, an incipient interiority for the individual, over which that individual exerts his or her control.

Even though construed as a language in Enlightenment thought, the body's gestures begin to signify that which cannot be spoken. This unique role for gesture prepares the way for a complete separation between dance and text that occurs in the early decades of the nineteenth century. Dance becomes imbued with a dynamic charisma, and text is assigned the ability to interpret and theorize about the ephemeral yet magnetizing presence of the dance. So powerful is this attribution of mutually exclusive functions for dancing and writing throughout the nineteenth and twentieth centuries that its historical specificity has only recently been questioned. But what if we allow movement as well as words the power to interpret? What if we find in choreography a form of theorizing? What if learning to choreograph, the choreographer learns to theorize, and learning to dance, the dancer assimilates the body of facts and the structuring of discursive frameworks that enable theorization to occur? What if the body of the text is a dancing body, a choreographed body?

This essay responds to these questions by reading two historical texts, two classic dance histories, as a choreographer might, looking for evidence of theories of relationships between body and self and one body and another body that could be choreographed. What permits this reading is a general assumption that theories of representation can translate, even if imperfectly, from one form of discourse to another. That is, literary conventions that enable such maneuvers as the framing and organization of an argument, the delineation of a subject, or the indicating of an authorial presence have choreographic equivalents. Such conventions theorize relationships between subject and surround or between subject and mode of expression in the same way that choreographic conventions theorize the body's relation to subject and to the expressive act. For a given historical period, the contents of these forms often, although not always, move in unison alongside one another.

In order to ex-press choreographic equivalents from these two historical texts, to press the texts for live and moving versions of themselves, I have treated them as if they were scores for dances. The act of comparing two such different textual forms with two such similar contents foregrounds the places where theory operates, and thus where a translation to choreography(-as-theory) could occur. The right-hand column of text represents the effort at one such translation. In that column the textual stances taken in the two histories toward their subjects find choreographic articulation in sets of parameters for two dances, one corresponding to Menestrier's text and the other to Cahusac's. The abstract guidelines for dance-making that are set forth in the right-hand text convert as literally as possible the text-making procedures discussed in the analysis of two histories conducted in the left-hand column of text.

Of course my interpretation of the histories as "scores" relies heavily on yet another set of "texts." These texts are the imaginary dances I have fabricated in response to fragmentary historical evidence that documents dances from the time of Menestrier and Cahusac, and also in response to live concerts by choreographers attempting to reconstruct historical dances for performance in the present. Out of these texts, some written and some performed, I have developed my own imagined versions of the court ballets that Menestrier saw and directed and of the action ballets that Cahusac watched emerge during his lifetime. These imagined dances impinge on my efforts to detect the theoretical moves made in the histories, and they also influence profoundly the shaping of the corresponding choreographic directives. The right-hand column thus responds choreographically to the histories, but also performs as an intertext, a kind of choreographer's notebook filled with ideas that coalesce past and present images of dancing into the general features of two distinct dances, one choreographed in response to Menestrier's world and the other to Cahusac's.

SUBJECT-ING DANCE

Constructing the Subject

Des ballets anciens et modernes recounts the actual history of dance in only thirty pages. The rest of the 332-page treatise is taken up with an examination of the ballet, using citations from classical and contemporary philosophers as well as descriptions of actual performances to illustrate the arguments. The text proceeds at a lively pace, shifting imperceptibly from theory to description to citation to opinion. Rarely is there any marking of the different kinds or levels of analysis. Comments of theoretical preeminence, such as the criteria for an adequate subject or the relationship between dance and painting, are often found buried, midparagraph, undistinguished from the descriptions of that which surround them. Nor does Menestrier offer any summary or conclusion. The manuscript ends abruptly with the description of a newly invented Italian card game, part of the discussion of literary and other sources of subjects of ballets.

Cahusac's history, although equivalent to Menestrier's in length, is more ambitious historically and cross-culturally. He discusses dances of Mediterranean antiquity, including those of Egypt and Turkey, as well as Greece and Rome, and his treatment of ballet occupies only half the book. Chapters typically conclude with a few summary sentences, or with Cahusac's opinions about the relative merits of the particular type of dance. The history follows in precise segments the development of dance until the last few chapters, where Cahusac considers briefly the main elements of ballets, in general—their actions and characters. He concludes with a sum-

An evening-length dance incorporating various kinds of sources and involving different levels of abstraction. It presents surreal sequences of images, seemingly magical transitions from one landscape or set of characters to another. The performance progresses without developing toward an obvious climax, nor does it offer a summary, celebratory conclusion.

A five-act work unified by a clear plot consisting of a beginning, a middle created around a dramatic knot that moves the action forward toward a climax, and an ending. It may begin or conclude with a celebratory section that consists of portraits of distinct dance traditions, each of which is transformed into the homogeneous style of the production through an insistent emphasis on the visual characteristics that each dance form exhibits.

mary plea for continued improvement in dancing and dance-making.

Defining History

Prefaces to the two histories place distinctive frames around their project. Menestrier's preface is taken up with lengthy descriptions of two ballets—one reprehensible for its indiscriminate presentation of profane and gaudy images, and the other, his own *L'autel de Lyon* (1658), meritorious for the restraint and appropriateness with which it develops a single theme. Cahusac's preface, instead of examining dances or choreographic principles, refutes the aesthetic theories found in other dance histories, in particular that of Abbé du Bos's *Réflexions critiques sur la poésie et sur la peinture.* Cahusac's critique of his predecessor situates his own work within a tradition of inquiry whose purpose it is to reflect on the continuing failures and successes of dance. Where Menestrier sees in history the opportunity to reinterpret and restate a set of aesthetic principles of interest to both historians and choreographers, Cahusac casts himself as one of a group of specialists capable of evaluating "objectively" the intention of a given dance. In doing so, he sets history apart from choreography as an impartial documentation of its accomplishments and errors. History, an indispensable reference for choreographers who, because of the practical nature of their work, cannot take time to reflect on their own aesthetic decisions, creates a picture of dance's development for choreographers to evaluate.

Early in his first chapter Menestrier sets forth the principles of his historical method—to determine the origins of things with briefness and exactness through an

The performance is conceived and produced for a singular occasion. Because of its commemorative function, it draws members of the community into the dance and even the dance-making. They actively interpret the dance as it is composed, embedding its form with symbolic structures and re-deciphering their meanings while it is performed.

The performance occurs as part of the institutionalized art offerings of the society, for general edification but not for any specific occasion. Dancers perform for viewers who are set apart in a related but separate sphere. Rather than interpret the performance, viewers evaluate its success using clearly specified aesthetic criteria. Just as dancers train to perform, so viewers educate themselves as to the levels of perfection a dance can attain.

Dance movements, like costumes, scenery, music, and

examination of the names things have been given. A thorough consideration of these names, Menestrier argues, will establish the foundation of the art so that its various parts can be studied and related to the whole. Menestrier then proceeds to outline not the contents of the book, but the source materials for this study. He proposes to treat with clarity and order the names given to dance by the Hebrews, Greeks, and Romans, as well as the definitions offered by Aristotle, Plato, and others. These very definitions will lead to an understanding of choreographic practice.

Cahusac, in contrast, assumes that the origins of dance are common knowledge, its history a set of incontestable facts. Historical research, the organization and comparison of facts about the past, needs no methodological justification. What does require comment, in Cahusac's estimation, is his own aesthetic evaluation of the dances he writes about. Where the Abbé du Bos argued that dancing in his time achieved complete perfection and also that it was different in every respect from dances of antiquity, Cahusac is concerned to show the continuity between classical and contemporary forms and also the superiority of the most recent developments in ballets. Cahusac thus separates, in a way that Menestrier does not, "historical" information about dances of the past from his own "didactic" views on the relative merits of dance in his own and earlier times. And he advises his readers that he has supplemented the facts with his own judgments, which are, he admits, the specific product of his own time.

dialogue, are selected for their metaphoric appropriateness. They should all relate harmoniously by each emblematizing the most essential elements of the subject being represented. Dance movement has the status of a name—a referent with a history and usage that are open to explication.

Taxonomies constituted by the simple and complex and the true and false organize all dance movement. The selection of steps conforms to the guidelines for tasteful proportion and lively yet clear rhythmic and spatial articulation. Selection of gestures—detailed schemata for the representation of human attitudes and feelings—is based on how well the movements look like, even as they perfect, their quotidien referents. Gestures and steps, distinct categories of movement, each have the status of facts. They are incontestable; only their use can be evaluated.

Re-viewing the Dance

Differences in the overall structures of the two volumes are reinforced by the authors' distinctive approach to the description of a specific ballet. Both historians make detailed references to several of the same performances, always with consistent differences in emphasis. Where Menestrier is concerned to point up the symbolic significance of characters and acts, Cahusac focuses on the way things looked. Take, for example, their accounts of the ballet *Les montagnards* (1631), which, both argue, was significant because it introduced a new kind of subject matter—concerned with peasant life—into the courtly tradition. Both texts begin their descriptions of the ballet with the same sentence: "The theater depicted five large mountains" (Menestrier 79; Cahusac 3:5), and both continue by explaining that each mountain symbolized a type: windy; resonant because inhabited by Echoes; wooded; luminous; and cloudy. Cahusac adds to this observation that the middle of the stage constituted a field of glory recently seized by the inhabitants of all five mountains. According to both authors, Foolish Rumor, costumed as an old woman, then entered, riding an ass and carrying a wooden trumpet. Cahusac provides a footnote explaining her trumpet as an allusion to an old proverb; Menestrier notes the allusion in the text itself. Cahusac describes the old woman delivering a speech that revealed the subject of the ballet. Menestrier notes instead that the first part of her recitation was delivered to the animal she was riding and the second part to the audience. Menestrier then goes on to quote her speech in its entirety.

At this point the styles of the two narratives diverge dramatically. Menestrier proceeds as follows:

> After this pleasant speech, the Winds came forth from the windy mountain carrying windmills on their heads and bellows in

All events and actions in the performance take place under the auspices of an unquestioned, overarching set of relations that reference a moral order of cosmic proportions.

Events elaborate the logic of human reaction and interaction. Each action requires motivation and, in turn, provokes a response. The full sequence of actions creates a moving portrait of life.

All features of the production—dancing, text, music, costumes, scenery—carry equal weight, and all are sublimated to the project of representing a larger moral, political, and aesthetic their hands that whistled like the Winds. Echo then gave a speech and led in the inhabitants of the resonant mountain, all dressed like bells. (80)

Cahusac describes the same action in these terms:

> Then, one of the mountains opened and a whirlwind sprang forth. The quadrilles that composed this act were dressed in the color of flesh; all of them carried windmills on their heads and, in their hands, bellows that when shaken produced the whistle of the winds.
>
> The nymph Echo made the opening speech for the second act and led in the inhabitants of the resonant mountains. They carried tamborines, a bell as a head ornament, and their clothes were covered with small bells of varying pitches that together created a joyful and lively harmony. The ensemble adapted itself to the meter of the songs played by the orchestra, in following the cadences of the dance movement. (3:6)

Whereas Menestrier only provides information that would be helpful in interpreting the identity of the characters and the meaning of their actions, Cahusac emphasizes the visual appearance of the performance. His description contains many more phrases portraying the characters and also more active verbs indicating the quality of the movement. Furthermore, Cahusac is concerned to delineate structural features of the ballet—Echo's speech commences the second act.

The same kinds of differences reappear throughout the rest of the descriptions. Menestrier completes his report in three long sentences, one for each act; Cahusac requires five short paragraphs. Menestrier mentions only the main characters and actions and concludes with a comment on the new reputation for mountain people created by the ballet. Cahusac methodically lists

order. Movement, sound image, texture, and mass all convey their messages equivalently.

The visual impression of the dancing, the way it looks, takes primacy over kinesthetic or aural forms of information. The visual has factual rather than hermeneutic value. Dancing illustrates, makes visible, both music and text.

Dancers work to fit into the ensemble, to make the overall statement evident through their careful and astute execution of the choreographic directions.

Dancers show themselves aware of performing before others. Their actions are shaped so as first the act and then the principal characters, costuming, and actions. As his description proceeds, he also begins to introduce evaluative phrases: "ingenious steps," "this grand spectacle," and even a footnote that comments, "the wooden leg and dark lantern, props of the Lie, are two ideas quite new and amusing" (3:7).

Menestrier's version of the ballet records its main features in order to educate viewers as to the relationship between the ballet's subject, the enactment of that subject, and its moral impact. After quoting the opening recitatif as an overview of the ballet's intent, he seems concerned only to explain key symbolic figures and paraphernalia so that viewers can augment their understanding of the principles of representation. Cahusac, in contrast, replicates his history's functional division of information into chapters in his precise classification into acts of all the action. His description assembles the distinct elements presented on stage into vivid, discrete images. The meaning of these images is self-evident. Once they have been described in all their detail, it remains for the narrator to evaluate their originality and effectiveness. Menestrier offers a set of codes so that readers/viewers can live out and through danced ideas; Cahusac provides visual information so that his audience can compare and improve upon images of life.

Menestrier's account of *Les montagnards* occurs at the end of his discussion of three types of plot structure for ballets—philosophical, poetic, and romantic—and pivots the narrative into a comparison between dance and painting (for which there are also three types). Cahusac mentions the ballet in his chapter titled "Festivals in which dancing played a major part given at the French court between 1610 and 1643."

to be viewed from one perspective, and they deliver those actions with daring showmanship to the viewing eye.

Bodies have sculptural presence. They are round and dripping with emblems; they create masses of potential energy that release into kinetic trajectories that modulate between fast and slow, high and low, and quick and sustained.

Bodies look like two-dimensional cutouts frozen in picture-perfect tableaux that depict a touching scene. Then they suddenly exhibit extraordinary plasticity, darting through space as they display intricate coordinations of hands, feet, and head.

Characters reiterate a set of static structural relationships among types of characters. Individual actions link to evoke a harmonious balance between lively and sedate moods and good and evil presences. Characters' actions do not cause change in circumstances; rather changes occur as the action

He attests to the low aesthetic standards that had developed at court during this period as a result of the assumption that French ballets were superior to all others. For him the ballet's greatest significance lies in its reception—the initial derisive response of the snobbish nobility and the subsequent triumph of a ballet composed in the Italian style. His analysis of the ballet ends the chapter; it is followed in the next chapter by a discussion of similar festivals at other courts in Europe.

reaches designated moments in a preordained plan. Their form is lyric.

The dancer's identity resides in the interstices between the local choreographic moment and the larger moral, aesthetic, and political order of which it is a part.

Dance's Facts and Fictions

In Menestrier's history, *Les montagnards* exists as one among many stories of dances, some good and others inadequate, which can be told about this fine art. In Cahusac's history the ballet occurs at a particular moment in the narrative trajectory that follows the decline and subsequent regeneration of dance. The quality of dances, Cahusac points out, had deteriorated during the reign of Henry IV to the point where "pleasantries of the vilest and worst taste took undisputed possession of the Palaces" (3:4). *Les montagnards* signals the coming of a new era of choreographic genius which officially begins as Louis XIV takes the throne. This dramatic story replicates on the larger scale of dance history: the initial glory of classical Greek and Roman dance is followed by the fall into decadence during the Middle Ages, and the rise *toward* greater glory witnessed by the author and his contemporaries. Unlike Menestrier's history, extending seemingly without end into the flat, continuous terrain formed by past and present, Cahusac's history delineates epicycles of refinement and vulgarity as part of the single dramatic progress of civilization.

Individual phrases of movement that rise and fall nest within larger sections of dance which likewise reach toward and then fall away from climaxes. Characters' aspirations and struggles reveal the unfolding plot. The overall narrative structure conforms to that of tragedy or comedy. Suspense is followed by resolution repeatedly. Variations on the simple plot trajectories show the choreographer's inventiveness, just as innovations in vocabulary usage demonstrate choreographic skill.

The epistemological assumptions that enable Cahusac to separate facts from opinions and to verify facts on the basis of visual appearance also permit him to posit a universal rather than a particular origin for dance. The *fact* of dance exists prior to the various social forms it has assumed. For Cahusac, dance results from a natural correspondence between gesture and all the feelings of the soul. Along with song, dance paints in an unequivocal though clumsy manner all the situations of the soul. The soul's feelings, although they dictate what the gesture will be, do not motivate the gesture. Instead, Cahusac suggests a metonymical relationship between body and soul—they exist side by side. The body's gestural representations of the soul can thus be compared one with another and with an abstract visual image of the soul itself. The act of comparison takes place on the two-dimensional framed canvas, the site of the body's paintings, analogous in structure to the proscenium stage itself.

Whether the dancer transforms into the character and lives out the character's actions or, instead, learns to approximate perfectly the look of those actions becomes a question of acting technique.

For Menestrier, dance does not originate in the individual soul but in the social body. Dance as it was known in Menestrier's time developed out of ancient group practices, with their inherent political and religious as well as aesthetic connotations. The body's gestures thus represent aspects of social life rather than individual feeling. They reenact, rather than paint, life's events. They exist as social facts in a world to be interpreted by all who witness them. The body does not display the world but alludes to it in ways that can be likened to, but not measured against, one another.

The dance provides a map to assist the viewer in navigating through the rest of life. The dance surrounds viewers as much as they surround it. The dance is a commentary.

For Menestrier, dance's history consists of a body of stories, and the historian's art lies in the appropriate arrangement and interpretation of these stories so as to achieve a balanced and judicious account of the past. Cahusac's history, in contrast, adorns a body of facts with a refined set of opinions. More sociological than hermeneutic in orientation, the historian's project is one of comparing life and its images and presenting the best organization of images possible by selecting and arranging an existing body of knowledge. Although Cahusac might discover new facts, he would never admit responsibility for having created them. Facts remain neutral, aestheticized, and amoral within a past that separates the evidential from the evaluative so as to provide objective criteria for the ordering of historical events.

For Menestrier, the original dancing body cannot be separated from the dances it performed. In ancient times, as in his own, the dance, and not the body, is the medium of expression. Through the dance, all participants reinterpret their own life situations. In contrast, Cahusac's original dancing body learns to interact, to dance, with others so as to exhibit dance which in turn provides society with a model for refined and decorous conduct. Menestrier's history, like Menestrier's dancing body, offers to choreographers, viewers, and readers the opportunity to peruse endless stories, some meandering and some coherent, in an effort to comprehend the rules that transform bodies into ideas and life into dance. Cahusac's conception of history offers instead a method for evaluating dance, one that sensitizes readers to the degenerate and enlightened elements of which it has been composed over the years. Cahusac's readers are thereby inspired to attain the sensibility necessary to distinguish between an imaginative performance and a lifeless one.

The production impresses and inspires with its brilliance, cleverness, and virtuosity. The dance's proscenium frame both isolates and factualizes the performance. The dance is an appraisal.

The dance reconfigures images of life.

The dance re-presents images of life.

The dance relies on a universal code to create images appropriate to a particular context.

The dance employs a universal language to portray a particular situation.

DANCING THEORY

Bodies of texts, like dancing bodies, are subject to disciplinary actions that cultivate them in specific ways. These two dance histories and the dancing bodies
they describe take shape in response to distinct distributions of power that impel
their presentations' structure and content. Menestrier envisions his own role and
that of dance as extensions of both religious and royal authority. The free play of
interpretations invited by his text and its dances is enabled by the absolutist
control of a king who embodies divine authority and a divinely inspired system
of interpretation. Cahusac, in contrast, imbues artists and scholars with an individual ingenuity consonant with Enlightenment values, yet this emphasis on individual initiative is accompanied by new configurations of disciplining control.
Individuals must internalize values of fact and fiction which authorize their dis-
tinction-making. It is as if the proscenium itself supplants the royal figure watching the dance and individual audience members use this prosthetic device to
guide the organization of their viewing labor. The story ballets that they see
displayed onstage, like the taxonomized treatment of dance's history, replace the
opera-ballets' endlessly similar commentaries on dance and text. The segmented,
carefully shaped body with its hierarchies of accomplishment takes over from the
body capable only of innumerable analogies to other moving things.

In each of these choreographies of power the body retains a certain integrity. It
functions neither as a sentimentalized disappearing act nor as an awesome source
of magical inspiration. Both Menestrier and Cahusac evoke a body that has
agency and that can participate actively in the production of meaning. Yet in the
reduction of the body to fact, Cahusac's history initiates a distinction between the
verbal and the bodily in which bodies lose their capacity to theorize. For Cahusac, bodies cannot theorize relationships between time and space or individual
and group; they can only pronounce the fact of those relationships. Cahusac's
approach to history thus establishes grounds on which text can claim exclusive
rights to theory.

The body of this text teaches itself to choreograph through its interactions with
both dance histories. It throws itself into dancing alongside them and returns,
ambidextrous, fragmented, replete with fantasized limbs and unusual boundaries.
It has learned some new moves, the most intriguing of which is the ability to turn,
to trope, from fact into metaphor and back again. In this turning it performs as
evidence of theory and at the same time evidence for theory. The choreography
for this double-bodied dance, this dance by bodies of facts and bodies of fictions,
gives theory new explanatory power just as it makes dancing theory more
evident.

NOTES ‒ ‒ ‒ ‒ ‒ ‒ ‒ ‒

1. Claude François Menestrier, *Des ballets anciens et modernes selon les règles du théâtre* (Paris: Chez René Guignard, 1682), 8–9 (author's translation).

Born at Lyon in 1631, Menestrier became a member of the Jesuit College as a scholar specializing in religious heraldry and ceremony. Like other Jesuits who recognized the educational opportunities afforded by performances, he became heavily involved in their study and production. He traveled widely throughout France and Italy, witnessing many ballets, weddings, festivals, banquets, tournaments, entries, and pageants of all kinds, and, as a close friend of those Jesuits who had worked with Count Filippo D'Aglié San Martino at the Savoy court in Turin, he heard about even more. Menestrier documented these performances in some 160 books and pamphlets, including two major theoretical works, *Des représentations en musique anciennes et modernes* (1681) and the companion volume considered here, *Des ballets anciens et modernes selon les règles du théâtre.* An authority on ceremonial symbolism, Menestrier was also in demand as a choreographer and composed numerous processions, ceremonies, and ballets, many of which are described in his writings. For a concise summary of Jesuit involvement in ballet, see Margaret McGowan, *L'art du ballet de court en France, 1581–1643* (Paris: Editions du Centre National de la Recherche Scientifique, 1963).

2. Louis de Cahusac, *La danse ancienne et moderne* (Paris: Chez la Haye, 1754), 17 (author's translation).

More a devoted critic of dance than practitioner or philosopher, Louis de Cahusac was born in 1706 at Montauban. He studied both law and literature before moving to Paris at the age of twenty-seven. Once there he began to write librettos for opera and dance. His most successful productions were collaborations with the composer Jean-Philippe Rameau: *Les fêtes de polymnie* (1745), *Les fêtes de l'hymen* (1747), *Zaïs* (1748), and *La naissance d'Osiris* (1754). His history of dance, *La danse ancienne et moderne* (1754), and his entries for the *Encyclopédie* are his only known scholarly works.

3. Exceptions to this general format are the chapter titles "On Figures," "On Movement," "On Harmonie," "On Paraphernalia," and much later in the text, "On the Number of Parts in a Ballet" and "On Games and Divertissements." These titles appear in capital letters, centered on the page, and have the effect of segmenting and emphasizing those portions of the text. They are not consecutive, however, nor do they seem more significant than other chapters, whose titles appear in the margins.

Notes on Contributors

ANN COOPER ALBRIGHT is a dancer and feminist scholar who has taught and performed in Philadelphia and New York, and is currently an assistant professor in the dance and theater program at Oberlin College, Ohio. Combining her interests in dancing and cultural theory, she teaches dance, performance studies, and women's studies courses that seek to engage students in both the practice and the theory of the body. When she is not running after her two-year-old daughter, Albright writes for various publications, including *Contact Quarterly, Women and Performance*, and *Dialogue Magazine*. She is a recipient of a 1992 Ohio Arts Council Individual Artist Award in Dance Criticism and is working on a book about the body and identity in contemporary dance.

BARBARA BROWNING, assistant professor of English at Princeton University, has danced professionally in Brazil, France, and the United States. The essay in this volume is part of a larger project on the social history of Afro-Brazilian dance. She is also completing a book on literature in the Yoruba diaspora. Her poetry has appeared in *Yale Review, Literary Review*, and *Minotaur*.

ELIZABETH DEMPSTER is currently a lecturer in dance at Victoria University of Technology, Melbourne. A founding member of the Dance Exchange company, she is active as a choreographer and performer. Her choreographic work has been presented throughout Australia, in London, and elsewhere abroad. She is the founding and continuing editor of the journal *Writings on Dance*. Her scholarly work in the areas of feminism and dance has been published in Verso's Questions for Feminism series (*Grafts*) and by Deakin University Press.

JACQUES DERRIDA teaches at L'École des Hautes Études en Sciences Sociales.

SUSAN L. FOSTER, choreographer, dancer, and writer, is professor of dance at the University of California, Riverside. Her book *Reading Dancing: Bodies and Subjects in Contemporary American Dance* (University of California Press, 1986) received the 1986 DelaTorre Bueno Prize for scholarship in dance. Her current work concerns the development of gendered bodies in the danced narratives of late eighteenth- and early nineteenth-century French ballet.

MARK FRANKO, dancer/choreographer/scholar, is associate professor of dance at the University of California, Santa Cruz. In 1994 he was visiting associate professor in the Department of Performance Studies, Tisch School of the Arts, New York University, and a Getty scholar at the Getty Center for the History of Art and the Humanities. His company, Novantiqua, has performed in the United States and Europe since 1985, and he is the author of *Dance as Text: Ideologies of the Baroque Body* (Cambridge University Press, 1993), *Objects of Movement: Radical Dance and Aesthetic Modernism* (Indiana University Press, 1995), and *The Dancing Body in Renaissance Choreography* (Summa, 1986).

J. ELLEN GAINOR is an associate professor of theatre arts at Cornell University. She is author of *Shaw's Daughters: Dramatic and Narrative Constructions of Gender* (University of Michigan Press, 1991) and is currently completing *The Plays of Susan Glaspell: A Contextual Study* (University of Michigan Press, forthcoming), co-edited with Linda Ben-Zvi. She is editor of *Imperialism and Theatre* (Routledge, 1995) and co-editor of two other collections in process, *Performing America: Cultural Nationalism in American Theatre* and *Theatre and Reproductive Rights*. She received her training in international ballroom dance under the late Neil Clover, and currently studies with Dee Quinones and Steven Dogherty.

ELLEN W. GOELLNER did her graduate work in English at the University of Chicago, and teaches in the American Studies Program and the Department of English at Princeton University. She has studied modern dance in Baltimore, New York, and Chicago. Currently she is at work on a study of William Faulkner invoking both dance and narrative theory.

FELICIA MCCARREN is assistant professor in the Department of French and Italian at Tulane University, and taught previously at Stanford University and the University of California at Los Angeles. She is the author of *The Female Form: Gautier, Mallarmé and Céline Writing Dance* (University of Michigan Press, 1992) and has translated Michel Serres's *Rome: The Book of Foundations* and Philippe Lacoue-Labarthe's *Mùsica Ficta (Figures of Wagner)* for Stanford University Press. She is currently working on a book about dance and hysteria, and a multimedia project.

CHRISTIE V. MCDONALD is professor of Romance languages and literatures at Harvard University. She is the author of *The Dialogue of Writing* (W. Laurier University Press, 1984), *Dispositions* (Ville de LaSalle, Hurbubise HMC, 1986), and *The Proustian Fabric* (University of Nebraska Press, 1991), and editor for *The Ear of the Other, Otobiography, Transference, Translation: Texts and Discussions* with Jacques Derrida (Schocken Books, 1985).

MICHAEL MOON teaches English and gay studies at Duke University. He is the author of *Disseminating Whitman: Revision and Corporeality in Leaves of Grass*

(Harvard University Press, 1990) and co-editor of the journal *American Literature*. He is completing a study of queer performance in the twentieth century, of which the essay in this volume is a part.

JACQUELINE SHEA MURPHY writes about violence, narrative, and performance in nineteenth- and twentieth-century American literatures and has studied dance most of her life. She is the author of short stories and of articles on Leslie Marmon Silko and Sylvia Plath, and has taught writing and literature in the English department at the University of California, Berkeley, and in the writing seminars department at Johns Hopkins University.

GAYLYN STUDLAR is associate professor of film studies at Emory University. She is author of *In the Realm of Pleasure: Von Sternberg, Dietrich, and the Masochistic Aesthetic* (University of Illinois Press, 1988) and numerous essays on film theory and history, and on feminist-psychoanalytic approaches to film. She is also co-editor of *Reflections in a Male Eye: John Huston and the American Experience* (Smithsonian Institute Press, 1993). Her most recent work centers on masculinity and stardom.

Index

Page numbers in *italics* denote illustrations.
When not otherwise designated, titles in *italics* refer to choreographed dance works; choreographers' names follow in parentheses.